THE
COMPETITION WALLAH

AMS PRESS
NEW YORK

THE

COMPETITION WALLAH.

BY

G. O. TREVELYAN, M.P.

SECOND EDITION,

WITH OMISSIONS AND CORRECTIONS.

London and Cambridge:
MACMILLAN AND CO.
1866.

Library of Congress Cataloging in Publication Data

Trevelyan, George Otto, Sir, bart., 1838-1928.
   The competition wallah.

   Reprint of the 2d ed., with omissions and corrections, published in 1866 by Macmillan, London.
   1. India—Description and travel—1859-1900.
2. Trevelyan, George Otto, Sir, bart., 1838-1928.
I. Title.
DS413.T815 1977   915.4'04'31   75-41272
ISBN 0-404-14782-8

Reprinted from an original in the collections
of the University of Chicago Library

From the edition of 1866, London
First AMS edition published in 1977
Manufactured in the United States of America

AMS PRESS INC.
NEW YORK, N.Y.

PREFACE.

THOSE who read these letters with attention cannot fail to perceive that my most earnest desire and most cherished ambition is to induce Englishmen at home to take a lively and effective interest in the native population of their Eastern dominions; and with that view to lay before them a plain statement of the feeling which is entertained towards the population by the European settlers in India. This is a task which cannot be undertaken by an anonymous writer. On a matter so momentous evidence will not be received from a witness whose character and antecedents are unknown. On all the great questions which now agitate Anglo-Indian society the civilians and the settlers are at odds: so that men naturally reject the testimony of an author whom the larger half of his readers and reviewers believe to be a civilian. The admiration expressed in the fourth letter for the gallantry of Macdonell and Mangles, and the recital of the advantages of a public career in India contained in the fifth, were successively attributed to the predilection of the author for his own Service. This was of little consequence: but not so with the ninth letter, which exposes at length the horrible tone adopted by a certain class of Anglo-Indians regarding the murder of natives by Europeans. This exposition consists almost entirely of extracts from the Anglo-Indian journals themselves: and yet it was styled "a burst of civilian hatred against the Independent Settler" by no less a journal than the *Spectator*, which had noticed the previous letters most favourably and courteously. The tenth of the list is chiefly an attack upon the proposed Criminal Contract Law: the facts of which are drawn almost entirely from the writings of the advocates of that law. Nothing would have given me greater pleasure than a criticism, however hostile, in the pages of the *Spectator*, since my dearest object is to excite the interest of the English people in these questions so vital to India; but the only notice bestowed upon me was that "the " Competition Wallah is writing on a subject on which " a civilian always loses his senses, and pleads his bro- " therly affection for natives as a reason for his cousinly " spitefulness to all settlers."

PREFACE.

I am not a civilian, nor a prejudiced witness: for having sailed from England in a state of such entire ignorance with regard to Indian subjects as effectually to preclude the very existence of prejudice, during my first three months I lived much in the indigo district; and my hosts and friends, whether official or non-official, were for the most part advocates of the Contract Law, and opposed to the policy of the Home Government. By the end of that time I was a rabid Anglo-Saxon. But, with increasing knowledge of the country, my opinions underwent a gradual but complete change. My faith in the principles of the anti-native party was first shaken by the violence and ferocity of the anti-native journals, the sure symptom of an unjust and unhealthy cause. Nine months more, spent in travel and study, and in free and familiar intercourse with all classes of men, European and native alike, have strengthened and confirmed those opinions which are expressed at length in the latter half of this book. I entreat adverse critics from this time forward not to set down my sentiments to the score of civilian spite, but to show that I am wrong in my facts; that the European settlers cherish a kindly feeling towards the children of the soil; that they speak and write of them as equals in the eye of the law—as fellow-men and fellow-subjects; that they do not stigmatise them as "niggers," and treat them little better than such; that they do not regard as execrable hypocrisy the sentiment that "we hold India for the benefit of the inhabitants "of India."

Something has been added to the book, and something altered. Much bad prose and worse rhyme has been omitted from the earlier letters : and yet a great deal remains so interwoven with more important matter that it cannot be expunged, of which I am heartily ashamed already, and expect to be still more ashamed in years to come. Such, however, must be the case with every young author, unless he be rarely precocious or uncommonly self-satisfied. It may be hoped that some pardon will be granted to youth and inexperience, and some to the excitement and emotion of one who has lived among scenes of social oppression and injustice which his readers have not known even by hearsay. These letters will not have been written in vain if, by their means, the natives of India obtain some portion of English sympathy and English justice.

2, CLARGES STREET,
April, 1864.

PREFACE TO THE SECOND EDITION.

THE alterations and omissions in the Second Edition aim at making this book not less faulty, but less unreadable. I have struck out nothing that is merely bad, but much that is dull. The only exception is in the case of some remarks which have brought upon their author the charge of religious bigotry, and of spite towards the Catholic faith. My readers will, I think, allow that religious bigotry is not my crying sin. I do not, however, hesitate to expunge a passage which has given offence to men whom I deeply respect, and whose claims for justice and tolerance I shall ever support to the extent of my ability.

8, GROSVENOR CRESCENT,
September, 1865.

CONTENTS.

                                        PAGE

LETTER OF INTRODUCTION 1

LETTER I.
THE TWO SYSTEMS 5

LETTER II.
AN INDIAN RAILWAY 18

LETTER III.
A GOVERNMENT SCHOOL AND AN OPIUM FACTORY 41

LETTER IV.
A STORY OF THE GREAT MUTINY 64

LETTER V.
A JOURNEY, A GRAND TUMASHA, AND THE TRUTH ABOUT THE CIVIL SERVICE CAREER 94

LETTER VI.
A TIGER-PARTY IN NEPAUL 133

LETTER VII.

ABOUT CALCUTTA AND ITS CLIMATE; WITH SERIOUS INFERENCES 167

LETTER VIII.

ABOUT THE HINDOO CHARACTER; WITH DIGRESSIONS HOME . . 210

LETTER IX.

BRITISH TEMPER TOWARDS INDIA, BEFORE, DURING, AND SINCE
THE MUTINY 238

LETTER X.

CHRISTIANITY IN INDIA 282

LETTER XI. AND LAST.

EDUCATION IN INDIA SINCE 1835; WITH A MINUTE OF LORD
MACAULAY 317

LETTERS

FROM A

COMPETITION WALLAH.

LETTER OF INTRODUCTION.

To the Editor of Macmillan's Magazine.

DEAR SIR,—Though feeling some hesitation in approaching (metaphorically) the editorial sanctum, there are occasions when diffidence is out of place; and I think that you will allow that this comes under that category. But, without any further preface, I will plunge at once *in medias res*, and tell you my whole story from the very beginning.

The gentleman (and scholar), whom I wish to introduce to your notice, is Mr. Henry Broughton, my earliest and most attached friend. Throughout our school career—which we passed together in the classic groves and along the banks of Radley—to call us Damon and Pylades would have been to " damn with faint praise." Together we chased the bounding ball; together we cleft the yielding wave; together we studied; together we attended Divine worship; together we should have passed the hours of the night, had not the regulations of that excellent institution confined us to our separate cubicles. Our characters were admirably fitted to supply what was wanting in the other. My mind was of the class which developes late, and which, while it gives abundant promise to the observant eye, too often fails to be appreciated by those immediately around. His reached its maturity early. I was the more thoughtful and the intellectualler of the two; he the more practical and the quick-sighteder. I ofttimes found myself unable to express the high thoughts that welled inside me; while he carried off all the school-prizes. In the fulness of time we followed each other to college—to the college ennobled by more than one enduring world-wide friendship—to the college of Tennyson and Henry Hallam. In our new phase of life we were still as intimate as ever at heart, though, outwardly speaking, our social spheres diverged. He lived with the men of action; I with the men of thought. He wrote and talked, wielded the oar and passed the wine-cup, debated on the benches of the Union high questions of international morality and ecclesiastical government. I conversed with a few kindred souls about, or pondered out in solitude, the great problems of existence. I examined myself and others on such points as these : Why were we born? Whither do we tend? Have we an instinctive consciousness? So that men would say, when they saw me in the distance, " Why was Simkins born? Is he " tending hither? Has he an instinctive consciousness " that he is a bore?" I gloried in this species of intellectual persecution. I was the Socrates, Broughton the Alcibiades, of the University. His triumphs may be read in the Cambridge Calendar and the club-room of First Trinity : mine are engraven deep in the minds which I influenced and impressed with my own stamp. However, to come to the point, as we were lounging in the cloisters of Neville's Court on an evening in March, 1860, the conversation happened to turn on an Indian career. Broughton spoke of it with his wonted enthusiasm, maintaining that the vital object to be looked for in the choice of a line of life was to select one that would present a succession of high and elevating interests. I, on the contrary, was fired at the idea of being placed with almost unlimited power among a subject-race, which would look up to me for instruction and inspiration. What a position for a philosopher! What for a philanthropist! Above all, what for a philosophic philanthropist! We forthwith sent in our names for the approaching competitive examination. For the result of that examination I do not pretend to account. Broughton, who was lamentably ignorant of modern literature; who was utterly unable to "give a "brief summary of the opinions held by, and a sketch "of the principal events in the life of Heraclitus, Dr. "Darwin, Kant, or Giordano Bruno;"—Broughton, who, when asked for the original source of the quotation, "When Greek meets Greek," said that when Greek met Greek he probably inquired whether he intended to vote for Prince Alfred, Jefferson Davis, the Duke of Saxe Coburg, Panizzi, or any other man; Broughton, I say, passed third on the list, being beaten only by a student from Trinity College, Dublin, and a gentleman educated at Eton, where he resided exactly three weeks, and a private tutor's, with whom he passed seven years. As for myself, I have since been convinced that an examiner, whose name I willingly suppress, was shocked by my advanced opinions on the destination and progress of our race. This fact, together with a certain dash and freedom of style which continually peeps through, and which is more prone to disgust than to fascinate those with whom my fate lies, sufficed to exclude me from among the successful candidates. Our readers may possibly have heard, when the fire burns low on a winter night, and ghost-tale succeeds ghost-tale, and the trembling circle draw closer in round the blazing-hearth—on such an occasion my readers may have heard a story of two friends who made a compact in life that, if one of them died first, he should appear to the other and disclose to him what he knew of the secrets of the grave. While the result of the examination was still pending, we agreed, in imitation of these friends, that, if one only of us survived the ordeal, he should write to his home-staying comrade a full account of his Indian experiences. Broughton has been true to our contract; and, knowing that you had formerly expressed your willingness to insert a production of his pen (you may remember that your wish was conveyed in the same letter in which you informed me—with thanks—that you could not find space for my article on "The " Subjectivity of Buckle"), I determined to transmit you his letters for publication.

Sincerely yours,

Trin. Coll. Cant.   CHARLES SIMKINS, B.A.

P.S.—I send you under cover a trifle which has occupied a few of my idle moments. It is somewhat in the vein of Browning. If you think the imitation too pronounced, or if, on the other hand, the originality of the little thing appears too marked to be graceful in a young author, pray do not hesitate to reject it.

LETTER I.

THE TWO SYSTEMS.

CALCUTTA, *Jan.* 24, 1863.

DEAR SIMKINS,—Indian travellers usually commence their first letter by describing their earliest impression upon landing in Calcutta. With some it is mosquitoes; with others, Warren Hastings; while others, again, seem divided between an oppressive consciousness of heathendom and hot tiffins. My prevailing feeling was negative: it was the absence of Dundreary. The sense of relief at being able to ask a question without being told that it was "one of those things that no fellah " could understand," was at first delightfully soothing. On the whole, the current English slang is at a discount in the market here.

I did not write during the first fortnight, as I was in very low spirits, and nothing encourages that state of mind so much as trying to communicate it to others. There is no doubt that the situation of a young civilian has much in it that is very trying. His position is precisely that of a new boy at school. I was continually expecting to hear the familiar question, " What's your " name, you fellow ?" Nobody, however, seemed to care enough about me to ask. There are so many young civilians that older residents cannot afford to show them attentions until they have earned themselves an individuality. Every one has been a " student " in his day, with the same hopes, the same aspirations, the same anxiety about passing in Persian. Just as the magnates of undergraduate life at the University refuse to see in an ardent freshman the future Craven Scholar or Member's prizeman; even so the judges of the High Court and the Secretaries to Government are slow to extend their favour and encouragement to budding Metcalfes and possible John Peters. As a set-off, however, against the insignificance of student life, there is the certainty that each year will bring with it an increase in importance and social position. A civil servant of ten years' standing, who has not plenty of friends and a sufficiency of admirers, must either be singularly undeserving or exquisitely disagreeable.

The sensation of loneliness is much aggravated by the present system of selecting and training the members of the Indian Civil Service. In old days a Writer came out in company with a score of men who had passed the last two years of their English life in the same quadrangle as himself. He found as many more already comfortably settled, and prepared to welcome and assist their fellow collegian; and, in his turn, he looked forward to receiving and initiating a fresh batch at the end of another six months. Haileybury formed a tie which the vicissitudes of official life could never break. In the swamps of Dacca, in the deserts of Rajpootana, amidst the ravines and jungles where the Khoond and the Santhal offer an intermittent but spirited opposition to the advance of civilization and the permanent settlement, wherever two Haileybury men met they had at least one set of associations in common. What matter if one wore the frock-coat of the Board of Revenue, while the other sported the jack-boots and solar topee of the Mofussil Commissioner? What matter though Brown swore by the Contract Law and Sir Mordaunt Wells, while Robinson was suspected of having lent a sly hand in pushing about the Nil Durpan? Had they not rowed together on the Lea? Had they not larked together in Hertford? Had they not shared that abundant harvest of medals which rewarded the somewhat moderate exertions of the reading-man at the East Indian College? This strong *esprit de corps* had its drawbacks. The interests of the country were too often postponed to the interests of the service. But the advantages of Haileybury outweighed the defects.

Our situation is very different. Few of us are lucky enough to have more than two or three acquaintances among the men of our own years: and, while our seniors persist in looking on us as a special class, we have no bond of union among ourselves. At Cambridge you must have observed that freshmen regard freshmen with a peculiar suspicion and shyness; and I sometimes think that it is the same with the novices of the Civil Service. It is some time before we acquire the aplomb, the absence of which characterises the reading-man of the University. I use the word "aplomb" in order to avoid your darling term "self-consciousness," that treasured discovery of a metaphysical age. When a man describes himself as "self-conscious," I always think of the American fugitive bawling out to an officer who attempted to rally his regiment, "For Heaven's "sake, do not stop me; I am so fearfully demoralised." The stories against the Competition Wallahs, which are told and fondly believed by the Haileybury men, are all more or less founded on the want of *savoir faire*. A collection of these stories would be a curious proof of the credulity of the human mind on a question of class against class. They remind one of nothing so much as of the description in "Ten Thousand a Year" of the personal appearance, habits, and morals of the supporters of the Reform Bill.

For instance :

Story showing the Pride of Wallahs.—A Wallah being invited to dinner by a member of Council, went out before the whole company.

Story showing the Humility of Wallahs.—A Wallah, on a visit to the Lieutenant-Governor of Bengal, being urged to sit down, replied that he knew his place better. (Be it observed that the Lieutenant-Governor denies the story with all its circumstances.)

Their want of familiarity with polite society.—A Wallah, having occasion to write to the daughter of a man high in office, addressed her as :

Miss White,

&c. &c.

Barrackpore.

Some anecdotes are more simple, such as : a Wallah, riding on a horse, fell into a tank ; or, a Wallah, seeing a rifle, thought it was a musket.

The idea entertained by the natives is droll enough : they say that another caste of Englishmen has come out. A common complaint among the magistrates and commissioners up country is, that many of the young men who have lately joined lack the physical dash and the athletic habits that are so essential in India. When some three or four Englishmen are placed over a province as large as Saxony, an officer who cannot drive a series of shying horses, or ride across country, is as useless as a judge who suffers from headache in a badly-ventilated courthouse. A commissioner of Police told me that on one occasion, when a district in Bengal was in a very inflammable state on account of the Indigo troubles, he marched up in hot haste with a strong force, and requested the civil officer to meet him on the way. To his ineffable disgust that gentleman came to the rendezvous in a palanquin. It was not by travelling about in palanquins that Wake and Mangles and their fellows, in the midst of a hostile population, with small hope of succour, bore up against frightful odds through the long months of the great mutiny. It is impossible to believe that any class of Englishmen are deficient in natural courage ; but familiarity with arms and horses can only be acquired by men constantly exercised in field sports ; and to field sports the new civilians are not addicted as a class. The individual members of an imperial race settled in small numbers throughout a subject population must be men of their hands. What the Enniskilleners were in Ireland, what the soldiers of Cortes were in Mexico, that are our countrymen in India. It is well for a Mofussil civilian that he should have cultivated tastes and extended views ; but it is well likewise that he should be ready at need to ride fifty miles on end without seeking for road or bridge, and that in villages and bazaars of the most evil reputation he should feel secure with a favourite hogspear in his hand, and a double-barrelled Purdey slung across his shoulders.

In the earlier days of the new system stories were frequently told against the competitioners, accusing them of the grave crimes of frugality and foresight. One competitioner had set up housekeeping with a dozen of beer and a corkscrew. Another was seen walking with his arm round his wife's waist in the bazaar. We no longer hear anything of this class of anecdotes, for the plain reason that society has come round to the competitioners, and acknowledged that they were in the right. If a young couple in the first year of wedded life cannot be happy without a carriage, their love can hardly be so warm as to justify their marrying on three hundred a year. Many of those who laughed loudest had bitter reason to regret the want of the prudence which they ridiculed. In old days, it was no uncommon thing for men of advanced life and high standing in the Service to be tormented with debts contracted during their first eighteen months in the country. With minds of a certain class, to have "turned your lac"—that is, to owe ten thousand pounds—was conventionally supposed to be a subject of mutual congratulation. Whether the contemplation of that achievement afforded equal pleasure to the father of a large family down a vista of thirty years may well be doubted. A civilian who has the self-command to live within his income from the very day on which he lands, after a very short time, will never know what the want of money is. But to live within his income is no easy thing for a student within the Calcutta ditch. To him iced champagne is as pleasant, and native hack-coaches are as dirty, and promising colts in the last batch landed from the Cape are as good bargains as to any collector and magistrate in the receipt of nineteen hundred rupees a month. It is sweet to quaff Moselle-cup on Sabbath afternoons in the Botanical Gardens; sweet to back one's opinion with fifty gold mohurs within the palings of the Grand Stand; sweet—oh, passing sweet!—to whisper soft somethings in the ear of the beauty of the cold season as you rein in your chafing Arab by her carriage on the course. Facile is the descent of Avernus; subservient is the native banker; easy is it, and withal somewhat dignified, to borrow on official prospects. But it will not be so pleasant a quarter of a century hence, when Harry, poor fellow, has to be written to and told to give up the Balliol Scholarship because you cannot afford to pay his college-bills; and Tom must be kept on at that private school where he learns nothing, because Rugby is too expensive; and Margaret's marriage has to be put off another, and yet another year, because you cannot spare the couple of thousand for her settlements; and, worse than all, the little ones are growing paler and more languid every month, but the fares of the P. and O. are so heavy; and that infernal Baboo is becoming so insolent; and your head was not quite the thing last hot season; and mamma .... It is better to pinch a little, while one is young and hopeful; and the competitioners have discovered this principle, and are acting upon it honestly and well.

We must not close our eyes to the undoubted advantages of competition. Short of competition, the old system of appointment by individual directors is far the best that ever was devised. A gentleman in very high office out here, of great experience and excellent judgment, proposes that the Secretary of State should name twice as many candidates as there are vacancies, and that the half of these should be selected by a searching competitive examination. But it is impossible for a statesman, with his hands full of work, however well disposed, to make, on his own judgment, a large number of appointments. He must rely on the recommendation of others. He might, indeed, request the headmasters of the great public schools to send in the names of those of their best scholars who fancied an Indian career—which, after all, would only be an irregular competitive system under another name. But he would be far more likely to ask members of parliament, who were undecided which way to vote on the approaching stand-and-fall question, to assist him with their valuable advice in making the nominations. The prizes of the Civil Service are too rich to be placed in the lap of any one man. Suppose twenty vacancies, and a secretary for India with free opinions on the matter of patronage. What would be easier than to nominate twenty favoured candidates, and twenty youths who had failed three times running in the preliminary examination at Cambridge? The only chance for a man, without interest, would be to feign extreme incapacity; to get flogged at school and plucked at college; and then to burst on the horror-struck examiners with a flood of unsuspected information and latent genius. It would be necessary to imitate the elder Brutus, in order to deceive the Tarquin of the India Office.

Now, the system of appointment by directors worked well, because it was founded on the principle of personal responsibility. Each member of the board wished his *protégé* to do him credit. He chose the most pro-

ADVANTAGE OF THE OLD PLAN.

mising of his sons or nephews : and a public-spirited man would often go further and nominate the most likely young fellow of his acquaintance. The chief disadvantage lay in the fact that the lads, brought up in Anglo-Indian families, and among Indian associations, from an early age, looked upon India as their birthright, and failed to acquire the larger views and wider interests of a general English education. Any one who has observed boys closely cannot but remark the unfortunate effect produced on a growing mind by a special line of life constantly in prospect.

Is there, then, any plan which would unite the advantages of the old and the new systems? Why not appoint men by open competition, between the ages of, say, seventeen and nineteen, and afterwards send the successful candidates to an East Indian College at or near London? By choosing your civilians at an earlier age, you will get hold of a class who now slip through your hands. A man of first-rate powers, who has once tasted the sweets of university success, will never be persuaded to give up his English hopes. By the time he is five-and-twenty, when he has begun to estimate his position truly, and to see that a Univerity scholarship is not a certain step to the cabinet or the woolsack, then, indeed, he would be glad enough to take the Civil Service by the forelock. But at two-and-twenty, in the full conceit of a glorious degree, in the full view of a Trinity or Merton fellowship, who would consent to exchange the Common-room *in esse*, and Downing-street *in posse*, for the bungalow and the cutcherry ? Warren Hastings and Sir Charles Metcalfe were among the best scholars of their time at Eton and Westminster. If they had once worn the gown, once known what it was to be the pets of the Union Society and the favourites for the Medal among the knowing ones at the scholars' table, they would have been lost for ever to India. Under the existing system, such men are lost to her for ever. Put the limit of age some three years earlier, and you will have a fair chance of getting a Metcalfe every other year, and a Hastings once in a decade.

Such a college as I propose would retain all that was good in Haileybury, without its capital defect—an excessive *esprit-de-corps*, a way of thought too exclusively Anglo-Indian. A set of lads, fresh from the great public schools, imbued each with the traditions and tone of the place in which he had been brought up, the heroes of Bigside, the aristocracy of the Philathletic Club at Harrow, would be in no danger of turning into a community of young Quihyes. Future judges of the Zillah Court, with livers as yet unenlarged, would drive their eight-oar past the Plough with all the zeal of Caius and something of the dash of Third Trinity. Sucking assistant residents would vie with any in acquiring that style, so exquisitely compounded of Pope's "Odyssey" and Brady-and-Tate, which used to characterise the Cambridge Prize Poem, until the heir of England inspired the University lyre. Such an institution would obviate all the defects in the present system, that are so strongly felt both by its enemies and its well-wishers. It would again unite the members of the Civil Service, in the most indissoluble of ties; and would prove an admirable corrective of a pedantic, unpractical turn of mind, or of a sedentary effeminate habit of body. The innate evils of a close college would have no existence among a society of young fellows, picked by merit from the great places of education, and planted within easy reach of Lincoln's Inn and Westminster Hall.

I have been very long and dull about my competitioners, but it is consoling to think that you would have been much duller. You may take your revenge by writing eight sides upon any subject in which you are interested, excepting only the American war and the destinies of our race, provided that you prepay the letter. My next shall be more amusing, as I start this day week on a visit to my cousin, the collector and magistrate of Mofussilpoor, in Bahar; so that you shall hear something of up-country life. Go on and prosper in your mission of reforming society by your pen. I have no doubt that, before many months are out, I shall hear of your having left something so written that the world will very willingly let it die. Be assured that my affection for yourself, and my indifference to your theories, continue unchanged.

"Jecur, non animum mutant qui trans mare currunt."

It is not worth while altering the line for your benefit, as you never had a strong opinion on the question of quantities. It has sometimes occurred to me that your having fallen short of excellence as a writer of Latin verse may be partially accounted for by your neglect of prosody.

Ever yours,

H. BROUGHTON.

P.S. You asked for a description of life on the overland route. I send you the prologue written for a play we acted on board Captain Weston's ship, the *Nemesis*, on the evening of the day on which we stopped at the coral island of Minnicoy, to pay a visit to the poor people who had been wrecked in the " Colombo " some six weeks before. It will tell you as much as it is good for you to know about the habits and pastimes of the " P. and O." travellers.

>   Fair dames, whose easy-chairs in goodly row
>   Fringe either bulwark of the P. and O ;
>   Whose guardian angels with auspicious gales
>   Swell the brood bosom of our outward sails,
>   Or, as a metaphor more strictly true,
>   Direct the revolutions of our screw ;
>   As the long day wears on, and nothing brings
>   To break the dull monotony of things,
>   No fresh delight, no genial Christmas fun,
>   Save water-ices or a casual bun,
>   Just like our watches, as we eastward go
>   We're growing slower still and yet more slow.
>
>   In search of sport these join the circle full
>   That smokes and lounges round the game of "Bull,"
>   Chaff if Smith get a B, and marvel when
>   Jones, flushed with triumph, scores a lucky ten.
>
>   Those train their muscles, spite of bruise and rub,
>   With two old dumb-bells and a broken club,
>   And, like true heroes, undergo in play
>   Work that were cheap at five rupees a day.
>
>   Some loftier natures court a nobler care,
>   And sit in judgment on the bill of fare,
>   Sigh for fresh butter and abuse the ghee,
>   Sneer at the ox-tail soup and praise the pea,
>   And for discussion find a boundless field
>   In Irish stew hermetically sealed.
>
>   Then blame us not if we exert our powers
>   To charm away *ennui* some two short hours.
>   Excuse our faults. For time most sorely prest
>   We've done but roughly, though we've done our best.
>   To dye our lover's waistcoat in a hurry
>   We stole a spoonful of the purser's curry,

And left the after-dinner wine and fig
To pick the hemp that forms our villain's wig.

Is there one here who, when his spirits droop,
Recalls his broken slumbers on the poop ;
Roused from the rugged plank on which he lay
By humid Lascars ere the break of day ?
Is there a maid who lives in nightly dread
Lest some dire cockroach drop from overhead,
And in the fevered fancies of her sleep
Sees the foul insect towards her pillow creep ?
Let them to-night, while laughing till they cry,
Lay cares and cockroaches and Lascars by.
If thoughts of those we left on Minnicoy
Infuse some bitters in our cup of joy,
Let us at least this consolation rest on,
Through their mishap we sail with Captain Weston.

While friends at home through dank Tyburnia's fog,
Their flanks protected by a trusty dog,
A stout alpaca o'er their shoulders spread,
Alert and armed, are marching back to bed,
And scheming to avoid, as best they can,
The fell embraces of "the nasty man ;"[1]
Here shall the mermaids who pursue in play
Our track of phosphor stretching miles away,
When burst of merriment and jocund stave
Come floating by across the Indian wave,
Cock up their tails and cry, "Full well we know
"Some lark's afloat on board the P. and O."

[1] This is the professional title of the gentleman who actually gives the hug.

LETTER II.

AN INDIAN RAILWAY.

BANKIPORE, *alias* PATNA,
Feb. 7, 1863.

DEAR SIMKINS,—A man gains more new ideas, or, which comes to the same, gets rid of more old ones, within his first month on Indian soil than during any equal period of his life. It is consequently very hard for him to realize that many things, which are familiar to himself, are strange to his English correspondents. A dashing comedy by Mr. Tom Taylor, with life in an up-country station for its subject, in the style of "the " Overland Route," would do more to unite the sympathies of England and India than the Red Sea Telegraph, or the Army Amalgamation Scheme. A few days before my departure a youth of that class which you persist in alluding to as " our mutual friends," who had already undergone the rite of ordination, and might therefore be considered qualified to impart instruction to his fellow-men, asked whether I should not be a full fortnight on the voyage between England and Calcutta! On the same occasion, a gentleman much distinguished in the University Curriculum was speaking of a friend in Bengal who had been pushed forward by "a man called

"Grant." I inquired, "Do you refer to Sir John Peter?" "I don't know about that," he replied, "but I am sure "that the man's name was Grant." The effect of this out here is much the same as that which would be produced at home by hearing Lord Monteagle described as having been in old days "a Mr. Rice," or Lord Lyveden spoken of as "formerly Smith of the Board "of Control."

But it is not only the absence of ideas in common that renders correspondence an arduous task. Almost as serious an obstacle is the want, so to speak, of a common language. Anglo-Indians are, naturally enough, wont to interlard their conversation with native words, though this is the case less in Calcutta than elsewhere. The habit is so universal that a Governor-General fresh from home complained in a published order that he could not understand the reports of his own officials. An Englishman may keep his ground in Parisian salons, and pass for a very sensible, intelligent fellow, by a copious though judicious use of "*par exemple.*" In the same way, a man who is a thorough master of the word "Pucka," may hold his own in any society in India. "Pucka" literally means "ripe," and is used to express the notion of perfection and completeness. A man who is good at all points, whom Aristotle would have denominated "a cube without blame," is more concisely described out here as "pucka." A permanent barrack is "pucka," as opposed to a thatched hut. The arrangements for a shooting party are "pucka" when the pale ale does not run short, and the bore of the station is prevented from coming by an attack of dysentery.

The adjectives or verbs which are imported into conversation from native sources are comparatively few; but, in the case of names of things, the English word is often entirely shoved out of the field. All India outside the Mahratta Ditch is the Mofussil; Sport is always Shikar; and an Order always a Hookum. A civilian of old standing, who was desirous of pleasing me by praising my University, told me that the "compounds" of some of the colleges were charming. The same gentleman complained that, when he was travelling on the Continent during his furlough, he found it impossible to avoid mixing up Hindustani with his French or German. On one occasion he astonished an ardent imperialist, with whom he was holding a dispute in a railway carriage, by exclaiming, "*Ah, monsieur, votre Empereur n'est pas pucka du tout, du tout, du tout!*" There is nothing that enchants people out here so much as the mistakes in the languages made by new arrivals. The native name for soda-water is Belattee Pawnee, which, being interpreted, means, "English water." This arises from an idea which prevails in the Hindoo mind that it is the ordinary water of the English rivers bottled for exportation. Never shall I forget the enthusiastic delight occasioned by my talking of "bi-carbonate of "Belattee." In fact, a charitably-disposed griffin will not unfrequently commit intentional inaccuracies in order to give the greatest possible amount of pleasure with the least expenditure of wit. A young officer lately convulsed a dinner-table by proclaiming that he was going to shoot tigers in the Cummerbunds—a triumph which was afterwards dimmed by a competitioner, who stated that at one time it had been his intention to have taken hookums. The natives have met us halfway in the matter of language. I am told that the current Hindustani has been much anglicized within the last twenty years. Besides borrowing the form of the sentences, they have adopted many of our words, and altered them in the most curious manner to suit their own effeminate pronunciation. This is ordinarily done by the insertion of a vowel before our harsher combination of consonants. Thus, "Tank "Square" becomes "Tanky Square," and "Stewed Duck" "Ducky stew." "Champagne" seems to have troubled them most. They have turned it into your singular, and call it "Simkin."

Towards the end of last month I applied for, and obtained, six weeks' leave, after passing in the first of my two languages. It is a fact worthy of note, that the men who fail are very generally dissatisfied with the manner in which this examination is conducted, while the men who succeed seem, on the whole, inclined to think that there is not much amiss. On the evening of the 31st I left Calcutta by train, with the intention of living a week at Patna with Major Ratcliffe, who is on special duty there, and then passing the rest of my leave with my cousin, Tom Goddard, at Mofussilpore. Ratcliffe is a Bengal Club acquaintance, who gave me first a general, and then a most particular invitation to stay with him up country. There is something stupendous in the hospitality of India. It appears to be the ordinary thing, five minutes after a first introduction, for people to ask you to come and spend a month with them. And yet there is a general complaint that the old good-fellowship is going out fast ; that there are so many Europeans about of questionable position and most unquestionable breeding, that it is necessary to know something of a man besides the colour of his skin before admitting him into the bosom of a family.

There is something very interesting in a first railway journey in Bengal. Never was I so impressed with the triumphs of progress, the march of mind. In fact, all the usual common-places genuinely filled my soul. Those two thin strips of iron, representing as they do the mightiest and the most fruitful conquest of science, stretch hundreds and hundreds of miles across the boundless Eastern plains—rich, indeed, in material products, but tilled by a race far below the most barbarous of Europeans in all the qualities that give good hope for the future of a nation—through the wild hills of Rajmahal, swarming with savage beasts, and men more savage than they; past Mussulman shrines and Hindoo temples; along the bank of the great river that cannot be bridged, whose crocodiles fatten on the corpses which superstition still supplies to them by hundreds daily. Keep to the line, and you see everywhere the unmistakable signs of England's handiwork. There are the colossal viaducts, spanning wide tracts of pool and sandbank, which the first rains will convert into vast torrents. There are the long rows of iron sheds, with huge engines running in and out of them with that indefiniteness of purpose which seems to characterise locomotives all over the world. There is the true British stationmaster, grand but civil on ordinary occasions, but bursting into excitement and ferocity when things go wrong, or when his will is disputed; who fears nothing human or divine, except the daily press.

There is the refreshment-room, with its half-crown dinner that practically always costs five and ninepence. Stroll a hundred yards from the embankment, and all symptoms of civilization have vanished. You find yourself in the midst of scenes that Arrian might have witnessed; among manners unchanged by thousands of years—unchangeable, perhaps, by thousands more. The gay bullock-litter bearing to her wedding the bride of four years old; the train of pilgrims, their turbans and cummerbunds stained with pink, carrying back the water of the sacred stream to their distant homes; the filthy, debauched beggar, whom all the neighbourhood pamper like a bacon-hog, and revere as a Saint Simeon —these are sights which have very little in common with Didcot or Crewe Junction.

A station on an Indian line affords much that is amusing to a curious observer. Long before the hour at which the train is expected, a dense crowd of natives collects outside the glass-doors, dressed in their brightest colours, and in a wild state of excitement. The Hindoos have taken most kindly to railway-travelling. It is a species of locomotion which pre-eminently suits their lazy habits; and it likewise appeals to their love of turning a penny. To them every journey is a petty speculation. If they can sell their goods at a distance for a price which will cover the double fare, and leave a few pice over, they infinitely prefer sitting still in a truck to earning a much larger sum by genuine labour. A less estimable class of men of business, who are said to make great use of the railway, are the dacoits, who travel often sixty or seventy miles to commit their villanies, in order to escape the observation of the police in their own district. Every native carries a parcel of some sort or kind; and it often happens that a man brings a bundle so large that it cannot be got in at the door.

At length the barrier is opened, and the passengers are admitted in small parties by a policeman, who treats them with almost as little courtesy as is shown to Cook's tourists by a Scotch railway official. When his turn comes to buy a ticket, your true Hindoo generally attempts to make a bargain with the clerk, but is very summarily snubbed by that gentleman; and, after an unsuccessful effort to conceal a copper coin, he is shoved by a second policeman on to the platform, where he and his companions discuss the whole proceeding at great length and with extraordinary warmth.

Natives almost invariably travel third-class. At one time a train used to run consisting entirely of first and third-class carriages. Every first-class passenger was entitled to take two servants at third-class prices. It was no uncommon thing for well-to-do natives to entreat an English traveller to let them call themselves his servants for the sake of the difference in the fares. The most wealthy Hindoos would probably go first-class if it were not for a well-founded fear of the Sahibs; and therefore they share the second-class with our poorer countrymen. In fact, in spite of the fraternity and equality which exist in theory between the subjects of our beloved Queen, the incompatibility of manners is such that English ladies could not use the railway at all if native gentlemen were in the constant habit of travelling in the same compartment. If you ask how

THE SAHIB ON A JOURNEY. 25

our countrymen manage to appropriate to themselves the first-class carriages without a special regulation to that effect, I ask you in return, How is it that there are no tradesmen's sons at Eton or Harrow? There is no law, written or unwritten, which excludes them from those schools, and yet the boys take good care that if one comes he shall not stay there very long.

To return to the scene at our station. Suddenly, in the rear of the crowd, without the gates, there arises a great hubbub, amidst which, from time to time, may be distinguished an imperious, sharp-cut voice, the owner of which appears to show the most lordly indifference to the remarks and answers made around him. A few moments more, after some quarrelling and shoving about, the throng divides, and down the lane thus formed stalks the Sahib of the period, in all the glory of an old flannel shirt and trousers, a dirty alpaca coat, no collar, no waistcoat, white canvas shoes, and a vast pith helmet. Behind him comes his chief bearer, with a cash-box, a loading-rod, two copies of the *Saturday Review* of six months back, and three bottles of soda-water. Then follows a long team of coolies, carrying on their heads a huge quantity of shabby and nondescript luggage, including at least one gun-case and a vast shapeless parcel of bedding. On the portmanteau you may still read, in very faint white letters, " Cal-" cutta. Cabin." The Sahib, with the freedom and easy insolence of a member of the Imperial race, walks straight into the sacred inclosure of the clerk's office, and takes a ticket, at five times the price paid by his native brethren. Meanwhile, his bearer disposes the luggage in a heap, rewards the coolies on a scale which seems to give them profound discontent, and receives a third-class ticket from his master's hand with every mark of the most heartfelt gratitude. If there happen to be another Sahib on the platform, the two fall to talking on the extreme badness of the road in the district made by the Supreme Government, as opposed to those constructed by the local authorities. If he is alone, our Sahib contemplates the statement of offences committed against the railway rules and regulations, and the penalties inflicted, and sees with satisfaction that his own countrymen enjoy the privilege of being placed at the head of the list, which generally runs somewhat thus :—

" John Spinks, formerly private in the —th Foot,
" was charged before the magistrate of Howrah, with
" being drunk and disorderly on the Company's pre-
" mises, in which state he desired the station-master to
" run a special train for him, and on this being refused,
" he assaulted that official, and grievously wounded
" three native policemen. On conviction, he was sen-
" tenced to three months' imprisonment."

" David Wilkins, who described himself as a pro-
" fessional man, was charged with being drunk and
" disorderly, and with refusing to leave a railway car-
" riage when requested to do so. He was reprimanded
" and discharged."

Then comes a long series of native misdemeanours, chiefly consisting in riding with intent to defraud.

At length the train arrives. As the traffic is very large, and there is only a single line (though the bridges and viaducts have been built for a double line), the trains are necessarily composed of a great number of trucks. First, perhaps, come eight or ten second-class carriages, full of pale panting English soldiers, in their shirt-sleeves. Then one first-class, of which the *coupé* is occupied by a young couple going to an appointment up-country. They have become acquainted during the balls and tiffins of the cold season at Calcutta, and were married at the end of it. Perhaps they may never see it again until the bridegroom, who seems a likely young fellow, is brought down from the Mofussil to be put into the Secretariat. They have got a happy time before them. India is a delightful country for the first few years of married life. Lovers are left very much to themselves, and are able to enjoy to the full that charmingly selfish concentration of affection which is sometimes a little out of place in general society. When the eldest child must positively go home before the next hot season, and ought to have gone home before the last—when aunts, and grandmothers, and schoolmistresses at Brighton, and agents in London have to be corresponded with—then troubles begin to come thick. The next compartment is filled by a family party—a languid, bilious, mother; a sickly, kindly, indefatigable nurse; and three little ones sprawling on the cushions in different stages of undress. In the netting overhead are plentiful stores of bottles of milk, bread and butter, and toys. Poor things! What an age a journey from Calcutta to Benares must seem at four years old! In the third compartment are two Sahibs smoking, who have filled every corner of the carriage with their bags and trunks, the charge for luggage in the van being preposterously high out here. Our Sahib, who is too good-natured to disturb the lovers, and who has no great fancy for children as fellow-travellers, through the dust and glare of a journey in India, determines to take up his quarters with the last-mentioned party. The two gentlemen object very strongly to being crowded, although there is full room for eight passengers; but our Sahib is a determined man, and he soon establishes himself, with all his belongings, as comfortably as circumstances will admit, and before very long the trio have fraternized over Manilla cheroots and the Indigo question. Behind the first-class carriage come an interminable row of third-class, packed to overflowing with natives in high exhilaration, stripped to the waist, chattering, smoking hubble-bubbles, chewing betel-nut, and endeavouring to curry favour with the guard—for your true native never loses an opportunity of conciliating a man in authority. Though there does not appear to be an inch of room available, the crowd of new comers are pushed and heaved in by the station-master and his subordinates, and left to settle down by the force of gravity. In an incredibly short space of time the platform is cleared; the guard bawls out something that might once have borne a dim resemblance to "all right be-"hind," the whistle sounds, and the train moves on at the rate of twenty-five miles an hour, including stoppages.

If one of the pleasures of travel be to find a preconceived notion entirely contradicted by the reality, that pleasure I enjoyed to the full at Patna. A city of nearly three hundred thousand inhabitants, the capital of an immense province, one of the earliest seats of Batavian commerce, connected with the history of our race by the most melancholy and glorious associations; —I expected to pass through a succession of lofty streets, of temples rich with fretwork, of bazaars blazing with the gorgeous fabrics of the Eastern loom; in fact, through such a scene as you described in your unsuccessful prize poem upon "Delhi." Somewhere in the centre of this mass of wealth and magnificence I depicted to myself a square or crescent of architecture less florid than elsewhere, but more nearly approaching to European ideas of comfort. This was to be the quarter appropriated to the English residents. Here were to be their shops and factories, their courts, their offices, and the churches of their various persuasions. Such was the picture which I had composed in about equal proportions from the "Arabian Nights" and Macaulay's Essay on Lord Clive. Now for the original.

We were due at Patna at 2 P.M., and, punctual to the time, the engine slackened its pace. There were no signs of a town to be seen; nothing but a large collection of mud huts standing in small untidy gardens, and shaded by a great number of trees. We arrived at the station, and I alighted, and collected my things —a course of conduct which appeared to excite some surprise among the English passengers, none of whom left the carriages. The natives got out in herds, and the platform was instantly covered with a noisy multitude, who surged round my baggage, which I had placed in front of me as a species of breakwater. After some minutes the train moved off, and the station-master came up and demanded my ticket. I asked him whether I could get a conveyance to take me to Major Ratcliffe's. "No. There were no conveyances at the "station." Would he send some one to the nearest hotel to order me a fly? "Quite impossible. The "nearest hotel was at Dinapore, twelve miles off." At length, the awful truth began to dawn upon my bewildered intellect. Patna was the native town; Bankipore, the civil station, was six miles farther on; and Dinapore, the military station, six miles again beyond that. The railway people were very civil, and procured a couple of bullock-carts for my luggage. As it was so early in the day, there was nothing for it but to wait at least three hours before the sun was low enough to allow me to venture on a six-mile walk; and an Indian waiting-room is a perfect black-hole of dulness. In a road-side station at home, there are a few objects out of which an intensely active mind may extract some particles of amusement. First, there is the Bible provided by the *Society for Promoting Christian Knowledge*, for the edification of people who may have missed the train —a circumstance not generally conducive to a devotional state of feeling. On the fly-leaf you find something of this sort:—

' You who upon this holy book
With Reverenshal eyes do look,
Seek for and gladly pluck the fruit
Contained within this holy truth.

(Signed) John Hopkins,
Aged 28,
Little Marlow,
Near Boston,
Lincolnshire."

Then, in another hand :

" The Bible does not need the recommendation of John
" Hopkins, aged 28."

The writer of this last sentence appears to be the local
Voltaire, for he is attacked in a series of appeals to his
conscience, all more or less illegible, for the most part
commencing, " O Scoffer—." Then, in the absence of
a refreshment-room, you may feast your mental palate
on the list of perishable articles in the tariff of goods—
" Eggs, Fruit, Fish, Game ;" or you may shudder over
the diabolical character of the man who can transmit
" Phosphorus, Gunpowder, Lucifer-matches, or other
" Combustible Articles," without declaring the nature of
the package. Finally, you can walk into the village,
and examine the small shelf of books which are kept
for sale at the general shop ; where the mistress of the
establishment, in answer to your request for something
new, offers you " Uncle Tom's Cabin," with the assurance
that a gentleman told her that it was " quite the go in
" London now-adays." I had nothing to beguile the
time except the conversation of a stoker in a state of
what I once saw described in a novel by a female
hand as " doubtful ebriety :"—a mistake in etymological
analogy, for which I had been prepared a few pages
before, by finding a misogynist called a " womanthrope."
I abandoned myself accordingly to my own reflections,
which, as there was nothing to reflect, soon became
sufficiently dull; the only point which actively occupied my mind being the extreme helplessness of a stray
European in India. His way of life is so essentially
different from that of the population, that the country

outside the European stations might as well be desert for all the accommodation it can afford him. He cannot eat the ordinary native food, or sleep under a native roof. The serais, or inns, are mere filthy sheds; and he might walk through miles of bazaar without seeing an article which would add to his comfort. Fortunately, no Englishman of decent habits and trustworthy character need long be an outcast in Bengal.

As soon as the evening shades began to prevail I proceeded to take up my wondrous tail, which consisted of two curious bullock-cars—so contrived that by great skill it was possible to place in them about one-fifth of the weight which the animals could draw—and three coolies, each conveying with apparent ease half again as much as both the vehicles together. Our way lay at first through groves of palms, and patches of poppy and various sorts of lentil, interspersed with wretched mud huts, at the doors of which numbers of children were intently engaged in the only recreation indulged in by the Hindoo infant, that of making dirt-pies. I was much impressed by the portentous development of stomach among the younger ones, and by their dress, which consisted simply of a strip of red tape, which I presumed to be a delicate compliment to the Imperial Government. However, their wrists and ankles were covered with silver ornaments; in consequence of which custom the decoying and murdering of children is one of the most common crimes out here. Along the gutters wandered the hideous foul Indian pig. It is only necessary to watch the habits of the animal for five minutes to understand why the eaters of swine-flesh are held unclean throughout the East. In this

A VILLAGE IN BAHAR.

respect Englishmen have adopted what is generally looked upon as an Oriental prejudice; and no pork appears on a Calcutta table except such as has been sty-fed by hands in which the host reposes the most perfect confidence. Add a few bullocks sprawling in a roadside pool; a few thin-legged peasants half-dressed in a single garment of coarse cotton, sitting on their haunches in an attitude which can be imitated by no European who is not a practised athlete, sharing the alternate pipe, or cleaning their teeth with a bit of stick, the end of which they have previously chewed into a brush; a few slim mysterious poles of about twelve feet high, ornamented with bits of coloured rag; a few pariah dogs; and not a few smells; and you will have a very fair notion of a village in Bahar. But where are the graceful maidens with pitchers balanced on their stately heads? Where are the lovely daughters of Hindustan, from whom Southey drew his conception of the charming heroine of the Curse of Kehama? Echo, alas! answers: "In the zenanas of wealthy baboos." At any rate, they are not to be seen on the roads. In fact the village women are so stunted and unattractive that, so far from appreciating the taste of those Sahibs in whose eyes they have occasionally obtained favour, one finds it difficult to imagine how they ever find husbands among their own people.

After a time we got into the main line of bazaar, which extends from the farther extremity of the city of Patna to the English station of Bankipore. Do not let the name "bazaar" conjure up reminiscences of the Pantheon, or the fond infantile associations which cluster round the corner of Soho Square, or those subterraneous chambers which form the basement of the chaste and classical gallery of Tussaud—that unfrequented fancy-mart where, at the unwonted apparition of a visitor, the stallkeepers duck under the counters as rabbits disappear at the approach of a man in tight corduroy trousers and an old velveteen coat. An Indian bazaar is a narrow street of one-storied hovels, each with a small verandah, of which the floor is raised about two feet above the level of the road. The fronts are generally of wood, carved in tawdry patterns, dirty beyond anything that cold western imaginations can conceive. Into the filth and darkness of the inner room behind the shop no European, save a police-officer, or a sanitary commissioner, would dare to penetrate. The proprietor sits in the verandah surrounded by his stock-in-trade, which consists of a dozen bags of various sorts of grain; or as many baskets of sweetmeats, made of sugar and rancid butter; or three or four pounds' worth of silver anklets and charms; or a few piles of coloured handkerchiefs of the coarsest English manufacture. There is very little difference between the appearance of the town and country populations, and an utter absence of the picturesque costumes which, in the markets of Cairo and Alexandria, almost realize our ideas of the Bagdad of Haroun Alraschid.

There were already some ten minutes of daylight left when I arrived on a scene which amply repaid me for the dust and discomfort of the preceding hour and a half. On the left of the road lay an expanse of turf of some thirty acres, encircled by a race-course, an institution without which our countrymen seem unable to support existence in India. Surrounding the plain stood the residences of the officials, each in its own enclosure of from three to ten acres of lawn and garden. There is a strong family likeness between all houses in the Mofussil. A one-storied building, covered with plaster of dazzling whiteness, relieved by bright green blinds, surrounded on all sides by a broad verandah. Two lofty spacious sitting-rooms, with so wide an opening between that they almost form one hall, extend through the centre of the house from front to back, while either end is occupied by bedrooms, each with a bath-room attached. The servants sleep in sheds scattered about the compound; and the cooking is carried on in an outhouse, which gentlemen who are particular about their eating sometimes connect with the dining-room by a covered passage. The Sahib, generally speaking, has a sanctum of his own, where a confusion reigns which surpasses anything which could be found in a Lincoln's Inn garret, or the chamber in an English country-house appropriated to the son and heir. The walls are ornamented with mouldering antlers and dusty skulls of boar and tiger, the trophies of unmarried days; a map of the district, a ground-plan of the station, a picture of Rugby Close in 1843, and a print of Lord Canning, cut out from the *Illustrated London News*, marked with the generic sulkiness which characterises the portraits in that remarkable periodical. The furniture consists of a table overflowing with papers and pamphlets, which constantly encroach on the small corner reserved for an ink-stand and blotting-pad, in spite of a species of temporary dam formed by a despatch-box and two bags of wadding; a dressing-table and appliances which would be scorned by a Belgravian footman; a camp-bed, so light as to allow of its being placed at will within range of the punkah; half-a-dozen cane chairs, and a vast leather couch, where the Sahib spends the half hour after his early morning walk, alternately dipping into the *Englishman*, and sharing his tea and buttered toast with a favourite terrier. In one corner stand two splendid smooth-bores, stamped with the name of Westley Richards, and a double-barrelled rifle by the same hands; a long native gun, studded with glass beads, the muzzle shaped into a dragon's mouth; a blunderbuss, a couple of hog spears, a heavy hunting-crop, and two driving-whips; and the ancient family Joe Manton solemnly presented to the young writer by his anxious parent the day before he left the East India Docks in the Lord Minto, 1,200 tons, some fifteen years since. The other three corners are heaped with a chaos of salt-reports, minutes, blue-books, codes and translations of codes, and letters of every size and age, filed and unfiled, tied up with string, whipcord, boot-laces, or the frail, foul, execrable red-tape of India, which has done more to break the hearts and health of English-bred Governors-General and Financiers than the mists of the Hooghley or the stenches of the Black Town.

By a careful inspection of the furniture and knick-nacks in the drawing-room, a close observer may be able to name with confidence the three years which his host passed at home on furlough. In one house there is a prevailing sense of Great Exhibition. Everywhere you see views of the interior and exterior of the building, crowded with Turks and Albanians, Highlanders and Esquimaux, with here and there an individual in the hat and coat of modern civilization directing the attention of a female on his arm by pointing his stick at some interesting object in mid-air. On the table lie some Great Exhibition tokens. Till I came out here I never could conceive who bought those most futile and meaningless articles of commerce. In the bookshelves stands a long row of volumes of the Illustrated Catalogue, blazing with blue and gold. In other families, pictures of Solferino and the entry into Milan, maps of Sicily, and portraits of Cavour and Garibaldi, testify that the furlough of your host coincided with the struggle for Italian Unity. There is something touching in these memorials; for they remind one that, however devoted our countryman may be to the interests of the race which is entrusted to his charge, the objects dearest to his inmost heart lie far away, beyond the glaciers of the Hindoo Koosh, and the seething waves of the Red Sea.

On my right hand a smaller open space, likewise covered with grass, ran some way back from the road. On one side stood a church, as pretty as anything can be which is coated with yellow plaster, surrounded by a portico formed by means of graceful flying buttresses; on the other a row of low barracks, swarming with native policemen in bright blue tunics and scarlet turbans. At the end farthest from the road was the collector's office, or cutcherry, encircled by a rude fortification thrown up in the crisis of 1857. I was much interested in this, the first evidence I had met with of the great mutiny. A mere ditch and mound overgrown with prickly pear, a man could walk over it without changing step. And yet it was behind such slender defences as this, that in many an isolated station a dozen or two of the Imperial race stood at bay for months before a hundred times their number of infuriated enemies, disciplined by English skill, and armed from English arsenals. In those dreadful days this was the refuge for the Europeans from every one of the six or seven districts in the Patna division: from every one except Arrah, where eight or ten civilians and railway officials, with a handful of stout Punjabees, were defending a billiard-room against the levée-en-masse of a province, supported by three strong regiments of regular infantry.

It is five years since my attention was directed to this country by the "Siege of Delhi" at Astley's. I had been persuaded by Jack Whiffin, of whom the "fast set" at Radley consisted, to run up to town for a lark— which eventually resulted in his premature departure from that seminary of moderately sound learning and uncommonly religious education. Our lark comprised Astley's, a visit to Cremorne (which, to our intense though unexpressed relief, we found closed, as I am told is the case in the winter months), an ineffectual search after the Cider-Cellars, and a supper at a Covent Garden hotel, of a dozen oysters, a roast goose, an apricot-tart and custard, and a bottle of what Jack pronounced to be "a fine dry fruity sherry." That evening, from seven o'clock till half-past nine, we gazed with rapture on what we religiously believed to be an accurate and life-like picture of Indian habits. The play opened with a scene representing a number of sepoys off duty. A Brahman—who reminded one alternately of a Druid and a Jew pedlar—was handing about Lotus-flowers as a signal for revolt. This slight verbal error of Lotus-

A LIVE ZEBRA.

flowers for brass Lotahs was pardonable—shared as it was by the most imaginative and oriental of England's statesmen. To them entered an officer, and began to form the men into line; whereupon two sepoys fired at the chandelier, and one into the prompter's box, which proceeding was unaccountably followed by the fall of the officer. The *coup d'œil* of the next scene was very fine. It displayed "the mountain-pass of Barrackpore," up which were painfully winding supplies for the beleaguered garrison of Cawnpore, consisting, according to the bill, of "cavalry, infantry, artillery, buffaloes, a "LIVE ZEBRA." What part this singular animal was destined to play in the great events which followed, I do not know. Perhaps it was intended as a remount for General Windham. Now, Barrackpore is on the Hooghley, within six leagues of Calcutta, and the country, for two hundred miles round, is as flat as the beer in the refreshment-rooms in the Great Exhibition. The principal part in the capture of Delhi, and in the operations which preceded it, was played by a comic Irish sergeant, who appeared to have emancipated himself entirely from all discipline, and—perhaps from an unmerited distrust of the powers of the regulation rifle— went to action armed with a shillelah. Among other feats he danced the jig of his country with an extremely attractive lady's-maid (whom he subsequently led to the altar), without hat or bonnet, under the mid-day Indian sun—an act of daring which alone should have sufficed to procure him the Victoria Cross. Cawnpore was relieved, at the very moment that the women and children were about to be butchered, by Sir Henry Havelock's showing himself on horseback on the top of a precipice

overlooking the cantonment; at which stupendous apparition all the sepoys dropped down dead, with the exception of four, who were reserved for immediate execution. Just then in rushed a youth of some eighteen years of age, attired in a frock-coat, a black silk hat, evening trousers, and an enormous blue scarf, described in the programme as " Mr. John Peters, a Commis-
" sioner," who cried out, " Spare these good men! They
" are innocent! Are you not, my poor fellows?"

"Yes, Sahib. We were forced into the mutiny by
" others."

" You have not been concerned in any atrocities, have
" you?"

" Oh no, Sahib! "

Hereat John Peters is highly delighted, and enters on a general disquisition about the quality of mercy, which he represents, with great truth and originality, as not being strained; when, by some mysterious process, the guilt of the culprits is established, and they are sentenced to be blown from guns; which is done by tying them to the muzzles of the cannon, and letting down the curtain, from behind which four reports are heard after a short interval.

Ever yours,

H. BROUGHTON.

LETTER III.

A GOVERNMENT SCHOOL AND AN OPIUM FACTORY.

MOFUSSILPORE, *Feb.* 12, 1863.

DEAR SIMKINS,—I libelled Patna somewhat in my last letter. Ratcliffe drove me in on two different occasions, and we spent one long day in poking about the town, and another in the opium factory, which is second only in importance to that of Benares. There is a mile or two of very singular street architecture. The Mahommedans live here in great numbers, and everything belonging to them is picturesque all the world over. We visited a Mahommedan foundation, something between a college and a monastery, which boasted a good deal of shabby magnificence. It is very richly endowed, and the loaves and fishes are kept strictly among the founder's kin. The head of the family for the time being is *ipso facto* President, and he had apparently distributed the college offices with great impartiality among his brothers. The Fellows were certainly *bene nati*, and may have been *mediocriter docti* for all I knew. There was no doubt that they fell short of the All Souls' standard in the other particular.

We were led through a long series of quadrangles built of white stone, with the shrine of some devotee of ancient days standing in the centre of each, on the brink of a pretty little ornamental tank. Some of the courts were used as hospitia for pilgrims, others as schools for the younger members of the institution, others again as combination-rooms and studies for the Fellows. As all Mahommedans are strict teetotallers, it is hard to imagine how they spend their time in the combination-room. They probably talk about the dangers of setting aside the founder's will, and the presumption of the young men in wishing to have the mosque fines reduced. At present they were in a violent state of excitement, because the local authorities were thinking about appointing a species of University Commission, to inquire into the management of their revenues. Behind the courts lay a spacious garden. The whole establishment would have presented a very pleasing appearance, had not everything been in a disgraceful state of dirt and decay. At length we came to a large pile of buildings, on the roof of which we mounted, and found ourselves at the door of a chapel, in which sat the Master of the College. From the time that he succeeds to that office he may never descend to the level of the earth, so that, if a set of reforming young Fellows got a footing in the society, they might introduce all sorts of innovations with impunity, as long as they kept to the ground-floor. Fancy if, as a condition of holding his present position, the Master of Trinity was never allowed to come down from the roof of Neville's-court, even if he saw us playing cricket on the bowling-green! The old fellow was very civil—so much so, that I felt half inclined to give him some advice about throwing open his scholarships, but was deterred by my imperfect acquaintance with the language.

These premises are the head-quarters of religious enthusiasm at the great festival of the Mohurrum. Last year the ferment was such that a strong force of police was stationed close at hand, and the officers of the party kept watch through a whole day and night in a tower opposite the great gate. I was told that the mass of the crowd who went about bawling "Hussain and Hussan," were Hindoos; but it is idle to draw any conclusion from a fact of this nature. Englishmen out here are very fond of saying that there is no strong religious feeling among the natives; that the fetters of caste are maintained by our own mistaken tenderness for the prejudices of the country, and by the idleness of our domestics, who object to perform duties that belong to another class, not because they are bigoted, but because they are lazy. Nothing is easier than to pick up a hundred stories of servants who have been detected feasting on ham and champagne, though in the Menu code, the crime of drinking strong liquors comes next in turpitude to throwing the parings of your toe-nails at a Brahmin; of villagers who have used the same cup as a European traveller; of learned men who have laughed at the received Hindoo theories of astrology and geography. Yet all this does not prevent either the votaries of the Prophet or the worshippers of Vishnu from rushing to any extreme of ferocity, or self-sacrifice, if they believe their religion to be in danger. More than once some insult to custom, or to rites which to us appear insignificant, but by them are held dearer than life itself, has aroused a passive but stubborn resistance, followed by a savage outbreak of fanatical wrath and devotion. In the days when a great deal of the tailor entered into the composition of a genuine military officer, the authorities introduced into a regiment stationed at Vellore, a turban, which, in the diseased imagination of the soldiery, resembled a hat. The idea got about that they were to be forcibly turned into topee-wallahs, hat-fellows, a synonym for the hated name of Frank or Christian. The most respectable among the men remonstrated; and the commanding officer, who, naturally enough, considered that plumes and facings were of infinitely greater moment than the faith of the human beings committed to his care, answered their petition by flogging and degrading them as seditious rascals. When the outraged sepoys had risen as one man, when hundreds of Europeans had been butchered in a single evening, it began to occur to our colonels and brigadiers that a persecution of the warriors, by whose aid we kept down the Mahrattas and Pindarees, for the sake of some regulation frippery, was as mad a scheme as forcing the leopard to change his spots, or a man-eating Bengal tiger his stripes.

Time rolled on and the lesson was forgotten. Some few, who smelt the hurricane in the air, raised their voices in warning, only to be taunted with credulity and timidity. The earnest expostulations of one to whom the latter taunt could hardly be applied, the victor of Meeanee, were passed by with respectful neglect. Again recurred the same indications of a coming storm; again the native soldiers entreated their superiors not to put a force upon their conscience; again their request was treated as a crime. Then, with the suddenness and fury of an Eastern tempest, burst forth the madness of superstition in all its full horror. In a moment, in the twinkling of an eye, many a pleasant English homestead was laid waste. Many a family lamented their nearest and dearest, slain by forms of death as frightful as anything that fiction or the Spanish Inquisition ever invented. More dreadful still, there were families in which none was left to lament another. Through tens of thousands of square miles, our authority, which but just now seemed at last secure against any shock, was overthrown and scattered to the winds. Our treasuries and magazines were sacked, our barracks and court-houses burnt to the ground. Our officers fled for their lives through the districts which they had ruled with absolute authority; while tenderly-nurtured ladies, with their little ones on their knees, travelled night after night along by-roads and through jungles, and crouched all day in native hovels.

Then came the great vengeance, at which the world still shudders. The blaze of Oriental fanaticism, which at one time threatened to baffle all our efforts to subdue its ravages, at length yielded to the courageous perseverance, and the unconquerable energy of our race. Yet, though the fire has been got under, the embers glow with as fierce a heat as ever, and the crust of ashes is not so thick but that the flames break out with ominous frequency. Only the other day, in a village within the borders of a State under British protection, a report got about that two unfortunate men, father and son, had buried some cow-beef in their garden. The mob of the place, set on by the most wealthy and influential people of the neighbourhood, assembled at the suspected cottage, tied the poor wretches by their feet to the bough of a tree, and swung them to and fro, beating them all the time with the heavy murderous staves carried by all Indian peasants. They were then cut down, and branded from head to heel with hot iron, mounted on donkeys with their faces to the tails, led round the village under a shower of stones, and finally pitched down dead in front of their own door. What more could the celebrated majority in the Oxford Convocation do to their Greek Professor, if they had the power as well as the will?

The nature of religious enthusiasm is the same everywhere. It is not always the most zealous champions of a Church who observe most exactly all that their Church ordains. Philip the Second was living in open defiance of the teaching of his own religion, all the while that his emissaries, in the name of that religion, were burning, and butchering, and racking, and ravishing his misguided subjects over the seventeen provinces of the Netherlands. The conduct of our own James the Second proves how easy and comfortable it is to eject and suspend men from livings and fellowships for non-conformity to a faith, at a time when one is disobeying some of its precepts. But there is no need to ransack history for analogies. When we predicate the indifference of the natives to their religion from their neglect of its observances, they might well retort and say: "The English are not so strict as they might be. "Last Sunday our Sahib would not do Poojah in the "morning because it was so hot; and, when the hour "of afternoon prayer arrived, he was at tiffin with the "judge Sahib, and could not dishonour the table of his

"host by going away. Nor does the Sahib eat the food
"that his religion prescribes. On Good Friday there
"were no hot cross buns at breakfast. The only thing
"hot and cross was the Sahib himself. And the Sahib
"does not pay respect to his Brahmans. He only once
"set food and wine before the holy man from the bar-
"racks; and I heard him tell the brigadier Sahib that
"his Mollah was no better than one devoid of under-
"standing. And the brigadier Sahib stroked his beard
"and replied, 'Haw, demmy, yes. More he is. Haw!'"
No one can deny that this is not an unfair picture of
many of our countrymen; and yet men of this class are
among the first to resent any outrage on the religion of
their country, real or imaginary. The most hot opponents of Cardinal Wiseman and his bishops were not
all the most regular church-goers. Then why should a
Mussulman gentleman, who is occasionally overcome by
the charms of iced Moselle, or a Hindoo Zemindar, who
is sometimes scandalized at the ignorance and cupidity
of his priests, be the more likely to be pleased at seeing
his religion held up to ridicule, and his hundred millions of brethren devoted to damnation, in a tract or a
sermon?

From the college we passed on to a more common-
place, but far more useful institution, the Government
School. The buildings appropriated for the purpose
are, in most instances, beggarly enough; but the class
of scholars, and the character of the instruction given,
place them far above the level of Government Schools
in England. We had the curiosity to question a Form
of some two dozen boys on the profession and standing
of their respective fathers. Half of them were the sons

of public *employés*, and full a fourth of Zemindars, who answer in social position to the French "Rentier." Every here and there sat, glittering in gold and jewellery, the child of a rajah who counts his income by lacs. The little fellows are sometimes very pretty and intelligent, and are always dressed with great taste in very brilliant colours, for the natives are much addicted to petting their young children. It is now a trite observation that, up to a certain time of life, the Hindoo boys show greater cleverness and capacity than Europeans of the same age. James Mill observes that "they display "marvellous precocity in appreciating a metaphysical "proposition which would hopelessly puzzle an English "lad." This is high praise as coming from the father and preceptor of John Stuart; for it is hard to conceive a metaphysical proposition which could have hopelessly puzzled John Stuart at the most tender age. Their turn for mathematics is truly wonderful. A distinguished Cambridge wrangler assured me that the youths of eighteen and twenty, whom he was engaged in teaching, rushed through the course of subjects at such a headlong speed that, if they went on at the same rate, they would be in "Lunar Theory" by the end of six months. But it is allowed with equal unanimity that, at the period when the mind of young Englishmen is in full course of development, the Hindoo appears to have already arrived at maturity, or rather effeteness, and begins to degenerate rapidly and surely. There is nothing which gives such deep discouragement to those who have the instruction and improvement of the race most at heart.

It is often said that a liberal education is valued only

as a stepping-stone to Government employ; that, as in everything else, the natives look upon it merely as a question of rupees. But this is very unfairly put. As well might you throw it in the teeth of the parents of all the boys at Harrow and Marlborough that they sent their sons to a public school in order to enable them to get their living in the liberal professions. A very respectable proportion of the Government scholars come from the homes of independent and opulent men, and would never dream of looking to official life for their maintenance. And, after all, why is it worse for a native gentleman to send his child to school, to qualify him for the office of a treasurer or deputy judge, than for an English gentleman to engage a crammer to turn his son into a walking encyclopædia against the next Indian competitive examination? But the habit of sneering at our dark fellow-subjects is so confirmed in some people, that they lose sight of sense and logic—if logic be anything else than sense—whenever the subject is introduced.

The headmaster asked Ratcliffe to examine the first class, which consisted of twelve or fifteen boys of about the same age and height as the sixth form at a public school. In everything else, however, they were sufficiently unlike the heroes of Eton and Rugby. The effeminate habits of the higher classes in Bengal had already told fatally on their physique. Slouching, flabby, spiritless, the whole lot together could not stand up to Tom Brown for a single round, and would as soon think of flying as of running a hundred yards. The members of the moneyed class in the Gangetic provinces are the most helpless, feeble set of beings in the universe.

If one of them can ride a shambling pony, daubed all over with splotches of white paint, to and from his office, without tumbling off, he considers himself to have done quite enough to establish his reputation as a horseman. Their only amusements in boyhood consist in eating immense quantities of the most sickly trash, and in flying kites—which latter pastime, in another and more popular sense, is the principal occupation of their riper years. What wonder if, long before they come of age, they have lost all trace of the pleasing features, and graceful shape which may often be observed among the younger children? The youths before us appeared to be too old for pets, since they were not attired with any remarkable elegance. "Young Bengal" has adopted a most unsightly mongrel costume, compounded of a native tunic and ludicrously tight European trousers. Bearing in mind the class at home who especially affect tight trousers, I imagined at first that "Young Bengal" was horsey; an idea which the sight of him, outside a horse, effectually dispelled. There are often gaps in the first class caused by the absence of the scholars on their frequent honeymoons. In fact, where an English boy finds it expedient to "run up to town to see the den-"tist," a young Hindoo asks for leave to go and get married.

The class was engaged on "The Deserted Village." Each scholar read a few lines, and then gave a paraphrase of them in the most grandiloquent and classical English. I sat aghast at the flowery combination of epithets which came so naturally to their lips; not knowing at the time that the natives who have been brought up at the Government schools, having learnt our language from Addison and Goldsmith, use, on all occasions, the literary English of the last century. They talk as Dr. Johnson is supposed to have talked by people who have never read Boswell, as seems to have been the case with the authors of "Rejected Ad-"dresses." The passage before us was that beginning—

"Ill fares the land to hastening ills a prey—"

an excellent sample of that mild conventional sentimental Conservatism, which to so many minds is the constituent idea of poetry; and which appeals to man in his maudlin moments throughout all ages and in every clime. There was something exquisitely absurd in hearing a parcel of young Bengalees regretting the time when every rood of ground in England maintained its man, and indignantly apostrophising trade's unfeeling train for usurping the land and dispossessing the swain. And yet, was it more truly incongruous than the notion of English boys in the latter half of the nineteenth century upbraiding the descendants of Romulus with their degeneracy and luxury; calling on them to fling into the nearest sea their gems and gold, the materials of evil; and complaining that few acres are now left for the plough; though, if that implement resembled the one described by Virgil in the first Georgic, it is, perhaps, as well that the field of its operations was limited? Ratcliffe created a general agitation by asking whether commerce was really a curse to a country. These young Baboos, destined, many of them, to pass their lives in the sharpest and most questionable mercantile practice, seemed to consider any doubt on the subject as perfect heresy; until one of them, who expressed himself in a manner more nervous and less ornate than his fellows, solved the difficulty by stating that "the poets often told lies." One youth, at the bottom of the class, on being requested for a definition of what Goldsmith meant by "unwieldy wealth," amused me much by replying, "Dazzling gawds and "plenty too much elephants." On the whole, the facility with which they used a tongue which they never hear spoken, except in school, was very creditable to the system.

The other day, a captain, in a native regiment, showed me a letter sent him by a sepoy in his company, who, having been punished for a civil offence, thought it necessary to give a plausible explanation of the matter to his officer. It had evidently been written for him by a friend who had received his education at a Government school. It appeared from this production, that the sepoy and some of his comrades took it into their heads to pay a visit to the town near which they were stationed; so they got leave for a few days, and on the evening of their arrival " set forth from our lodging and " traversed the streets with unwearied steps. By " chance, I discerned at a window a pleasing dame, from " whose eyes shot the dart of love. Not being able to " resist the dart, I approached the lattice, and courted " and wooed her as a lover should. While we were " engaged in our dalliance, there came by a banker who " had formerly been her swain. The banker, seeing his " Phyllis smiling on another, could not contain his ire, " but passed on breathing immediate vengeance." The upshot of the matter was that the injured rival brought a charge of theft against the sepoy, and, "by dint of "tortuous perjury and forensic chicanery," succeeded in getting him imprisoned for three months.

A Calcutta daily paper complained lately that native correspondents were so long-winded and verbose, that they omitted nothing that could bear upon the subject, except the point of it, and gave as a specimen a communication from one of them concerning the abuses at a school for Hindoo children. The writer begins by saying that "there is not a single soul which will not echo "back the emotions that spontaneously arise in our "breasts, when we consider the heavy chains under "which the little innocent sufferers are made to groan." He then proceeds to declare himself inadequate to the task he has undertaken, and exclaims—"Would to God "there were half a dozen Ciceros and Burkes here to "give vent to our feelings!" Half a dozen Ciceros! What an overwhelming thought! Ninety-six books of Letters to Atticus! Thirty Verrine Orations! Six De Finibi! The human faculties are too weak to seize the conception in all its immensity. Yet, who can feel the want of any amount of Ciceros or Burkes when he meets with such a sentence as the following?—"Not to "mention the damp, ill-ventilated, dismal cells, with "bare, unprotected, naked roofs, upon which the young "pupils, panting after fresh air and light, go during a "recreation hour, and plentifully enjoy the short period "of their amusement, by running and frisking in the "meridian sun, heedless and unwarned of the danger of "tumbling over into a gaping well beneath, or some "such pitfalls of death, artfully kept there for a sup- "posed good purpose." The peroration of the complaint is magnificent—"Friends and patriots!" exclaims the writer, "what shall we do when the future hopes and "glories of our nation are at stake? Where shall we "fly for a refuge, when the cries of infants groaning "under the yoke of a bondage worse than slavery haunt "us from all sides?" &c. &c. If a kindly Providence had ordained that Mr. Bellew should be born a Yankee, is not this something like the style in which he would address an audience of his countrymen on the Fourth of July?

The opium factory at Patna is an enormous mass of buildings of the most durable construction, from the roof of which there is a commanding view far up and down the Ganges. It was erected by the Dutch long before the English name became great in Bahar. There is something very interesting in the traces of the Mynheers. They seem to have preceded us everywhere by a century, and have passed away, leaving behind them monuments solid, homely, and ponderous, like themselves.

There could not be a worse month than February for a visit to the factory, for the stock of last year has by this time all been sold off, and this year's opium has not yet begun to come in. However, there was a little of the drug left at the bottom of the vats, and, fortunately for me, some chests which had been damaged on the voyage down the Ganges had been sent back to be repacked. Your studies, my dear Simkins, have for so long been directed towards the higher regions of thought, and your ideas about all material objects are so essentially vague, that I firmly believe your notion of the raw material of opium vacillates between cocoanuts and juniper-berries. I, therefore, shall not scruple

CULTIVATION OF OPIUM.

to give you a short sketch of the manufacture of that commodity, in the style of the enlightened Magnall, on whose tomb might be inscribed:—

> "Nullum fere scientiæ genus non epitomavit.
> Nullum quod epitomavit non obscuravit."

Do not wince at "epitomavit." It is an excellent word, and is used by no less an author than Treb. Poll. xxx. Tyr. It was likewise a favourite with Veg. Ren., a very nice writer, who flourished towards the close of the fourth century (A.D.).

The ryot, who answers to an uncommonly small farmer, makes an agreement with Government to furnish a certain quantity of opium at about four shillings a pound, receiving something more than a quarter of the money in advance. Now, this would be a losing game for the ryot, if it were not for the peculiarity of the crop—most of the labour being done by the women and children of the household, who would be otherwise unemployed. As it is, the natives consider it a privilege to be allowed to grow opium. At the proper season, the whole family turn out in the evening, armed with a species of three-pronged knife, and make an incision in each of the poppy-heads which have sufficiently ripened. During the night a juice exudes, which is carefully scraped off and preserved. This is repeated three times with each flower. Then the leaves are gathered up and formed into a sort of cake, for a purpose which shall be hereafter described, and the stalks are stacked and put by; no part of the poppy being without its use. The whole produce is then delivered in to the factory at Patna or Benares.

Here the opium goes through a series of processes which may generally be described by the epithet "refining." At any rate the result of them is that quantities of scum and dregs are separated from the more valuable portion, though even this refuse has a considerable value of its own. Who has not experienced the distress of being forced to trace an article throughout all the stages of fermenting, and precipitating, and puddling? In the eyes of the visitor every operation bears a hideous resemblance to every other. In all he gazes upon a mysterious liquid, lying apparently in a perfectly quiescent state far down in a frightful iron tank, over which he walks trembling on a single sloppy plank, preceded by a foreman of oppressive intelligence, and followed by two of the hands, who attend partly as an excuse for leaving their work, and partly from a faint hazy instinct of beer looming in the future. After the opium has been duly prepared comes the operation of making it into balls. The workman who is employed on this duty is seated at a board, and is provided with the materials for each ball separately—a fixed quantity of the precious drug, some refuse opium, and a certain portion of the coagulated mass of poppy-leaves, all measured out with scrupulous care. With the leaves he forms a bowl about three-quarters of an inch in thickness, using the refuse copiously as glue. In the cup thus fashioned he places the opium, and finishes off the ball with wonderful skill and celerity, consuming exactly the regulation amount of his materials. The balls are about the size of a man's head, and are sold by the Government at an average rate of seventy-six shillings each. They are packed by forties in a chest, the dried stalks of the poppy, reduced almost to powder, being poured into all the interstices, and are sent down to Calcutta to be disposed of by public auction; whence they go forth upon their mission of soothing John Chinaman into a temporary forgetfulness of the rebels who plunder him, and of the Anglo-Chinese force which protects him; and deluding his soul with visions of a Paradise where the puppy-dogs and rats run about ready-roasted; where the birds' nests are all edible, and the pigs all die a natural death; where the men have all short names and the women all short feet; where everybody has just succeeded in the competitive examination for the governorship of a province, and has a right to order everybody else three hundred strokes of the bamboo on his bare soles.

What a book might be made of " The Confessions " of an English Opium Agent!" It is the most romantic of manufactures. Everywhere the drowsy scent of the poppy prevails, and lulls the pleased visitor into a delightful consciousness of oriental languor and boundless profits, and into a sweet oblivion of the principles of competition and Free Trade. That little lump of black putty, which was bought a few days ago at forty pence, beneath the magic touch of the Government becomes an equivalent for a bouncing sovereign. What is this alchemy which can turn silver into gold? which can extract yearly six millions net from the pockets of an alien, often a hostile, nation? Regard with awe those dark sticky globes, lying so snugly in their bed of kindred straw! These are the cannon-balls with which to extract tribute from the stranger! " Such an " immoral traffic," say you? Let us get out of this sleepy lotus-eating atmosphere, and we will talk the question over at leisure.

If a practice is pernicious to the community, it is clearly the duty of a wise government to suppress it, with this condition—that the evils consequent on the suppression, or attempt at suppression, are not so great as to outweigh the benefits. When the English nation had been thoroughly convinced that slavery was a curse which must be got rid of at any risk, it cheerfully paid down as the price of its abolition twenty millions in cash, and the prosperity of our West Indian Colonies for many years to come. Never was money better laid out. We gave the devil such a beating as he had not got since Luther's first campaign, for one-tenth of what it cost us to lose America, and one-fiftieth of what we spent in avenging the execution of Louis the Sixteenth. On the other hand, though few people will deny that we should be better without the institution known as the " social evil" *par excellence,* still fewer are prepared to admit that affairs would be mended by the interference of the strong hand of power. Nothing could be more odious than that Government should meddle in matters which a wise father leaves to the conscience and discretion of his sons. The public scandal, the invasion of private liberty, the violation of houses, would be grievances far exceeding in importance any little success which might be gained for the cause of morality. Heaven preserve the streets of Liverpool and York from the condition of Oxford or Cambridge on the night of a grand Proctorial raid !

Gambling affords an instance in which the Government has wisely interfered, and wisely abstained from interference. It is impossible to put down the vice, or even to define it. What spectacle can be more innocent and touching than that of four subalterns sitting over a rubber at rupee points? And yet two files of privates playing for the same stakes would justly be considered gamblers of the deepest dye. Backgammon for sixpence a game is gambling among schoolboys. At the University it would be a recreation to which even the recital of the mistakes made by a freshman would be more preferable, to use the strongest comparative in existence. The only chance of getting at private gambling would be in an unlimited employment of spies, in the guise of club-waiters, billiard-markers, college-gyps, messmen, butlers, grooms, and barmaids. What Government could do, it did thoroughly. It forbade public gaming-tables. It prohibited individuals or Companies from making it their profession to play for money with any comer. The consequences were just what would naturally result from so judicious a course of conduct. Public feeling, not being shocked by any undue restraint upon opinion or practice, rejoiced to see hells stormed by the police, green-baize tables smashed, and foreign noblemen, with doubtful linen and patriotic opinions, turning the crank instead of the roulette-wheel, and reduced from picking aces out of their sleeves in St. James's Street to performing the same office by oakum at Brixton. The effect upon private habits was far wider and more lasting than could have been produced by a direct prohibition. High play became disreputable. Whist succeeded to hazard, and billiards to rouge-et-noir. Great Whig statesmen no longer came home to Herodotus after losing thirty thousand pounds, but read

Ricardo and Bentham without any such inauspicious preliminary to their studies.

In dealing practically with this class of questions, it should never be forgotten that no greater injury can be inflicted on society than the creation of a crime. Every prohibitory law makes so many new offenders. The exigencies of the public service absolutely require that a sum should be paid by the owner of certain goods at their entrance into the country. Henceforward, whoever introduces those goods without paying the dues becomes at once a criminal. He is a smuggler. He has broken the law, and is likely to turn at short notice into a pirate or a murderer. It is an old saying that poaching is halfway to sheep-stealing. There is a far more common phase of this portentous evil, which has not been noticed as it deserves. In almost all good books, so-called "sabbath-breaking" is classed in the same list as debauchery, drunkenness, and such like. A shop-boy who prefers the cricket-ground to a dull sermon, an overworked artizan who finds Hampstead Heath, or St. George's Hill a pleasanter resort on a July Sunday than Spitalfields or Drury Lane, feels a painful consciousness that he is committing what is denounced in nine tracts out of ten to be a sin, which must be repented of before the sinner can have any part in Him who said the Sabbath was made for man, and not man for the Sabbath. Poor fellow! He is not strong-minded enough or enlightened enough to claim his privilege as a Christian not to be judged with reference to New Moons or the Sabbath-day. He knows that every condemned felon, after having partaken (why do condemned felons always partake?) of his last mutton-chop and his penultimate cup of coffee, at the urgent importunity of the chaplain, confesses that Sabbath-breaking was his first step to the gallows.

If, then, any commodity in general use is undoubtedly deleterious, the Government is justified in putting a stop to the manufacture and sale of it. But if the circumstances of the case prevent the adoption of this course, then by all means tax that commodity as heavily as it will bear—that is to say, up to the point at which smuggling would be so lucrative as to offer an irresistible temptation. The most devoted lover of paradox would not dare to assert that a heavy tax has no tendency to check consumption. Who can doubt that, if the farmers of Devonshire and Sussex were allowed to grow tobacco, if Cavendish and Birdseye were imported at a registration duty of a farthing a pound, nine-tenths of the population of our isles would be blowing a cloud from morning till dewy eve ? Those, then, would smoke who never smoked before, and those who once did smoke would soon be well on their way to *delirium tremens.* In vain would Dean Close warn the men of " merry Carlisle," whom he certainly never leaves long without an excuse for merriment, not to make their mouth a furnace and their nose a chimney. Did it ever occur to you how very absurd is the employment of this rhetorical style in the discussion of questions purely physical ? When a man talks about my making my mouth a furnace, I always ask him why he makes his body a sewer. It is not too much to assert that, by taxing opium to the extent of six hundred per cent. on the prime cost, we diminish the use of it to one-tenth of what it would be if the drug were free. Do away with the monopoly in Bengal and Bahar, remove the transit duty on opium grown in the Native States, and, for every Chinese who is now insensible for a few hours three times a week, five will be in state of coma all day long: the whole nation will become one vast De Quincey; every one will neglect his work and loathe his food; the plumpest pug-dogs will wander along the streets of Canton with impunity; and the most measly porker will die unheeded at the very door within which, oblivious of his posthumous charms, the smoker is dreaming and inhaling away his appetite and health, his manliness and intellect. No one can logically assert that it is immoral to tax opium, unless he is prepared to maintain that we can, and should, put down with a strong hand the cultivation of the poppy.

Some say that it is criminal in the Government to recognise the vice. But taxing is not the same as recognising, and recognising is not the same as approving. There is an excise on brandy, and not on butcher's meat. Does this imply that the Cabinet recognises the fact of Britons being groggy, while it refuses to take cognizance of their carnivorous propensities? It is certainly a new and somewhat startling doctrine that taxation is a form of encouragement, that protection is afforded to a traffic by loading it with a strapping duty. If this be really the case, the two great English parties must change names. Free-traders must go about in top-boots and spacious waistcoats, and Protectionists must rush to the poll under the banner of the Big Loaf. Are we to give up six millions of income, and consent to demoralise the whole East, by allowing it to buy opium dirt cheap, in order that we may appear to ignore as a nation a practice the existence of which is patent to every individual? The colonel of a regiment once remonstrated with his chaplain, because he did not attend the hospital with due regularity. The clergyman answered that, whenever he went there, the only patients he found were men suffering from diseases engendered by drink and licentiousness, and that he did not choose to recognise those sins. And yet the sins in question continued to prevail in the cantonment, however much the worthy man averted his countenance. Happily Lord Stanley and Sir Charles Wood do not reason like this chaplain.

By this time, my Simkins, you must have had opium enough to send you asleep; so no more at present.

Sincerely yours,

H. Broughton.

LETTER IV.

A STORY OF THE GREAT MUTINY.

MOFUSSILPORE, *Feb.* 17.

DEAR SIMKINS,—Before leaving Patna I ran over to Arrah, and spent an evening and morning in visiting the scene of the most complete episode of the great troubles. The collector entertained me very hospitably, and I passed the night in "The House" in a more unbroken repose than others of my countrymen have enjoyed in the same room. I was rather ashamed of having slept so well. Would a Spartan have slumbered soundly on the tomb of the Three Hundred?—or a Roman, think you, beneath what Niebuhr does not believe to be the sepulchre of the Horatii, with no thought "on those strong limbs" which, according to that acute and able scholar, do not "moulder deep "below"? For Arrah is emphatically the Thermopylæ of our race—hallowed, no less than those world-famed straits, by superhuman courage and by memorable disaster.

All the associations there are concentrated within a small well-defined locality, which vastly increases the emotion that they excite. It is this, even more than the importance of the conflict, which draws so many tourists to Hougoumont. There is the farm-yard gate which the assailants forced open, and which four English officers and a sergeant shut in their faces by dint of hard shoving. There is the chapel half consumed by fire, and the crucifix with charred feet, and the loopholed brick wall which the French were said to have mistaken for a line of red-coats. Who—who, at least, with the exception of Sir Archibald Alison, cares to inspect the boundless flat expanse round Leipsic, where, for three autumn days, four hundred thousand combatants disputed the fate of Europe over a space of a hundred square miles? The interest of a battle does not depend on the number of squadrons and battalions engaged, nor on the extent of territory for which they contend, nor on the rank and power of the leaders, nor on the amount of the butcher's bill at the end of the day. We look to the character and worth of the individual actors, not to the breadth of the stage front and the multitude of supernumeraries. Naseby and Sedgemoor are to Borodino and Wagram what Fechter's Hamlet is to a play got up by Charles Kean, in whose eyes the main point of "Henry the Fifth" is the triumphal entry into the City, and the most important incident in "A Winter's Tale" a Pyrrhic dance which has no existence in the original. History takes small account of the millions of Assyrians, Egyptians, Medes, Huns, and Tartars, who have been driven as sheep to the slaughter to realize the *idée* of a despot, or have perished in obscure barbaric forays. But she will not soon forget those hundred and ninety-two citizens who, on the plain of Marathon, cheerfully laid down their lives for the city of the Violet Crown; those simple Dutchmen who died amidst the slush of their beloved dykes in many an amphibious struggle against Spanish tyranny and orthodoxy; those chivalrous mountaineers who flung themselves on the bayonets at Culloden in a cause which appealed to everything most romantic and irrational in our nature. To my mind there is no military operation on record which comes up to the retreat of Socrates from the defeat of the Athenian army at Delium. A sturdy, clumsy-built, common-looking man, with bare feet, walking off at a brisk, steady pace, spear on shoulder, turning up his snub-nose, and looking askance at the mingled mass of fugitives and pursuers which swept by on either side, engaged all the while in a discussion on the principle of evil with a fellow-citizen, who submitted to be bored for the sake of the protection of so intrepid a veteran. Then up rides Alcibiades, the ladies' pet, the darling of the popular assembly, covered with dust and blood, and without his helmet, and cries, "Cheer up, Socrates; for I will see "you safe home." A needless promise, because, in his own words, "the bearing of the man made it pretty "plain to all, far and near, that whoever meddled with "him would have reason to repent it."

Arrah lies twelve miles from the Ganges, between Patna and Buxar, which are both on the same river. To the eastward the Sone, which is in April a streak of water creeping through a wide desert of sand, and in July a torrent a mile broad and thirty feet deep, flows into the main stream at a distance of four leagues from Arrah and about five from Dinapore, which, as you doubtless remember, is the military station at Patna. The compounds of the European houses at Arrah are very extensive; and the most extensive of all is that in

THE HOUSE.

which stands the residence of the Collector. It is, as far as I can judge from recollection, four hundred yards long by three hundred broad. It is bounded in most parts by a crumbling ditch and the remains of a hedge of prickly pear. The Collector's house is large and commodious, with spacious, very lofty rooms; one-storied, like all dwellings in the Mofussil, but with the floor raised several feet above the level of the ground. On one side of the house is a portico; exactly forty yards from which stands a small whitewashed building, the basement of which consists of cellars, with open arches some four or five feet in height. A staircase in the interior leads to a single room, surrounded on three sides by a verandah. The dead wall faces the Collector's garden, which is thirty or forty yards off. It was formerly a billiard-room, and is now used for the accommodation of visitors when the great bungalow happens to be full. The house-top is reached by a ladder, and is surrounded by a parapet; but it is entirely commanded by the roof of the neighbouring building, from which the porch stands out like a bastion.

In the summer of 1857 there were stationed at Dinapore three regiments of native infantry—a force of at least twenty-five hundred bayonets. The composition of this brigade was such as to give grave cause for alarm. The men were all drawn from the notorious turbulent district of Shahabad, of which Arrah is the official capital, and were united by the bond of an undefined allegiance to Coer Sing, who was recognised as chieftain by the Rajpoots, or soldier caste, of that region. There is a strong family feeling in the native mind. Your head-servant fills your house with young barbarians from his own village, whom he brings up to Calcutta to try their luck in service. As soon as a Government *employé* is in receipt of a good income, relations and connexions pour in from all parts of India, and claim to live at his expense. In the same manner the old sepoys introduced into their company sons, nephews, and younger brothers; while any recruit who did not belong to the tribe was made almost as uncomfortable as a cockney in a crack Light Cavalry mess, and soon found it expedient to ask leave to change his quarters. The result was that the regiment had a tendency to turn into a clan, the members of which regarded each other with attachment and confidence, and carried out their common resolves with singular unanimity and secrecy.

The state of things at Dinapore excited profound uneasiness. For weeks previous to the catastrophe, letters appeared in the Calcutta daily papers urging the authorities to take measures to prevent an outbreak, which was regarded as now imminent. Unhappily, the brigadier in command at the station was one of that class known at the Horse-Guards as experienced officers of long standing in the service, and by the world in general as old women. It is our misfortune that the commencement of every war finds our choicest troops and our most precious strongholds at the disposal of men who won their first laurels at Salamanca or Quatre Bras, and who should have been content to have closed their career at Sobraon. It is a fact of serious import that the introduction of the rifle, the greatest military revolution of this century, was sulkily, peevishly, hysterically opposed by the majority of those who, in the

HOW NOT TO DO IT.

event of war, would have been at the head of our armies. The veterans of the Senior United Service Club might have sung if their feelings had allowed them—

> "Believe me, if that most endearing old arm,
>   Which we miss with so fondly to-day,
> Which never did Afghan or Sikh any harm,
>   Was to shoot straight for once in a way,
> It should still be the weapon for Guardsmen and Line,
>   Let the windage increase as it will;
> And we'd think the performance sufficiently fine,
>   If one ball in five hundred should kill."

Such a chief, to the cost of humanity, was in charge of Meerut on that day of evil omen, the first of many such, when the troopers of the Third Light Cavalry, having shot down their officers and burnt their barracks, galloped off unmolested to cut the throats of the English at Delhi. Such a chief was *not* in charge of Barrackpore at the crisis when foresight, calmness, and judicious severity broke up a battalion of murderous scoundrels, and saved the capital of India from the fate of Cawnpore. Hearsey at Meerut, Neill at Dinapore, and Outram at Allahabad, might have saved much of the good blood that was spilled, and much of the bad blood that remains.

Throughout July the insolence of the sepoys in the Dinapore cantonments, and the terror and discomfort of the European residents, waxed greater daily. At length the symptoms of sedition grew so unmistakable as to attract the notice of General Lloyd himself. Accordingly, on the morning of the 25th, he issued an order, enjoining the sepoys to return their percussion-caps at four o'clock that afternoon. This gave them just nine hours to pack up their clothes, ammunition, and wives, cook their rice, and get a wash, and march out of the station at their ease, in the direction of the Sone. When they had gone a mile or two on their way, a few round shots were sent after them, as a parting compliment, and then the General had plenty of leisure to sit down and reflect on the probable result of his masterly combinations.

Meanwhile the little community at Arrah did not regard with indifference the prospect of an event which caused so much apprehension at Calcutta. Those long July days could hardly have been to them a period of secure enjoyment. It was much if they could put force on themselves to get through their ordinary business. The women and children were sent to what, in those awful times, was considered a place of comparative security. Whatever might chance, at any rate, when the peril did come, the men should have to make provision for nothing that could be dearer than honour and duty. At that time the portion of the East Indian Railway in the neighbourhood was in course of construction—the embankment having been already thrown up, though the bridges were not yet completed. Mr. Boyle, the executive engineer of the company, resident at the station, happened to have a natural turn for fortification, which he subsequently had ample opportunity to gratify. This gentleman took it into his head to put what is now the Collector's outhouse in a state for defence, thinking that it might come in useful on an emergency. From time to time he sent in some bricks and mortar, and a few odd coolies, and devoted a spare hour or two to superintend the work. The arches of the cellars were solidly built up, and a thin curtain of brickwork erected between each pillar in the verandah on the first floor, with a judicious arrangement of loopholes.

On Saturday, the 25th of July, Mr. Wake, the Collector, received an express from Dinapore, bidding him to be on his guard, for that something was in the air. There followed a night of suspense, which was changed into terrible certainty by the arrival of a mounted patrol, who came in with the information that a strong force of sepoys had crossed the Sone, and that large numbers were still crossing. Then it became too evident that "some one had blundered." The moment had come when a resolution must be taken—hurried, but irrevocable. A few hours more, and the enemy would be upon them; the country-people in arms, the roads impassable, and the bridges broken up for thirty miles round. While their communications were still open, should they retreat on Buxar, and wait there till they could be brought back to their posts by the returning tide of European re-conquest? It was too late to avert the destruction of their property; too late to keep the town to its allegiance, and save the treasure and the public records. There was nothing which they could stow behind their slender defences—save the empty name of British rule. Was it worth while to run so frightful a risk for a shadow? Why, for an advantage so doubtful, expose their dear ones to anxiety worse than death—to bereavement and desertion in such a time and in such a plight? On the other hand, should they skulk off like outlaws through the province which had been entrusted to their care—where but yesterday their will was law—leaving the district ready to receive the rebels with open arms, and afford them a firm foothold on the South of the Ganges—another Oude, whence they might securely direct their future efforts against our power, which already tottered to the fall? If the rest of Shahabad must go—the authority of old England and of John Company—the most generous of masters—should be upheld, at least, within the walls of one billiard-room, which was to witness such a game as never did billard-room yet; a game at hopeless odds, amateurs opposed to professionals, fair play to knavery; a game where history stood by as marker, and where no starring could recover a life once taken; a game which one losing hazard would undo, one cannon almost inevitably ruin; but which Wake and his fellows, as with clear eyes, brave hearts, and steady hands, they awaited the opening stroke, were fully determined should not be a love game.

There was no time to be lost. Rice and flour sufficing for a few days' consumption, and what other provisions came first to hand, were quickly stored in the house. The supply of water which could be collected on such short notice, was alarmingly scanty. And then they made haste to enter their ark, before the flood of sedition and anarchy should engulph everything around. The garrison consisted of Herwald Wake, the Collector; young Colvin, and two other civilians; Boyle, the engineer, the Vauban of the siege; Mr. Hall, a civil surgeon; an official in the opium agency, and his assistant; a Government schoolmaster; two native public *employés*, and five other Europeans in various subordinate grades; forty-five privates, two Naiks, two Havildars, and one Jemmadar—names which so pain-

THE GARRISON.

fully bewilder an English reader of the list of killed and wounded in the Gazette after an Indian victory—true Sikhs all, staunch as steel, and worthy to be the countrymen of the heroes of Chilianwallah. Six-and-sixty fighting men by tale, with no lack of pluck and powder, but very badly off for meat and drink.

On Monday morning the sepoys poured into the town, and marched straight to the Treasury, from which they took 85,000 rupees in cash. After this indispensable preliminary, they proceeded to carry out the next step in the programme usual on these occasions—the slaughter of every one connected with the Government. It was very thoughtful of the Sahibs to have collected in one place, so as to spare Jack Sepoy the trouble of hunting them down in detail. It was best, however, to do the job in style; so a strong detachment was formed in column, and marched into the compound with drums beating and colours flying. It would give the men a good appetite for their curry to knock the dozen or so of quill-drivers and railway people on the head in the hole where they had taken refuge; and, if those unlucky Punjabees could not see on which side their chupatties were buttered, why, it should be the worse for them! But through every loophole in the brickwork on the first floor peered an angry Englishman, feeling at the trigger of his bone-crushing rifle, behind which he had stood the charge of many a tiger and buffalo—unless, indeed, he was one of the school of sportsmen who prefer a smooth-bore for anything under eighty yards; while in the cellars below, and beneath the breastwork on the roof, lurked half a hundred warriors of that valiant sect whom no other native army could look in the face. Just as the leading ranks were passing a fine tree, which grows a stone-throw from the house, they received a volley which laid eighteen of their number dead on the spot. As this made it evident that the Sahibs intended to die game, the mutineers, who had come out for a battue, and not on a storming-party, broke line, and dispersed behind the trees scattered about the compound, whence they kept up a desultory fire.

For long past Coer Sing had been watching the course of events with keen interest and a very definite purpose. This remarkable man came in for an abundant share of the abuse so indiscriminately dealt out to all who took part against us at that crisis. Coer Sing was described in the contemporary journals as a " devil," whose villany could be accounted for only on the theory that he was not " of human flesh and blood." The time for shrieking and scolding has now gone by, and we can afford to own that he was not a devil at all, but the high-souled chief of a warlike tribe, who had been reduced to a nonentity by the yoke of a foreign invader. " What am I good for under your dynasty ? " was his constant complaint to European visitors. He had already reached an age which in England is supposed to incapacitate for any employment short of the premiership. He well remembered the time when Scindiah and Holkar were not mere puppets of the Government of Fort William ; when the Mahratta still ruled at Poonah and Nagpore ; when, what with Pindaree raids, and the long contest for the Helen of Odipore, and the extremely bellicose attitude of non-interference adopted by the Company, a dashing partizan leader, with a few thousand stout Rajpoots at his back, was good for a great deal in

AN HINDOO DUNDEE.

the estimation of Central India. He fretted, like the proud Highland chiefs, when reduced to insignificance by the severe and orderly sway of the Southron. Surely, a people whose favourite heroes are Lochiel and Rob Roy Macgregor may spare a little sympathy for the chieftain who, at eighty years old, bade fill up his brass lotah, saddle his elephants, and call out his men, inasmuch as it was up with the pugrees of Coer Sing; who inflicted on us a disaster most complete and tragical; who exacted from the unruly mutineers an obedience which they paid to none other; who led his force in person to Lucknow, and took a leading part in the struggle which decided the destinies of India; who, after no hope was left for the cause North of Ganges, did not lose heart, but kept his men together during a long and arduous retreat in the face of a victorious enemy; and, as the closing act of his life, by a masterly manœuvre baffled his pursuers, and placed his troops in safety on their own side of the great river, when friend and foe alike believed their destruction to be inevitable. On that occasion a round-shot from an English gun smashed his arm, as he was directing the passage of the last boatfuls of his followers, contrary to the habit of Eastern generals, who ordinarily shun the post of danger. The old warrior, seeing that his last hour was come, is said to have cut off his shattered limb with the hand that remained to him, and to have died of the loss of blood which ensued. But his army had not lost the impress of his skill and energy. During several months they maintained themselves at Juggdeespore, harassing with daily incursions the English garrison at Arrah, whose head-quarters were in a fortification laid out by the recently-developed genius of Mr. Boyle; they repulsed with heavy loss a detachment sent to dislodge them; and finally laid down their arms under the general amnesty, after having defied our Government during more than a year of continuous fighting. Two facts may be deduced from the story of these operations—first, that the besiegers of the house at Arrah were neither cowards nor bunglers; and next, that it was uncommonly lucky for us that Coer Sing was not forty years younger.

Such, then, was the man who now claimed to take command of the levies of Shahabad by hereditary right. He brought with him a mighty following, and recruits poured in by hundreds and thousands daily. The sepoy veterans, who were living on pensions in their native villages, came forward to share the fortunes of their ancient regiments in greater number than in other districts. "That old fool, Coer Sing," was reported in the Calcutta papers to have held a review of eight thousand armed men, besides the three regular battalions. There was one cry throughout the province—that now or never was the time to shake off the oppression of the stranger. When once they had put to the sword the Sahibs in the billiard-room, all would go well. But the Sahibs in question manifested a very decided disinclination to be put to the sword, so that it became necessary to put the sword to the Sahibs. The siege was pressed forward with vigour. Bullets rained on the defences night and day alike. The sepoys bawled out to our Sikhs that, if they would betray the Sahibs, they should receive a safe-conduct and five hundred rupees apiece. The Sikhs, in return, requested them to

ANXIETY.

come nearer and repeat their liberal offers—a compliance with which invitation resulted in the unfortunate agents of Coer Sing finding that, when they approached within earshot, they were within musket-shot as well.

Meanwhile, the most painful solicitude, which was fast deepening into despair, prevailed at Dinapore and Calcutta, and wherever else the tidings of the great peril of our countrymen had penetrated. The first intelligence received at the capital was conveyed in a letter which appeared in the *Englishman*, dated the 27th of July, containing these words: "Mr. Boyle "and the magistrate sent me a message to find a safe "place. The Arrah people proposed to defend Mr. "Boyle's fortification. If they have done so, I hope for "the best, but dread the worst. What can a handful "of Englishmen do with hundreds of lawless soldiers?" A correspondent writes on the 29th: "We have no "news as to the English cooped up in Mr. Boyle's "fortification, whether they are in existence or not." And again: "God knows what the fate of the unfortunate people at Arrah has been." Towards the middle of the week it was determined at Dinapore to make an effort to raise the siege. An expedition started, consisting of nearly three hundred and fifty men of the 37th Queen's regiment, sixty Sikhs, and some young civilians who volunteered to accompany the party. Unfortunately, Captain Dunbar, the officer appointed to the command, was quite unfit for such a duty, his military experience having been gained in a paymaster's bureau. The force was put on board a steamer, and sent up the Ganges. It was the height of the rainy season, and much of the country was under water.

Accordingly, on arriving nearly opposite Arrah, the troops left the steamer, and embarked in some large boats, in which they followed the course of a nullah, which brought them some miles nearer their point. By the time they were landed, evening had already closed in. The officers present, who knew something of night service, importuned their leader to bivouac on a bridge at some distance from Arrah, to give the soldiers their rum and biscuit, with a few hours' sleep, and then march in at daybreak. They urged on him the extreme danger of taking a small party of tired men in the dark through an unknown region swarming with foes who were thoroughly prepared for their reception. The answer was: "No. They expect us at Arrah, and "I shall not think of halting till we get there." This was a reason which it was hard for Englishmen to gainsay. So the order was given to move on, and the men threw their firelocks over their shoulders, and set off on the march, the Sikhs forming the advance-guard. Almost incredible to relate, Captain Dunbar had not sufficient foresight to throw out flankers. It never seems to have occurred to him that a march at midnight through three miles of bazaar and mud-wall, grove and garden, to the relief of a place beleaguered by ten thousand armed men, had need to be conducted with any greater caution than a change of quarters from Calcutta to Dum Dum.

A short league from the Arrah Collectorate, on the right hand of a man travelling towards the town, stands a large Hindoo temple, in grounds of its own. Just before reaching this point, the way, which has hitherto passed through open fields of rice and poppy, runs for

THE CONSEQUENCE. 79

some three hundred yards between belts of trees about fifty feet in width. The road lies along an embankment raised considerably above the level of the surrounding country. The Sikhs had already passed, and the straggling array of English soldiers were plodding along the defile, half asleep, with weary legs and empty stomachs, when the darkness of the grove on either side was lit up as by magic, and a crashing fire poured into their ranks. Exposed on the top of the causeway, their bodies standing out against what dim starlight there was, they afforded an easy mark to their invisible enemies, who swarmed in the gloom below. During the first minutes many were struck down, and at that short range there were few wounds which did not bring death. Then, by a sort of instinct, the men deserted the road, and collected in groups wherever they could find cover. One large party took refuge in a dry tank, beneath the banks of which they loaded and discharged their pieces at random, as long as their ammunition lasted; while the flashes of their musketry enabled the sepoys to direct their aim with deadly accuracy. Another party occupied the temple, and throughout the night there went on constant skirmishing round the walls and in the inclosure of the garden. If the soldiers had been got together in one place, and made to lie down quietly in their ranks till the morning, they were still quite strong enough to perform the service on which they had been despatched. In spite of their heavy losses, they were quite as numerous as the force which eventually succeeded in relieving Arrah. But there was no one there of the temper of Nicholson or Hodson; no one who at such a moment dared to step forward and usurp authority in the name of the common safety. Split up into small sections, without orders from their superiors; ignorant alike of the fate of their comrades, the nature of the surrounding localities, and the number and position of their assailants; wasting their strength and powder in objectless firing, than which nothing is more sure to demoralise troops under any circumstances—in such plight our countrymen awaited the dawn of day.

Then, after a short consultation, the officers who survived got the men into some sort of order, and commenced a retreat upon the boats. But by this time the enemy, flushed with success, and increasing every minute in strength, redoubled their efforts to complete the ruin of our force. In front, in rear, on either flank hung clouds of sepoys, who kept up a withering discharge on the thin line of dispirited exhausted Englishmen. At first our soldiers replied as best they could; but soon every one began to think of providing for his own safety. Our fire slackened, ceased; the pace quickened; the ranks became unsteady; and finally the whole array broke, and fled for dear life along the road in the direction of the nullah.

Then came the scenes which have ever marked the rout of a company of civilized men by barbarian foes. Some of the fugitives were shot down as they ran. Others, disabled by wounds or fatigue, were overtaken and slain. Others again, who sought preservation by leaving the line of flight, were mobbed and knocked on the head by the peasants of the neighbouring villages. More than one unfortunate European, who, after having been pursued for miles, took to the water like a tired stag, was beaten to death with bludgeons from the brink of the pond in which he had taken refuge. All who remained on the ground in the vicinity of the temple, whether dead or alive, were hung on the trees which fringed the road. The Sikhs that day proved that they were still animated by the same spirit which had formerly extorted the respect of their conquerors in many a fierce and dubious battle in the open field. Setting shoulder to shoulder, they fought their way to the boats in unbroken order, and found that in such a strait the most honourable course is likewise the safest. Ross Mangles, a young civilian, whose father was chairman of the court of directors during that trying year, bore himself gallantly amidst the universal panic. He had joined the expedition purely out of love for Herwald Wake, and in the surprise of the preceding evening had been stunned by a bullet-wound on the forehead. His commanding appearance and cheery air now won the confidence of those immediately round him, and he succeeded in keeping together a small knot of men who supplied him with a succession of loaded rifles. As he was a noted shikaree, a dead hand at bear and antelope, the sepoys thought proper to keep their distance. Meantime he carried a wounded soldier on his back for six miles, laying him down tenderly from time to time when the enemy came too close to be pleasant. With threescore fellows of his own kidney at his side, Ross would have shaken his friend by the hand before night closed in, though Coer Sing stood in the way with all the mutineers in Bahar. The men of his term at Haileybury will long point with pride to the V.C. that follows his name in the list of the Bengal Civil Service.

On reaching the banks of the nullah, the soldiers, who had now lost presence of mind, self-respect, subordination, everything but the unbridled desire for safety, flung themselves into the water, and swam and waded to the boats, into which they crowded with all the unseemly hurry of an overpowering terror. As they struggled with the current, floundered in the mud, and scrambled over the gunwales, the sepoys plied them with shot at pistol-range, directing their especial attention to a barge which was prevented from effecting its escape by a rope twisted round the rudder. The men inside crouched at the bottom of the boat, not daring to show their heads above the bulwarks as a mark for a hundred muskets. Nothing could have averted the capture and destruction of the whole party, had not a young volunteer, Macdonell by name, climbed out over the stern, and unfastened the rope amidst a hail of bullets; an action which gave another Victoria Cross to the Civil Service.

And now all was over; and the survivors, bringing home nothing but their bare lives, returned in mournful guise, full of sad forebodings about the brave men whom they were forced to abandon to their fate. The people at Dinapore, when the steamer came in sight, as they strained their eyes to catch some indication of the result of the expedition, saw the deck covered with prostrate forms; and the dejection expressed by the air and attitude of those on board convinced them at once that all was not well. Of four hundred men who went forth, only half returned. The others were lying, stripped and mangled, along those two fatal leagues of road. Captain Dunbar, in the Pagan phrase ordinarily used on such occasions, atoned for his obstinacy with his life. When the news of this reverse reached Calcutta, there were none so sanguine as to retain any hope of deliverance for the little garrison at Arrah.

The opinion which prevailed in Calcutta certainly coincided with that of Coer Sing and his army. Throughout the night none of the defenders of the house had slept. They listened with sickening anxiety to the noise of the firing, now beguiling themselves into the idea that it was drawing nearer; now desponding, as it remained ever stationary; and again comforting each other with the theory that their countrymen had taken up a strong position in the suburbs, and would advance to their relief at break of day. Alas! they little knew what that day would bring forth. But, when morning came, and the reports of the musketry grew fainter and fainter, till they died away in the distance, their hearts sank within them. They were not long left in suspense; for the besiegers had no intention of keeping such good news to themselves, and they were speedily informed that the force from Dinapore had been cut to pieces, and that their last hope was gone. Yet not the last—for they still had the hope of dying sword in hand, instead of being tamely murdered like all who had hitherto put trust in the word of their treacherous and unforgiving Eastern foe. That foe now offered the whole party their lives, if they would give up Wake and Syed Azmoodeen Khan, the deputy-collector, a native for whom the Sahib of Sahibs, Lord William Bentinck, had entertained a great regard. This proposal having been rejected, nothing more was said about conditions of surrender, and both sides applied themselves to the serious business of the siege.

The enemy had fished out from some corner two cannon — a four-pounder, and a two-pounder — the smaller of which they placed at the angle of the bungalow facing the little house, while they hoisted the larger on to the roof. They adopted the plan of loading the gun behind the parapet, and then running it on to the top of the portico, and wheeling out an arm-chair fitted with a shot-proof screen of boards, on which sat a man who aimed and discharged the piece. It was then drawn back with ropes to be sponged out and recharged. This method of working artillery would perhaps be considered somewhat primitive at Shoeburyness or Woolwich; but, when employed against a billiard-room at a range of forty yards, the result might justly be described as a *feu d'enfer*. For some time the besieged fully expected that their walls would come tumbling down about their ears; but they soon took heart of grace, and set themselves manfully to repair the damage caused by breaching-battery, No. 1. Fortunately the store of cannon-balls was soon exhausted. The enemy eked it out by firing away the castors of Mr. Boyle's piano, of which the supply, however, was necessarily limited. Meanwhile, the sepoys had lined the garden wall, which at that time ran within twenty yards of the rear of the house. From this position their picked marksmen directed their shots at the loopholes, while from the trees around, from the ditch of the compound, from the doors and windows of the bungalow, an incessant fire was maintained throughout the twenty-four hours. If Mr. Boyle's fortification, like Jericho, could have been brought to the ground by noise, it would certainly not have stood long. The mutineers, in imitation of the besiegers of Mansoul, in Bunyan's "Holy War," seemed determined to try all the senses round, and to enter at Nose-gate if they were repulsed at Ear-gate. Poor Mr. Wake, who provided the material both for the attack and the defence, had placed his horses in an inclosure under the walls of the outhouse. These were now shot by the sepoys; and the Indian sun speedily produced effects which gave more annoyance to the garrison than the cannonade from the porch. But the contents of every knacker's cart in London might have been shot out under the verandah, without weakening the determination to resist to the last. Some ingenious natives set fire to a large heap of the raw material of red pepper on the windward quarter, with the view of smoking out the Sahibs. But a lot of genuine Qui-hyes, with their palates case-hardened by many pungent curries, were not likely to be frightened at a bonfire of chilies. Since the first day, the mutineers fought shy of any attempt to carry the place by storm: and not without reason: for, as a reserve to their trusty rifles, each Sahib had his fowling-piece, with a charge of number four shot for close quarters, lying snugly in the left-hand barrel. Then they had hog-spears, and knew how to use them. The charge of a forty-inch boar, rising well in his spring, was at least as formidable as the rush of a sepoy. They had revolvers, too, with a life in every chamber,—the weapon that is the very type of armed civilization. On the whole, the besiegers were not far wrong in regarding an attack by open force as a resource to be adopted only when all other devices had failed.

Meanwhile the temper of the people inside was as

true as the metal of their gun-locks. Englishmen are always inclined to look at the bright side of things, as long as there is a bright side at which to look; and the English spirit was well represented there. Young Colvin was especially cheerful himself, and the cause that cheerfulness was in other men. The whole party accommodated their habits to their circumstances with great good-humour. The Sikhs occupied the cellarage. The Sahibs lived and slept in the single room on the first floor, and took their meals, sitting on the stairs above and below the landing-place, on which the cloth was laid. On the wall above the hearth, Wake wrote a journal of the events of each day, in full expectation that no other record would be left of what had taken place within those devoted walls. One morning the Jemmadar reported that the water with which his men had provided themselves had all been drunk out. The Europeans offered to supply them out of their own store: but one Sikh obstinately refused to touch the same water as the Sahibs. He stoutly affirmed that he had rather die of thirst than give in to such a scandalous piece of latitudinarianism. It was not a time to disregard the whims and prejudices of any one of the gallant fellows, whom neither fear nor lucre could tempt to be false to their salt. So Natives and English together set to work to dig a well in one of the vaults, and within twelve hours they had thrown out eighteen feet of earth by four, a depth at which they found abundance of water. At the end of the week close observation convinced them that the sepoys were engaged in running a mine towards the back of the house. This justly gave them greater alarm than any other machina-

BLOCKADE.

tion of the enemy. But necessity is the mother of countermines ; and these amateur sappers soon made themselves as secure against the new peril that threatened them as their scanty means would admit.

And so they staved off destruction another day, and yet another. But a far more terrible foe than Coer Sing now broke ground before the defences. The house had been provisioned for a week, and a week had already passed. Neither rifle, nor spear, nor British courage, nor Native fidelity, would avail aught, when the rice and the flour had all been eaten. At Arrah, as at other Indian stations, where the residents know good meat from indifferent, there was an institution called a mutton-club, the sheep belonging to which were feeding about the compound under the hungry eyes of their owners. But no one could show himself for a second outside the walls and live. It might be a hundred, it might be a hundred and fifty hours, (for who could say beforehand how long human pluck and patience, when put to the test, could endure the last extreme of privation ?) but the dread moment was steadily drawing on, when death must come by famine or by the bullets of the enemy. In no direction could they discern a gleam of light. The only force that was near enough and strong enough to march to the rescue had been routed and disorganized. The English troops at Buxar were a mere handful, not numerous enough to guarantee the safety of the station. The days of miracles had gone by, and it seemed that nothing short of a miracle could deliver them. Unless it should come to pass that the angel of the Lord should go forth by night and smite the camp of the besiegers, they felt that this world, with its joys and troubles, would be all over for them ere but a few suns had set.

The English troops at Buxar certainly were a mere handful. But there was a man there who was neither a novice nor a pedant, neither a young soldier nor an old woman. Wherever hard knocks had been going within the last twenty years—and during that period there was no lack—Vincent Eyre had generally managed to come in for a liberal allowance. In the Afghan war, the roughest of schools, he had learnt to preserve an equal mind in arduous circumstances. When the intelligence of the outbreak, travelling with the proverbial speed of bad news, reached the station of Buxar, Eyre at once made up his mind to march, without waiting to hear whether an expedition had started from Dinapore. Perhaps he was unwilling to leave the fate of the garrison entirely dependent on the energy and promptness of General Lloyd. Perhaps he thought that a good thing like the relief of Arrah would bear doing twice over. His force consisted of a hundred and fifty and four English bayonets, twelve mounted volunteers, and three field-pieces, with their complement of artillerymen. The distance to be traversed was fifty miles as the crow flies; and, as the waters were out over the face of the country, and the population was in a state of open hostility, the march proved long and formidable. On the way, Eyre received tidings of the reverse sustained by Dunbar's detachment. It seemed foolhardy indeed to advance to the attack of an enemy who had just cut in pieces a force twice as strong as his own. But, according to his view of the matter, this consideration did not in any wise affect the result of his rea-

HOW TO DO IT.

soning. His axiom was that Arrah must be relieved. There was no one else now left to do the business; so of necessity it fell to him. He had not many soldiers, and would be glad to have more. He did not share the sentiment of King Henry at Agincourt. He would have been delighted to see at his back a thousand or two of those men at Aldershott who did no work that day. But, as he had only a few, he must perform the work with those few. So on he went, nothing doubting.

On the night of Sunday, the 2d of August, our force bivouacked at Googerajgunge. In the morning the enemy put in an appearance, and the march was one constant skirmish as far as Bebeegunge, where the road crosses a deep nullah. The bridge had been destroyed; and Eyre had nothing for it but to direct his course towards the railway embankment, along which he hoped to force his way to Arrah. This route, however, was barred by a wood, in and about which was drawn up Coer Sing's whole force—two thousand five hundred mutineers, and the *posse comitatus* of the province, estimated at eight thousand men. The rebels, whom their recent success had inspired with unwonted confidence, did not wait to be attacked. The sepoy bugles sounded the "Assembly," then the "Advance," and finally the "Double;" and their battalions, in columns of companies, charged our guns in front, but were driven back several times with great slaughter. Then they tried a surer game, and endeavoured to crush our line with a heavy point-blank musketry fire. "And "now," said Major Eyre, "we had as much on our own "hands as we could manage." Large numbers of the enemy stole round under cover of the trees, and raked our whole array from either flank. The men began to fall fast; and, in an army of nine or ten score combatants, men cannot fall fast for many minutes together without serious consequences. Our troops began to be disheartened, and to be painfully aware of the overwhelming odds against which they were contending. It was trying work receiving twenty bullets for every one they fired. At such a moment the man of sterling stuff feels that things cannot go well, unless he personally exerts himself to the utmost. It is this state of mind that wins foot-ball matches, and boat-races, and battles. Now or never, was the word. The order was given, and our officers ran forward, sword in hand, towards the point where the enemy stood thickest, with the men shouting at their heels. This appeared to the sepoys a most unaccountable proceeding; but they were not ignorant of the great military truth that "when two hostile parties " find themselves on the same ground one or the other " must leave it;" and, as our people kept coming nearer and nearer with the expression on their faces which the Sahibs always wear when they don't intend to turn back, they had no choice but to run for it. That charge saved Arrah. When once natives have given way, it is almost impossible to bring them again to the scratch. Coer Sing retreated, leaving on the ground six hundred of his followers, most of whom had been killed in the attack upon the battery; and our poor little force, which he had expected to devour at a single mouthful, gathered together the wounded, limbered up the guns, and with lightened hearts pressed forward on its mission of deliverance.

When the garrison looked out of their loopholes at

dawn, on the 3d, they were surprised at seeing none of the besiegers stirring in the neighbourhood. As they were not the men to wait tamely for what might befall them without doing something to help themselves, they sallied forth and took this opportunity to get some fresh air and replenish their larder. After a hard chase about the compound, they succeeded in capturing four sheep, which they brought back into the house amidst great rejoicing, together with one of the enemy's cannon. Presently the boom of guns was heard in the distance, and excited a strange hope which, but just now, they expected never again to experience. Towards evening the beaten rebels poured into the town in dire confusion. They stayed only to collect their plunder—in the sense in which the word is employed both by a Yankee and an Englishman—and marched off, bag and baggage, never more to visit Arrah, with the exception of a few who returned from time to time in order to be present at their own execution. On the morning of Tuesday, the 4th of August, there was not a sepoy within miles of the station. And then our countrymen came forth, unwashed, unshaved, begrimed with dust and powder, haggard with anxiety and want of sleep, but very joyous and thankful at heart: pleased to stand once more beneath the open sky, and to roam fearlessly through their old haunts, in which the twittering of birds and the chirping of grasshoppers had succeeded to the ceaseless din of musketry; pleased with the first long draught of sherry and soda-water, and with the cool breath of dawn after the atmosphere of a vault, without window or punkah, filled to suffocation with the smoke of their rifles. With what fervour must they have offered their tribute of praise and gratitude to Almighty God—not for having smitten Amalek, and discomfited Moab; not for having overthrown their enemies, and dashed in pieces those that rose up against them; not for having abated the pride of Coer Sing, assuaged his malice, and confounded his devices—but because, in His mercy, He so decreed, and in His wisdom so arranged the order of the world, that civilization should prevail over brute force, fair dealing over treachery, and manly valour over sneaking cruelty, that so all things might work together for our good and His honour!

There are moments when an oppressive sense of Nineteenth Century weighs heavy on the soul; when we shudder to hear Mr. Cobden pronounce that one number of the *Times* newspaper is worth the eight books of Thucydides. There are moments when we feel that locomotives and power-looms are not everything; that black care sits behind the stoker; that death knocks with equal foot at the door of the Turkey Red Yarn Establishment. Then it is good to turn from the perusal of the share-list; from pensive reflections on the steadiness of piece-goods, the languor of gunny-cloths, and the want of animation evinced by mule-twist, to the contemplation of qualities which are recognised and valued by all ages alike. It is good to know that trade, and luxury, and the march of science, have not unnerved our wrists, and dulled our eyes, and turned our blood to water. There is much in common between Leonidas dressing his hair before he went forth to his last fight, and Colvin laughing over his rice and salt while the bullets pattered on the wall like hail.

Still, as in the days of old Homer, " Cowards gain
" neither honour nor safety; but men who respect them-
" selves and each other for the most part go through the
" battle unharmed." Still, as in Londonderry of old,
the real strength of a besieged place consists not in the
scientific construction of the defences, nor in the multitude of the garrison, nor in abundant stores of provision and ordnance, but in the spirit which is prepared
to dare all, and endure all, sooner than allow the
assailants to set foot within the wall. Though but six
years have passed away, the associations of the events
which I have related begin to grow dim. So changeable
are the elements of Anglo-Indian society that not one
of the defenders of the fortification is now resident at
the station. Already the wall, on which Wake wrote
the diary of the siege, has been whitewashed; and the
inclosure, where the dead horses lay through those
August days, has been destroyed; and a party-wall has
been built over the mouth of the well in the cellars;
and the garden-fence, which served the mutineers as a
first parallel, has been moved twenty yards back. Half
a century more, and every vestige of the struggle may
have been swept away. But, as long as Englishmen
love to hear of fidelity, and constancy, and courage
bearing up the day against frightful odds, there is no
fear lest they forget the name of " the little house
" at Arrah."

Yours very truly,

H. Broughton.

LETTER V.

A JOURNEY, A GRAND TUMASHA, AND THE TRUTH ABOUT THE CIVIL SERVICE CAREER.

CALCUTTA, *March* 12.

DEAR SIMKINS,—I have lately witnessed some phases of life in India which have little in common with Calcutta grandeur and civilization. To begin with the travelling: I spent sixteen hours on the four hundred miles between the capital and Patna, and seventeen hours on the forty odd miles between Patna and Mofussilpore. And uncommonly odd ones they were. I started at ten P.M. on the 9th of last month in the time-honoured palanquin. My suite comprised sixteen bearers, two fellows with torches and four banghy-wallahs, who convey luggage in something resembling the received idea of the Scales in the zodiac. The performances of these thin-legged, miserable, rice-fed "missing links" are perfectly inexplicable according to our notions of muscular development. Four picked readers of Kingsley would find it hard work to bring along an empty palanquin at their own pace; whereas a set of sixteen bearers will carry you and your traps at the rate of four and four and a half miles an hour for twenty leagues on end. The powers of the banghy-wallahs are something portentous. Two of them took to Mofussilpore, turn and turn about, a gun-case and a carpet-bag containing, among other things, twenty-eight pounds of shot and three hundred and fifty bullets, going the whole way at a swing trot. And yet the physical conformation of these men is so frail, that a blow on the body is liable to cause instant death. It is commonly believed that this proceeds from the large size of the spleen: and, whether true or not, the theory has its advantages: for the lower classes of Europeans are a little too apt to be free with their fists, and the coolies who come in their way escape many a thrashing which would fall to their lot if their midriffs were less ticklish to meddle with. Recruits are always solemnly warned of this peculiarity in the Hindoo constitution by their comrades who have been some time in the country: and more than once a soldier, when seeking redress in a court of justice for a fraud or theft committed by a native, has excused himself for not having taking the law into his own knuckles, by reminding the magistrate of the thinness of the defendant's pericardium.

In the rainy season, the Ganges at Patna is a sheet of water six miles in breadth; but in February it flows along two channels on either side of a low sandy island. On arriving at the first branch of the river, the whole company got on board a large boat, and we were ferried across for the moderate remuneration of three mites a head. The bearers enjoyed the passage amazingly; handing about the fraternal hubble-bubble, and discussing whether the Sahib was a planter or a police-officer—to which latter opinion the majority eventually inclined, on the ground that he had black hair. We then crossed the island, and a little after midnight embarked on our second voyage. I fell asleep directly after we started, and awoke again at four in the morning to find the boat stuck fast on a sand-bank in the centre of the stream. The crew, three in number, were up to their middles in the water, in the last stage of exhaustion, vainly endeavouring to shove us off; while the other natives, twenty-two in all, reclined at their ease on the benches, waiting apparently till the first rains in June should set the vessel afloat. The appearance of my head from the door of the palanquin produced an instantaneous effect. The whole party fell to upbraiding each other with indolence and selfishness, until at length one individual, more public-spirited, or, perhaps, more weak-minded than the rest, slowly divested himself of his toga, and stepped over the bulwarks into the river. His exertions were not followed by any visible amelioration in our position, and, when this fact had been thoroughly realized by his companions, another lowered himself into the gulf with the most leisurely air of self-sacrifice. By the time it came to the Quintus Curtius, another half-hour had gone by, and I could stand it no longer. So I bundled the whole lot bodily into the water, and, after a great deal of sighing and grunting, we bumped gradually into a deeper channel, and arrived at the left bank without any farther mishap.

As it was now five o'clock, I resolved to get some breakfast at the dawk bungalow, which stood near the ferry. There was only one Sahib staying in the house; a fat civil servant, whom at first I mistook for Jos

Sedley. He was travelling in most luxurious style, with a complete *batterie de cuisine,* and at least a dozen servants. He turned out to be a capital fellow, and provided me with a complete breakfast—tea, fish, steak, and curry. When he learnt that I was a competition-wallah, he was highly delighted, and asked me whether I was a good scholar. Then, without waiting for a reply, he informed me that the classics were his hobby; that they had long formed his only recreation, with the exception of pig-sticking; and that his mind was so thoroughly imbued with the literature of Greece that it had become positively Hellenized. To this I replied that our nature gradually moulds itself till it resembles the object of our favourite pursuit; which was rather an unlucky observation, as he was wonderfully like a pig. However, he took the remark in a favourable sense, and proceeded to tell me that the study of the ancients was the passion of his mature years. He had not been remarkable for early proficiency: although, indeed, on one occasion, he had come within seven of the classical medal at Haileybury. He was at present engaged on a work, the scheme of which, he flattered himself, was both judicious and original. It was neither more nor less than the rendering of the " Lays of " Ancient Rome " back into the ballad poetry of which they are supposed to be translations. This, when complete, would, he observed, be a "$\chi\rho\hat{\eta}\mu\alpha\ \epsilon\hat{\iota}\sigma\alpha\epsilon\hat{\iota}$." He then repeated the opening lines of " Horatius," which ran thus :—

> " En! Lars Clusinus per ter tres Porsena **Divos**
> Jurat Tarquinios ne longa injuria vexet
> Se provisurum. Per ter tres Porsena **Divos**
> Jurat, et Auroram certam proclamat ubique.

H

> Et speculatores decurrere solis ad ortus,
> Solis et occasus jussit, Boreamque, Notumque,
> Et latè Tuscum agmen 'ad arma' vocavit, 'ad arma.'"

"Observe," he cried, "the repetition in the last line. "The first '*ad arma*' may be supposed to be the "summons to battle; the second is, as it were, the "universal answer of the people. Is it not life-like?" I replied that it might be like life, but that it certainly was not like the production of a Roman bard who lived more than three centuries before Virgil was born or thought of. I reminded him that the hexameter was borrowed from Greece at a later period than that imagined by Macaulay as the date of this poem, and suggested that the Saturnian metre would be more appropriate. He asked for a specimen, and I repeated the only lines in that measure with which I was acquainted:—

> "Et Nævio poetæ, cùm sæpè lædrentur,
> Dabunt malum Metelli: dabunt malum Metelli:"

an attack upon the poet which was called forth by the epigram:—

> "Fato Metelli fiunt Romæ consules:"

a satire, the point of which is so preternaturally mild, that it is difficult to account for the bitterness which it excited. Hereupon my companion's countenance assumed an air of thought, and he retired into his bedroom, whence he emerged after an interval of about an hour, with the information that he had re-written the commencement of the lay in a manner which undoubtedly displayed considerable powers of adaptation:—

"I AM ONLY THE EXPRESS."

> "Ab urbe rex amicus cùm sæpe pelleretur,
> Mox Porsenæ minacis cohors Etrusca Romæ
> Dabit malum superbæ ; dabit malum superbæ."

Almost immediately afterwards I set off again on my journey, not without painful misgivings as to what my friend would do now that he had used up all his model in the first three lines of his poem.

About half-way to Mofussilpore we came upon a native lying asleep under a tree at the side of the road. The bearers stopped, and informed me that he was a dawk runner, carrying the post, and that, whenever the Sahibs saw a dawk runner asleep or loitering, they always got out and beat him with their feet. On subsequent inquiry, I found that the statement was correct. The postmen are bound to travel at the rate of six miles an hour; but, in point of fact, they never go beyond a walk. If, however, an Englishman heaves in sight, they set off, and puff and blow like a pedestrian who is trying to look as if he were being outrun by Deerfoot. Not wishing to appear ignorant of the custom of the country, I alighted, and began banging the man about with my umbrella, and asked him what the Son of Morning he meant by his conduct. It turned out that my zeal was misplaced; for when returning consciousness disclosed to him the presence of a Sahib with an avenging alpaca, he looked up in my face with an air of reproachful innocence, and said: "Main dawk nahin hi. Main express hi." (I am not the dawk; I am only the express.)

The omnipresence of "hi" never fails to impress a new comer. As it forms the termination to four sentences out of five, he at first imagines that it is an interjection with a sense of command. He deduces this theory partly from the fact that at home the particle in question is exclusively employed by 'busdrivers as a preliminary to running over deaf people; and partly from the profusion with which the word is used out here by Englishmen in giving their orders to inferiors. He therefore tacks it on to the end of the name of any article which he may require, exclaiming with touching confidence, " Belattee Pawnee hi ! " " Beer Shrub hi ! " — a form of expression which simply amounts to predicating the existence of those luxuries.

At five o'clock in the afternoon we had still an hour's journey before us. As it was no longer too hot to be pleasant, I sent on the palkee and my luggage, and walked into the station alone. The last two miles lay through the Bazaar. I was surprised, and not much flattered, by the indifference to my presence shown by the ladies seated in the verandahs bordering on the road. Whether travellers by profession have a higher opinion of their own personal charms than any other class of men, I cannot say, but their books usually teem with passages in this style:

"The fair daughter of Mahomet, as the sound of " wheels reached her ears, drew over her stately head, " in playful haste, the veil which religion and custom " alike prescribe, but not so quickly as to rob the " stranger of one glance at her dark features and chiselled " brow, worthy of a home in the Paradise of the " blessed : " or,

" From behind the lattice issued from time to time " the noise of suppressed laughter, while a careful ob-

"server might note a gazelle-like orb peering through
"the framework in curious admiration of the ruddy
"countenance and stalwart form of the young Frank."

My own impression is, that a native female troubles herself as little about young Franks as a Yorkshire girl about young Gentoos. A recluse, who knew the world only from books, would imagine that all women were of exquisite beauty, and thought about nothing from morning till night except the admiration which they excited. This is only another form of the fable of the lion and the sculptor. If the immense majority of books had been written by women, the conventional idea would have attributed good looks and coquetry to men. Poetry would have been full of tapering moustachios and waving whiskers, and Apollos de Medici, and men, in their hours of ease, uncertain, coy, and hard to please. A strong proof of the rapid spread of cultivation and knowledge among English ladies is afforded by the fact, that much of the nonsense about bright eyes and cruel charmers with which the literature of a century ago is larded would not be tolerated by modern readers. We owe this to Miss Austen, Currer Bell, Harriet Martineau, and others of their sex, who have shown by indisputable proofs that women are good for something better than to point a sonnet or adorn an eclogue.

At every turn of the road I came upon a policeman in a bright blue tunic, tight yellow pantaloons, and a red pugree or turban. It is some time before the mind can grasp the conception of police, in a country where the cooks are all of the male sex, and where religion forbids the consumption of cold mutton. The absence of areas is compensated to a certain extent by the village well, whither the officer on duty retires occasionally to refresh himself with a drink and a flirtation. The police force is in a state of reorganization over the whole Bengal Presidency. Under the old system, the duties were left unperformed by a watchman in every village, and by a Thannadar, or Government officer, who was a person of no small authority, having Burkandazzes under him, and saying to this man, " Find " me a culprit, or I will give you a hundred lashes; " and to another, " Pay me down twenty rupees, and " I will let you have six hours' law;" and to the civil servant in charge of the district, " Sahib, the murderer " has escaped over the frontier disguised as a Fakeer." The new police has been constructed on the Irish model. They are entrusted with various services which once fell to detachments from the regular army; such as guarding prisons, escorting treasure, and such like. The inspectors and superintendents are taken for the most part from among regimental officers, and it is said that the tendency of the new force is become too decidedly military. The detective element is certainly rather weak at present; but it is better thus than that the constables who are supposed to check crime should be a gang of Jonathan Wilds, which was too often the case before the present reforms began to take effect. The same complaint is brought against the Irish police. The magnificent fellows who parade in pairs, rifle on shoulder, along the highroads of Mayo and Limerick, consider it a great feat to capture an illicit still once every two years in a region where nine-tenths of the whiskey on sale has never paid duty. In time of peace there is something droll in the mixture of dislike and contempt with which they are regarded by the country people. When the tourist finds himself obliged to wade a stream, the chances are that he will be told by his guide that there was a beautiful bridge two years ago, which the police broke down by marching over it in step. It is needless to add that this accusation is merely the form in which the popular sentiment has thought fit to express itself.

It was just dark when I arrived at the Collectorate. My cousin Tom welcomed me warmly, if warmth can be connected with anything pleasant in such a climate as this. In eastern imagery, the idea of comfort and solace is expressed by similes which imply protection from heat and glare. "Like the shadow of a great "rock in a weary land," would mean very little on Ben Cruachan or the Scawfell Pikes. If in the course of time the language of our countrymen in India adapts itself to their altered tropics, we shall talk about our hearts cooling towards a kindred nature, and our disappointment at meeting with a hot reception from an old friend.

There was a large dinner-party in the evening, and every guest on his arrival was duly acquainted with my having performed the last four miles of my journey on foot. It was very amusing to observe the incredulity with which this statement was received by some, and the hilarity which it excited in others. That ghastly allusion to the supposed poverty of one's feet, which apparently had just penetrated to Bahar, was freely drawn upon for my benefit. One or two old Indians were seriously put out at such a piece of enthusiastic folly; and a young assistant-magistrate, who had won the mile race at Eton, and who, in the long vacation before he came out, had discovered three passes in Switzerland, talked of my "superabundant energy" with the languid pity of an Oriental voluptuary. From the moment when he is cheated in the purchase of his first buggy by a third-hand dealer in Calcutta, to the time when, amidst an escort of irregular cavalry, he dashes through wondering villages in all the state of a lieutenant-governor, your true civil servant never goes a-foot on the highroad for a hundred yards together. And this does not proceed from indolence or effeminacy: for a Mofussil official, on the most dim rumour of bear or tiger, will carry his gun for days over ground that would heartily disgust an English sportsman. But horses and grooms and fodder are so cheap out here, and the standard of incomes so high, that no one need walk except for pleasure; and the pleasure of walking in Bengal is, to say the least, equivocal. During the whole of my stay in these parts, this feat provided a subject for inexhaustible chaff, with the smallest conceivable admixture of grain.

It so happened that the Rajah of Futtehgunge, which lies somewhere in the outskirts of this district, called at Mofussilpore on his way back from the Durbar, or levée, held by the Viceroy at Agra. He had invited all the English residents to a grand tumasha at his camp, which was to take place the evening after my arrival. A "tumasha" is anything special in the way of amusement; a feast, a ball, or a play. The word has a magical effect upon the native mind. On one occasion, a friend of mine prevailed upon his bearer to submit to an agonizing series of electric shocks, under the assurance that the proceeding was a " tumasha."

We left the Collectorate at nine at night, and drove to the tents, which were nearly half a mile off, between hedges of blazing lights, in three rows, one above another. The Rajah received us at the entrance of the pavilion; and, after mutual compliments, we seated ourselves on a row of arm-chairs on either side of the great man. The scene was very picturesque. The tent, which was of immense extent, open at the sides, was thronged with guards and retainers in the most gorgeous costumes, studded with gems which glittered and twinkled in the fitful flaring torchlight. In the darkness outside thronged the whole population of the neighbourhood. The centre was spread with a broad rich carpet, on which were seated the performers. First came a nautch, which afforded a striking example of the profound dissimilarity in taste between Asiatics and Europeans. I have witnessed the exhibition of Mr. Woodin; I have seen Charles Kean enact the lover in a sentimental comedy; I have a horrible dream of having sat through the explanation of the comic dissolving views at the Polytechnic Institution; but, though a being of awful experiences, I could not have believed in the existence of an entertainment so extravagantly dull as a nautch. A young lady not remarkable for her charms, dressed in a very splendid robe, which was several inches too long for her, came forward a few paces, stumbling over her skirts, and commenced a recitation in a singular and monotonous key, accompanied by three musical instruments of barbaric fashion, which I concluded to be sackbuts and dulcimers. She sang the praises of Tom Goddard, his early promise, his beauty, his high birth. She related how he excelled all his companions in manly exercises, and how the Moonshees, who conducted his education, foretold his future greatness. (The fact is, that he was the most notorious muff on Bigside, and that the Principal of Haileybury threatened him with expulsion at the end of every term.) Then she described how the deities of the sea made smooth the waves around the prow of the ship which bore him across the black water. (He was unable once to leave his cabin between Southampton and Alexandria.) How, when he sat upon the bench of judgment, all wondered at the precocious wisdom of the youthful sage, and how the rulers of the land vied to do him honour, and disputed with each other the possession of so bright a jewel. (He began his public career in the north-west, under a magistrate who reversed three-fourths of his decisions, and made it a personal favour that he should be removed to Bahar, where he turned over a new leaf.) She then spoke of the condition of the province over which he now extended his fostering care. She told us that the period of his government was the golden age of the district; that force and fraud were unknown throughout the borders; that the planter did not grind the ryot, nor the ryot write libels on the planter; that the fields were white with poppies, and that grain had fallen three seers in the rupee; that fuller vats foamed with bluer indigo, and more vigilant policemen watched over emptier jails. At this point of the eulogium, Tom, who had only the day before committed twenty-three dacoits, blushed visibly—a performance to which I had thought him unequal. All this while, two stunted girls had been coming forward at intervals of some minutes, who, after waving their arms in time to the music, turned short round and ran back to their places. Meantime, another woman, with a sword between her teeth and bells on her fingers, was throwing about her head and hands in most ungraceful contortions. And this is the famous nautch, on which natives of the highest class gaze in rapture for three, four, six hours together!

To the nautch succeeded the drolleries of a company of comedians, ten or twelve in number. The Rajah had prudently given them a hint to be careful, feeling that even greater reverence is due to collectors than to boys. The affair, in consequence, was grossly proper, but excessively childish and absurd. It began with imitations of various animals—the peacock amongst others—which was represented by an ancient man with a long white beard, evidently the Robson of the troupe, who held up a lighted torch behind him to represent the bird's tail, and ran round and round cackling like a goose as he was. After this a number of scenes were enacted, in which the old fellow always played the principal character. At one time he was an Arab stable-keeper, while the others were grooms, horses, and customers. On another occasion he was a magistrate in Cutcherry, who, when a knotty case is brought before him, sends it to be determined by the Joint Sahib (as the natives designate the joint magistrate) and calls for a light to his cigar. Finally, all the rest of the party lay down on their backs, and clapped their hands, while he passed a lighted torch over them. This was feebly supposed to suggest the idea of a pyrotechnical exhibition.

We were roused from the profound melancholy into which we had been thrown by this specimen of Eastern humour, by a summons from our host to take supper previously to witnessing a display of fireworks. A magnificent banquet was laid out in an adjoining tent. We each sipped a glass of wine, and, declining any more solid refreshment, proceeded to mount a sort of grand stand, which had been erected for our accommodation, leaving the feast to be devoured by two deputy opium agents and an Irish gentleman, who, according to his own account, was engaged on a tour for the purpose of collecting facts with a view to entering upon public life, but who was very generally supposed to be Haynes the murderer—a report that was eventually traced home to the assistant-magistrate, who had been persuaded by the stranger into purchasing a spavined horse. The dulness of the nautch certainly had not communicated itself to the fireworks. Rockets, wheels, flowerpots, fountains, Bahar lights, Roman candles, were fizzing and blazing in every direction. There was no attempt at effect or grouping. Men rushed about with torches, lighting anything that stood most convenient. Within twenty minutes a good two hundred pounds' worth of gunpowder must have flashed away into the illimitable. The whole entertainment could not have cost the Rajah less than four thousand rupees; and yet the same man would think ten rupees a year a very handsome subscription to the dispensary or the schools in his own town.

The motive for this profusion is evident enough. All

the world within a hundred miles will hear that the Futtehgunge man has induced the Sahibs of Mofussilpore to be present at a tumasha; and the Rajah of Doodiah, his dearest enemy, will not know a moment's peace until he has achieved the same honour. Under the feeble rule of the Mogul, these great landholders exercised an absolute authority within their own borders, and made war upon each other with considerable gusto. Since we have been in the country they have been forced to confine their rivalry to quarrels concerning precedence, and endless litigation about every imaginable subject. At one of Lord Canning's Durbars a dispute arose between two Rajahs, as to which should be presented the first. They agreed to refer the decision to an eminent member of the Council then present, who proposed that they should settle the point by the ordeal of tossing up. They answered that they would be quite ready to adopt his suggestion for that occasion only, but that the matter was one which concerned all time, and must not be lightly disposed of. Accordingly the Englishman whom they had appointed arbiter, went thoroughly into the question, studied their respective genealogies, and drew up a report which was generally allowed to be conclusive. The unsuccessful claimant retired almost broken-hearted.

Next day the servants of the Rajah came with the intimation that the great man would pay us a visit in the course of the morning. They brought Tom a dolly, which is the name given to the only description of present that Government servants are permitted to accept. A dolly consists of trays of provisions, the number of which is regulated by the rank of the person to whom the compliment is paid. Thus, a lieutenant-governor gets fifty trays, while I, as a hanger-on of Tom's, came in for a little dolly of ten. The size of the offering, however, is of no consequence at all, as the only article that an Englishman ever dreams of touching is the box of Cabul grapes, of which each dolly, great or small, contains one and only one. The huge unsightly fish, the heaps of greasy sweetmeats, and the piles of nondescript fruit and vegetables, are appropriated by your servants, who are in a state of plethora for forty-eight hours after, and of dyspepsia during the whole of the next week.

Towards noon the Rajah came with a following of eighteen or twenty cavaliers, mounted on raw-boned horses daubed with paint according to the taste of their riders, and about two score guards on foot, armed with halberts, sabres, and blunderbusses of that bell-mouth form which the Irish landlord knows so well. "Oft in "the stilly night" he descries a tall hat peering over a neighbouring stone wall, in company with that primitive weapon, which, after a laudable effort at missing fire, belches forth a shower of slugs and rusty nails and copper halfpence, as an instalment of the rint which has been withheld. Then he rides home cautiously, looking out for the gates which have been taken off their hinges and laid across his horse's track; and, while his wife picks the bits of old iron out of his back, he discusses with the police sergeant the identity of the man who has been compelled by a crisis in his affairs to borrow the village blunderbuss. A Government less powerful than our own might object to the troops of armed ragamuffins who live at the expense of the great noblemen of these parts. But it is well understood, that all this state is merely maintained with a view to keep up their position in the eyes of their countrymen. There is no one who gets so little fun for his money as your rich Hindoo. He lives in a wretched doghole, and feeds on rice and spices and sweetstuff, like the meanest shopkeeper. Yet he is always in debt, always mortgaging his land to planters, and screwing his tenants, and cheating and being cheated by his agents and bailiffs. The mass of his income goes to gratify what is neither more nor less than the genuine spirit of snobbishness. The Rajah of Doodiah has forty armed men in attendance:—he must have fifty. The Rajah of Nilpore keeps eighty riding horses :—he must keep a hundred, although he never stirs out except in a litter. And yet Thackeray will have it that snobbishness is the peculiar weakness of Britons!—the crying sin for which fire from heaven is to descend upon Brompton, and turn Islington into a sea of brimstone!

What is the champagne from the public-house round the corner, and the greengrocer in white cotton gloves making off with a cold chicken in his umbrella, to the gigantic ruinous pretension and display of a highborn zemindar? I hate this ignorant abuse of everything English. It is an ill novelist that fouls its own nest. Is it really the fact that in England, of all countries in the world, a titled fool can command the worship of society, while merit without a handle to its name is doomed to contempt and sixpenn'orth of beef from the cookshop? If Mr. Gladstone were a Hindoo gentleman of limited means, his rare mental gifts would certainly not compensate in the estimation of the community for his deficiency of rupees. If Mr. Roupell were the wealthiest landholder in Tirhoot or Chumparun he might accuse himself of forgery for thirty hours out of the twenty-four without losing an atom of his influence and power. But it is the same in everything. Though the marriage tie is more sacred in England than in any other European community;—though our literature is pure compared with the German, and prudery itself by the side of the productions of modern France;—there are writers who perpetually inveigh against our licentiousness and immorality. In spite of hospitals and refuges, and shoe-black brigades, and Lancashire Relief Funds, you would judge from the sermons of some clerical horse-leeches that there was neither charity nor humanity throughout our island. We are not inclined to self-glorification. We have no Fourth of July, and we do not desire to have one. But it is affectation to deny that, as nations go, we honestly strive to learn what our duties are, and to fulfil them to the best of our abilities.

The Rajah's address, like that of all Bengalee grandees in the presence of Englishmen, was a curious compound of solemnity and servility. He told us a little about the Durbar, and we told him a little about the Great Exhibition. He spoke of the approaching marriage of the Prince of Wales, and expressed his surprise at that ceremony having been deferred till the bridegroom was twice the age at which he himself had taken his first wife. He informed us that a report prevailed in Bahar to the effect that the Muscovites, assisted by the King of Roum, were on the point of sailing up the Persian Gulf to the rescue of Brigadier

AN ALARM.

Jefferson Lincoln. My cousin advised him to have his son vaccinated, and in return he made a wild attempt to get his assessment lowered. Tom pretended to mistake his meaning, and answered that the Government was inclined to regard with favour the zemindars who promoted the cause of popular education by example and pecuniary assistance. Upon this the Rajah, who found the conversation growing unprofitable, took his leave, and drove away amidst a salute from all the fire-arms in his train which were capable of going off on so short a notice. This proceeding raised the most lively apprehension in the breast of the Irish gentleman, who was in a state of feverishness tempered with belattee-pawnee after the dissipation of the previous evening. Under the impression that a mutiny was on foot, and that the Rajah, with all the native police of the district, was besieging the Collectorate, he rushed out in his nightshirt and drawers, with a gun cocked and loaded, and was with some difficulty prevented from shooting Tom's principal Sudder Ameen, an eminently respectable Baboo in high judicial employ, who happened to be the first native that came in his way.

The Indian Civil Service is undoubtedly a very fine career. Here is Tom, in his thirty-first year, in charge of a population as numerous as that of England in the reign of Elizabeth. His Burghley is a joint magistrate of eight-and-twenty, and his Walsingham an assistant-magistrate who took his degree at Christ Church within the last fifteen months. These, with two or three superintendents of police, and, last, but by no means least, a judge, who in rank and amount of salary stands to Tom in the position which the Lord Chancellor holds to the

Prime Minister, are the only English officials in a province one hundred and twenty miles by seventy.

You must not imagine, my own Simkins, that a collector in Bahar at all resembles the individual at home who comes round with a pen in his mouth, leaving a notification at his first visit, and a surcharge at his next, and finally bringing a wheelbarrow and pickaxe to cut off your water, neglecting at every stage alike to scrape his shoes before he enters your hall. The *employé* who rejoices in the full dignity of collector and magistrate, in addition to the special duty of handling the revenue and determining all questions connected with the Land Settlement, is the chief executive authority in the district to which he is attached. His freedom of action is controlled by none but the commissioner, who presides over a division of five or six districts, and whose immediate superior is the Lord Sahib or Lieutenant-Governor, who is inferior only to the Burra Lord Sahib or Viceroy, who owns no master save the Secretary of State, for whom the natives have not invented a title, and of whom they probably know very little, except they happen to be in the service of a planter, in which case they have heard that functionary anathematized by their master whenever indigo showed any symptom of heaviness, or the ryots of independence.

Work in India is so diversified as to be always interesting. During the cold season, the collector travels about his district, pitching his camp for a night at one place, and for three days at another; while at the larger towns he may find sufficient business to occupy him for a week. Tent-life in the winter months is very enjoyable, especially to a man who has his heart in his duties. It is pleasant, after having spent the forenoon in examining schools and inspecting infirmaries, and quarrelling about the sites of bridges with the superintending engineer in the Public Works Department, to take a light tiffin, and start off with your gun and your assistant-magistrate on a roundabout ride to the next camping-ground. It is pleasant to dismount at a likely piece of grass, and, flushing a bouncing black partridge, to wipe the eye of your subordinate; and then to miss a hare, which your bearer knocks over with his stick, pretending to find the marks of your shot in its forequarter. It is pleasant, as you reach the rendezvous in the gloaming, rather tired and very dusty, to find your tents pitched, and your soup and curry within a few minutes of perfection, and your kitmutgar with a bottle of lemonade, just drawn from its cool bed of saltpetre, and the head man of the village ready with his report of a deadly affray that would have taken place if you had come in a day later. Is not this better than the heart-sickness of briefs deferred; the dreary chambers, and the hateful lobby; the hopeless struggle against the sons of attorneys and the nephews of railway-directors; the petition to be put into one of the law offices, that you may eat a piece of bread? Is it not better than grinding year after year at the school-mill, teaching the young idea how to turn good English verses into bad Latin; stopping the allowances, and paring down the journey-money; crowding as many particles into an iambic as the metre will bear? Is it not better than hanging wearily on at college; feeling your early triumphs turn to bitterness; doubting whether to class yourself with the old or the young; seeing around you an ever-changing succession of lads, who, as fast as they grow to be friends and companions to you, pass away into the world, and are no more seen?

During ten months in the year the collector resides at the station. The Government does not provide its servants with house-room; but they seldom experience any inconvenience in finding suitable accommodation, for the native landlords make a point of reserving for every official the residence which had been occupied by his predecessor. No advance in terms will tempt them to let the judge's bungalow to any but the judge, or to turn the joint Sahib out of the dwelling which has been appropriated to joint Sahibs ever since that class of functionaries came into being. They charge a very moderate rent, which includes the cost of gardeners and sweepers for the use of the tenant. This is an effect of the passion for conferring obligations upon men in authority which exists in the mind of every Hindoo. The life of a collector in the Mofussil is varied and bustling even in the hot weather. He rises at daybreak, and goes straight from his bed to the saddle. Then off he gallops across fields bright with dew to visit the scene of the late dacoit robbery; or to see with his own eyes whether the crops of the zemindar who is so unpunctual with his assessment have really failed; or to watch with fond parental care the progress of his pet embankment. Perhaps he has a run with the bobbery pack of the station, consisting of a superannuated fox-hound, four beagles, a greyhound, the doctor's retriever, and a Skye terrier belonging to the assistant-magistrate, who unites in his own person the offices of M. F. H., huntsman, and whipper-in. They probably start a jackal, who gives them a sharp run of ten minutes, and takes refuge in a patch of sugar-cane; whence he steals away in safety while the pack are occupied in mobbing a fresh fox and a brace of wolf-cubs, to the delight of a remarkably full field of five sportsmen, with one pair of top-boots amongst them. On their return, the whole party adjourn to the subscription swimming-bath, where they find their servants ready with clothes, razors, and brushes. After a few headers, and "chota hasree," or "little breakfast," of tea and toast, flavoured with the daily papers and scandal about the commissioner, the collector returns to his bungalow, and settles down to the hard business of the day. Seated under a punkah in his verandah, he works through the contents of one despatch-box, or "bokkus," as the natives call it, after another; signing orders, and passing them on to the neighbouring collectors; dashing through drafts, to be filled up by his subordinates; writing reports, minutes, digests, letters of explanation, of remonstrance, of warning, of commendation. Noon finds him quite ready for a *déjeûner à la fourchette*, the favourite meal in the Mofussil, where the teatray is lost amidst a crowd of dishes—fried fish, curried fowl, roast kid and mint-sauce, and mango-fool. Then he sets off in his buggy to Cutcherry, where he spends the afternoon in hearing and deciding questions connected with land and revenue. If the cases are few, and easy to be disposed of, he may get away in time for three or four games at rackets in the new court of glaring white plaster, which a rich native has built, partly as a speculation, and partly to please the Sahibs. Otherwise, he drives with his wife on the race-course; or plays at billiards with the inspector of police; or, if horticulturally inclined, superintends the labours of his Mollies. Then follows dinner, and an hour of reading or music. By ten o'clock he is in bed, with his little ones asleep in cribs, enclosed within the same mosquito curtains as their parents.

The ladies, poor things, come in for all the disagreeables of up-country life. Without plenty of work, India is unbearable. That alone can stave off languor and a depth of *ennui* of which a person who has never left Europe can form no conception. In a climate which keeps every one within doors from eight in the morning till five in the evening, it is, humanly speaking, impossible to make sufficient occupation for yourself, if it does not come to you in the way of business. After a prolonged absence from home, reviews and newspapers become uninteresting. Good novels are limited in number, and it is too much to expect that a lady should read history and poetry for six hours every day. What well-regulated female can make dress an object in a society of a dozen people, who know her rank to a tittle, and her income to a pice; or music, when her audience consists of a Punkah-wallah and a Portuguese Ayah? Some ladies, as a matter of conscience, go very closely into the details of household affairs; but after a time they come to the conclusion that it is better to allow the servants to cheat within a certain margin, for the sake of peace and quietness; for cheat they will, do what you may. Oh! the dreariness of that hour in the middle of the long day, when the children are asleep, and your husband has gone to tiffin with the judge, and the book-club has sent nothing but Latham's "Nationalities of Europe," and three refutations of

Colenso (who seems to take an unconscionable amount of refuting, considering the size of his publication), and the English post has come in yesterday, with nothing but a letter from your old governess, congratulating you for being settled among the associations of the Mahommedan conquerors of India, and asking you to take some notice of her nephew, who is in the office of the Accountant-General of Bombay. It is very up-hill work for a lady out here to keep up her spirits and pluck, and her interest in general subjects. The race-week, the visit to her sister in the Punjab, the hope of being ordered down to Calcutta, the reminiscences of the sick-leave, and the anticipations of the furlough, are the consolations of a life which none but a very brave or a very stupid woman can endure long without suffering in mind, health, and *tournure.* If a lady becomes dowdy, it is all up with her; and the temptations to dowdiness in the Mofussil cannot well be exaggerated.

I know of no better company in the world than a rising civilian. There is an entire absence of the carping, pining spirit of discontent which is so painfully apparent in able men at home who find themselves kept in the background for want of interest or money. In most cases, the normal condition of a clever Englishman between the ages of twenty-two and thirty is a dreary feeling of dissatisfaction about his work and his prospects, and a chronic anxiety for " a sphere." If he is a master at a public school, he wastes a couple of hundred pounds at Lincoln's Inn or the Temple, in order to delude himself with the fond idea that he will one day exchange his desk in the fourth-form room for the more stirring cares of forensic life. If he still hesitates to surrender the ease and security of a fellowship, he compounds with his intellect by writing for the *Saturday Review,* and representing the liberal element in the governing body of his college. He takes to the law, only to discover that there are instincts in the human heart which even conveyancing will not satisfy ; to the Church—no, he does not take to the Church ; to literature, and finds himself in the plight of that gentleman, who

> " At thirty years of age,
> Writes statedly for *Blackwood's Magazine,*
> And thinks he sees three points in Hamlet's soul
> As yet unseized by Germans."

An Englishman cannot be comfortable if he is in a false position ; and he never allows himself to be in a true position unless he is proud of his occupation, and convinced that success will depend upon his own efforts. These agreeable sensations are experienced to the full by an Indian civil servant. It is impossible for him to have any misgiving concerning the dignity and importance of his work. His power for good and evil is almost unlimited. His individual influence is as great as that arrogated by the most sublime of Dr. Arnold's favourite præpostors during his first term at the university. He is the member of an official aristocracy, owning no social superior ; bound to no man ; fearing no man. Even though he may be passed over once and again by a prejudice in the mind of his commissioner, or some theory on the subject of promotion held by his lieutenant-governor, he is well aware that his advancement does not hang upon the will and pleasure of this or the other great man, but is regulated by the opinion entertained of his ability and character by the service in general. In order to rise in India, it is not necessary to be notorious. In fact, notoriety is rather a clog than otherwise. People out here are not easily bamboozled, and like you none the better for trying to bamboozle them. A civilian who is conscious of power does not seek to push his way into notice by inditing sensation minutes, or by riding a hobby to the death; but makes it his aim to turn off his work in good style, trusting for his reward to the sense and public spirit of his chief. There is nothing which men in power out here so cordially abominate as solemnity and long-winded pedantry. A ready, dashing subordinate, who, to use a favourite Platonic phrase, " sees things as they are," is sure to win the heart of every resident and chief commissioner with whom he may have to do. I have observed that, if ever a young fellow is spoken of in high quarters as an able and promising public servant, he is sure, on acquaintance, to turn out a remarkably pleasant and interesting companion. A collector or under secretary will sometimes get a little maudlin over his cheroot, and confide sundry longings for literary society and European topics; but he never speaks of his duties except in a spirit of enthusiasm, or of his profession without a tone of profound satisfaction. He no more dreams of yearning for " a sphere " than for a pentagon or a rhomboid. A magistrate had been mildly complaining to me that he found no time for scientific pursuits. " But, after all," he said, " who can think about butterflies or strata when " there are embankments to be raised on which depends " the famine or plenty of a thousand square miles; and "hundreds of human beings are waiting their trial in "jail; and millions are living and dying in ignorance, "for want of schools and teachers?" He must be a happy man who can talk of his daily occupations and responsibilities in such terms as these.

But, besides the blessings of absorbing work and an assured position, a civilian enjoys the inestimable comfort of freedom from pecuniary troubles. Intriguing mothers used to say that a writer was worth three hundred a year, dead or alive. It requires some self-denial, during the probation in Calcutta, to make both ends of the six months meet; but in the Mofussil a young bachelor has enough and to spare. Tom's assistant-magistrate keeps four horses, and lives well within as many hundred rupees a month. If a man puts off his marriage to within a year or two of the age at which he may take a wife in England without being disinherited by his great-uncle, he may always have a good house and plenty of servants, his champagne and his refrigerator, his carriage and buggy, an Arab for the Mem Sahib, and for himself a hundred-guinea horse that will face a pig without flinching. He will be able to portion his daughters, and send his son to Harrow and Oxford; and, while still in the vigour of life, he may retire to a villa at Esher, or a farm in his native country, with a pension of a thousand a year, and as much more from the interest of his savings. Bobus Smith, during the intervals of writing hexameters which put to shame all Latin verse of the present day, used to say that a man could not live in India on less than two thousand a year, and could not spend more than three thousand. An amendment which would insert the word "married" before the word "man," and alter the numbers to fifteen hundred and two thousand respectively, would be nearer the mark. In a climate where fresh air and cool water are bought for a price, a good income is essential to comfort; but, when comfort has been attained, there is no object on which money can be laid out. A man might subscribe to every charity and every newspaper without being two hundred pounds the worse at the end of the year. The sum which can be thrown away on horse-racing is limited by the paucity of the people who desire to win your gold mohurs or to lose their own. There is no temptation to display; for every member of society knows the exact number of rupees which you draw on the fifteenth of each month. A joint magistrate and deputy-collector who marries on nine hundred a year may count on being a full magistrate and collector at one or two and thirty, with an income of two thousand three hundred. In five years more, with industry and ordinary parts, he will be in receipt of three thousand a year as a civil and sessions judge; or, if he prefers to wait his time, he will have charge of a division, with a commissioner's salary of three thousand six hundred. Then there are the quartern loaves and the plump fishes; the chance of Bombay or Madras; the lieutenant-governorships, with an income of ten thousand pounds; the Council, with an income of eight thousand; the chief commissionerships, with an income of six thousand; the secretariat and the board of revenue, with something under five thousand a year. And these prizes are open to every subject of the Queen, though his father be as poor as Job subsequently to the crash in that patriarch's affairs, and though he does not number so much as the butler of a member of Parliament among his patrons and connexions.

To those who think that life should be one long education, the choice of a profession is a matter of the greatest moment: for every profession that deserves the name must draw so largely on the time and intellect of a man as to allow scant opportunity for general study. Therefore, any one who wishes to preserve a high tone of thought, and a mind constantly open to new impressions, must look for a calling which is an education in itself—that is, a calling which presents a succession of generous and elevating interests. And such is pre-eminently the career of a civil servant in India. There is no career which holds out such certain and splendid prospects to honourable ambition. But, better far than this, there is no career which so surely inspires men with the desire to do something useful in their generation—to leave their mark upon the world for good, and not for evil. The public spirit among the servants of the Government at home is faint compared with the fire of zeal which glows in every vein of an Indian official. During a progress through his province, a lieutenant-governor is everywhere followed about by magistrates, who beg with the most invincible pertinacity for a thousand rupees more towards this infirmary, for another one per cent. on the court fees towards that Cutcherry. Our modern quæstors are every whit as grasping and venal as the satellites of Verres and Dolabella; but it is for the benefit of their district, and not for their own pockets. It is this deep and pure love for his adopted country, transplanted to an uncongenial soil, which too often attaches to the retired Indian the fatal title of " bore," which unites all parties in the endeavour to keep him out of the House of Commons, and cough him down if he succeeds in forcing an entrance. It seems incredible to him that people should exhibit indifference towards subjects which have been his dearest care ever since he was punted up the Burrampootra to his first station ; that there should be men who shudder at the bare mention of the Annexation Policy ; who shift their chairs at the most faint allusion to the indigo troubles. But it is out here that the fruits of this noble and earnest philanthropy are manifested in their true light. It is a rare phenomenon this, of a race of statesmen and judges scattered throughout a conquered land, ruling it, not with an eye to private profit, not even in the selfish interests of the mother country, but in single-minded solicitude for the happiness and improvement of the children of the soil. It is a fine thing to see a homely old pro-consul retiring from the government of a region as large as France and Austria together, with a clear conscience and a sound digestion, to plague his friends about the Amalgamation Act and the Contract Law ; to fill his villa on the Thames or the Mole, not with statues and bronzes snatched from violated shrines, but with ground-plans of hospitals and markets and colleges, and translations of codes, and schemes for the introduction of the Roman character.

Whence comes this high standard of efficiency and public virtue among men taken at random, and then exposed to the temptations of unbounded power and unlimited facilities for illicit gain ? It cannot be peculiarly the result of Haileybury, for that institution, from its very nature, united the worst faults of school and college. The real education of a civil servant consists in the responsibility that devolves on him at an early age, which brings out whatever good there is in a man ; the obligation to do nothing that can reflect dishonour on the service; the varied and attractive character of his duties; and the example and precept of his superiors, who regard him rather as a younger brother than as a subordinate official. One black sheep, and two or three incapables, in a yearly list of forty or fifty names, is a large average. A young member of the secretariat, a dead hand at a minute, and the best amateur critic I ever came across, told me that, if he had been the eldest son of a man with broad acres in England, he should nevertheless be glad to have spent ten years in India for the sake of the training, moral and intellectual. The absence of bigotry and intolerance here is undoubtedly very remarkable. Where there is so much work to be done by any one who will put his hand to the plough, men have no time to quarrel about the direction and depth of the furrows. Because you drive a pair of oxen, and I an ox and a donkey ; because your share is curved, while mine is straight; am I, therefore, bound to mulct you of your hire, and pelt you off the fallows with clods and pebbles? Here, at least, the waste lands are plenteous, and the labourers are very few. Here, at least, we can well afford to leave each other to toil in peace. Jones has doubts about the Pentateuch ; but he has just sailed for England, leaving his health behind him in that pestilential district which he volunteered to take during the cholera, and where his theories on draining and burning jungle saved countless lives; and I really have not the heart to let him be anathema maranatha—a curse which a mind unlearned in Oxford theology would conclude, from the context, to have no bearing on the authenticity of the Book of Deuteronomy. In spite of Doctor Pusey, I cannot help greeting as a brother Protestant the little Danish missionary who has changed those blackguard murderous villagers of Kurnaum into Christians and payers of rent. Flanagan rides twenty miles every fortnight to Dinagegur to hear mass; but I can remember when he rode as many leagues, through the September sun, with my baby on the saddle before him, a musket-ball in his shoulder, and his cheek laid open by a sabre cut.

The drawbacks of Indian life begin to be severely felt when it becomes necessary to send the first-born home. From that period until his final retirement there is little domestic comfort for the father of the family. After two or three years have gone by, and two or three children have gone home, your wife's spirits are no longer what they were. She is uneasy for days after a letter has come in with the Brighton post-mark. At last there arrives a sheet of paper scrawled over in a large round hand, and smeared with tears and dirty fingers, which puts her beside herself. You wake two or three times in the night always to find her crying at your side; and the next morning you write to the agent of the P. and O. to engage places for a lady and ayah. At the end of the six months she writes to say that the doctor has insisted on Joey's going to Nice for the winter, and that she must stay to take him. Shortly after you receive a communication from your mother-in-law, to the effect that you must give Ann another summer in England, under pain of the life-long displeasure of that estimable relative. And so it goes on, till, after the lapse of some three or four years, your wife joins you at the Presidency in a state of wild delight at meeting you, and intense misery at finding herself again in India. Within the next two hot seasons she has had three fevers. She tries the hills, but it will not do; and at last you make up your mind to the inevitable, and run down to Calcutta to take your seat at the Board of Revenue and despatch her to England, with a tacit understanding that she is never to return. Then you settle down into confirmed bachelor habits, until one day in August, when all Chowringhee is a vast vapour-bath, you feel, in the region of your liver, an unusually smart touch of the pain which has been constantly recurring during the last eighteen months, and it strikes you that your clever idle son will be more likely to pass his competitive examination if you are on the spot to superintend his studies. So you resign your seat in Council, accept a farewell dinner from your friends, who by this time comprise nearly the whole of Calcutta society, and go on board at Garden Reach, under a salute from the guns of Fort William and an abusive article in the *Hurkaru* on your predilection for the natives.

But the returned Indian does not leave all his troubles behind him on the ghaut whence he embarks for England. In fact, it is not till after the first year of home-life that he begins to appreciate the dark side of the career in which he takes just pride. The first sight

SORROWS OF THE RETURNED INDIAN. 129

of turnip fields and broad-backed sheep; the first
debauch on home-made bread, and bright yellow butter,
and bacon which is above suspicion; the first pic-nic;
the first visit to the Haymarket Theatre; the first stroll
round the playing-fields with his pet son, the Newcastle
medallist of the year, are joys so fresh and pure as to
admit no doubt about the future or yearnings for the
past. But before long he is conscious of a certain
craving for the daily occupation to which he has been
accustomed since boyhood. He remembers, with fond
regret, the pleasure with which he plunged headlong
into the Settlement of the Rajbehar district on his
return from furlough in '47. Though far from a vain
man, he misses the secure and important position which
he has so long occupied. He feels the want of the old
friends with whom he lived during his prime; the old
habits and associations which are familiar to him as
Household Words; in fact, much more familiar, for he
left England just in time to miss the first number of
that exemplary periodical, and returned to find the
name and publisher already changed. It is a severe
trial for a leader of Calcutta society to become one of
the rank and file in the pump-room at a watering-place;
to sink from the Council-board to the Vestry, and from
the High Court to the Petty Sessions. It is a severe
trial, when settled down at Rugby or Harrow, seeing
that his boys learn their repetitions and get up in time
for morning school, quarrelling with their tutor, and
requesting the head-master to publish his Confirmation
sermon, for a man to look back to the days when he
coerced refractory rajahs, bearded the secretariat, and
did the Finance Minister out of a lac and half for his

K

favourite cotton-road. It is a severe trial to live among men who know not John Peter, who hold the opinion that the opium duty is immoral, and who are under the impression that a zemindar is a native non-commissioned officer. He must console himself with English air and scenery and books and faces, with the consciousness of a good work well done, and a good name handed on unstained to the children who are growing up around him.

Yours ever,

H. BROUGHTON.

P.S. I have some thoughts of publishing a translation of the Odes of Horace, adapted to the use of Indian readers. Here are three examples. If they meet your approbation I will set to work in earnest.

Lib. III. Carm. 7.

Quid fles, Asterië, quem tibi candidi
Primo restituent vere Favonii?

I.

My dear Miss White, forbear to weep
Because the North West breezes keep
  At anchor off Rangoon
That youth who, richer by a lac,
May safely be expected back
  Before the next monsoon.

II.

Beneath his close musquito nets
With love and prickly-heat he frets
  On Irawaddy's water,
Nor heeds a dame on board the ship,
Who lets no fair occasion slip
  For praising up her daughter.

III.

She talks of maiden's heart so true,
And angry brothers six foot two
   Demanding satisfaction.
And, as a last resource throws out
Hints very palpable about
   A breach-of-promise action.

IV.

She tells how Pickwick's glance of fire
Quailed 'neath an angry woman's ire :
   But let not that alarm ye.
He still remains as deaf as those
Who govern India to the woes
   Of Bengal's ill-used army.

V.

Fear not for him, but, thou, beware !
'Tis whispered (though I hardly dare
   To credit the assertion),
How very kind an ear you lend
To some young Civil Service friend
   Who lately passed in Persian—

VI.

Than whom no other wallah steers,
With less excruciating fears,
   His buggy down the course ;
Or chooses out a softer place,
And with a more seductive grace
   Drops off a shying horse.

Lib. IV. Carm. 8.

Donarem pateras grataque commodus,
Censorine, meis æra sodalibus.

If all my "woulds," dear Jones, were changed to "coulds,"
I'd deck thy bungalow with Europe goods ;
With bronzes which the awe-struck Baboo stops
To gape and stare at in Chowringhee shops ;
With flagons such as either Ross has won
In many a hard-fought match at Wimbledon ;
With Brett's chefs d'œuvres which Ruskins buy and praise
Amidst the scorn of petulant R.A.s.

Brave presents these, but how can I dispense 'em
With just four hundred odd rupees per mensem?
One potent gift I boast, one treasure dear,
The access to an editorial ear.
What gives old Time this lie, and keeps alive
In school-boy mouths the mighty name of Clive;
Preserves great Hastings from oblivion's flood,
And daubs poor Impey with perennial mud?
Why, just two articles in that Review
Where tawdry yellow strives with dirty blue.
Ne'er will the man on whom the press has smiled
Pine in Collectorates remote and wild.
'Tis not for him the beaten path to trudge
From Sub-assistant up to Zillah Judge.
And, when, persuaded by his wife to give her
The best advice in London for her liver,
He chooses a convenient month to start in
And hurries home to see Sir Ranald Martin,
These magic words perchance may thrill his breast,
"Sir Charles and Lady Mary Wood request—"[1]

LIB. I. CARM. 11.

Tu ne quæsieris (scire nefas) quem mihi, quem tibi,
Finem Dî dederint Leuconæ nec Babylonios
Tentaris numeros.

Matilda, will you ne'er have ceased apocalyptic summing,
And left the number of the beast to puzzle Dr. Cumming?
What can't be cured must be endured. Perchance a gracious heaven
May spare us till the fated year of eighteen sixty-seven.[2]
Perchance Jove's Board of Public Works the dread decree has passed;
And this cold season, with its joys, is doomed to be our last.
Let's to the supper-room again, though Kitmutgars may frown,
And in Lord Elgin's dry champagne wash all these tremors down:
And book me for the fifteenth walse: there, just beneath my thumb.
No, not the next to that, my girl! The next may never come.

[1] Sic Jovis interest
Optatis epulis.

[2] This is the date fixed by Dr. Cumming for the end of all things.

LETTER VI.

A TIGER-PARTY IN NEPAUL.

March 28, 1863.

My dear Simkins,—For some time past "my mind "has been divided within my shaggy breast," as to whether I should send you an account of our tiger-party in Nepaul. I was deterred by doubts of my ability to hit off that peculiar vein of dulness which seems the single qualification requisite for a sporting author. Why a pursuit of such absorbing interest should lose all its charms in the recital it is hard to say. Perhaps men are misled by the delights of a hard run or a successful stalk, and imagine that a bare unadorned narrative will best convey the idea of those delights to their readers. But this can hardly be the cause; for accounts of sport, for the most part, are characterised by carefully elaborated jocosity of a singularly insipid flavour. Sometimes the writer aspires to poetry; in which case he invariably talks about his Pegasus, and is mildly mythological, calling all ladies "Dianas," and speaking of the sun as "Phœbus." After describing the breakfast at the house of "Amphitryon," the meet on the lawn, and the scene at coverside, he proceeds somewhat in this strain :—

> " Across the fields proud Reynard goes,
> Amidst a hundred Tally-hos.

> Our Master kept the Cockneys back,
> Who pressed and jostled in the track.
> Right manfully his tongue he plies,
> And to perdition dooms their eyes.
> Three couple now are on the scent !
> 'Hark, forrard !' and away we went.
> 'Hark, forrard ! Forrard !' is the cry ;
> And like a flock of birds we fly,
> In breeches, scarlet-coat, and tops,
> Along the Dyke to Heywood Copse.
> As down towards Barton Wold we sail,
> The Cockneys soon began to tail,
> And all of them were missing, rot 'em,
> Ere yet we got to Brambly Bottom.
> The pace now told on every nag,
> Which proved the fox was not a 'bag.'
> Poor Captain Fisher broke his girth,
> And, like Antæus, came to earth,
> Though with his fall, I greatly fear, O,
> Ceased his resemblance to that hero.
> Briggs came a cropper ; and the earl
> Experienced an unlucky purl,
> But towards the front he showed again
> Before we entered Ditton Lane."

Who reads these productions? I had the pleasure of living among fox-hunters in England (having indeed myself described parabolas over more than one hedge), and can vouch that their taste in literature was as good as that of any other class of educated men.

It is bad enough that the athletic pursuits which are the special glory of England should be made the vehicle for such melancholy buffoonery ; but the more practical writers on sporting matters have very crude notions of what is readable. There are no authors who as a class so consistently ignore the precept of Horace which forbids to commence the history of the return of Diomede with the decease of Meleager, and to trace the Trojan

War from the double egg. Just as the chroniclers of the middle ages always began with Adam, every one who publishes a treatise on the habits and diseases of the dog seems unable to tell us what mash he recommends for a tired pointer, and whether he treats distemper with sweet oil or mustard and water, unless he has prefaced his remarks by informing us that the hounds of Theseus

> "Were bred out of the Spartan kind,
> So flew'd, so sanded;"

and that the poor Indian entertains the hope that, when he has been dispatched "to the equal sky," by firewater, and small-pox, and the other blessings brought to the door of his wigwam by advancing civilization, "his faithful dog shall bear him company." Whether this privilege, if extended to the whole of the canine race, would conduce to the greatest happiness of the greatest number of departed spirits, may reasonably be doubted. There is an officer residing in our boardinghouse who was the spirited proprietor of a bull-dog which I shot the day before yesterday with a saloon-pistol, and of which I sincerely trust that I have seen the last in this world and the next. There is no one who can bring out a work upon the game of cricket without introducing into his first few pages an allusion to the rhyme—

> "At football or at cricket,
> How neatly hur could prick it!"

impelled apparently by the same mysterious necessity which, in the case of the weak-minded gentleman in "David Copperfield," over-ruled his efforts to keep King

Charles I. out of his memorial. It is fortunate that this tendency is confined to one department of literature. Conceive what it would be if every medical publication commenced with Hezekiah's poultice of figs, every book on tactics and fortification with the battle of four kings against five, and every peerage with Duke Teman, Duke Omar, Duke Zepho, and Duke Kenaz!

Indian sport has perhaps suffered more in public estimation by villainously bad writing than any other branch of the gentle craft. People have been so overdone with howdahs, and bottled beer, and hair-triggers, and hair-breadth escapes, and griffins spearing a sow by mistake, that they had rather face a royal Bengal tiger in his native jungle than in the Sporting Magazine, and dread the name of a pig more than the most scrupulous Jew can abhor the reality. What reader of taste does not feel his heart sink within him when, as he flits through the leaves of a periodical, paper-knife in hand, he is aware of a contribution headed:

> "Pigs and their stickers;
> Or, How we keep it up in the North-West.
> By Nimrod Junior."

Mayhap as he cuts his way through Nimrod Junior's article, in the haste of an absorbing terror, he lights upon a page commencing: "'— your eyes, you young "greenhorn, keep to your own side,' and up dashes "Major W—, the gallant, the determined, his long "beard floating on the mid-day air, his glance beaming "as it beamed when he led the stormers over the glacis "at Mooltan. Fly, poor piggy, if thou wantest to re-see "thy porcine spouse! But faster flies thy pursuer, his "intellectual brow knit with eagerness, as he just feels

"the Pelham pressing the mouth of his four-year-old."
I will endeavour to steer clear of the Scylla of slang
and the Charybdis of bombast, and to set down on paper
a simple unvarnished history of some most pleasant
days passed in very good company.

The northern border of the district, of which Mofussilpore is the capital, lies some fifty miles distant from
the station. The province is bounded in this quarter
by Nepaul, or rather by the Terai, a slip of plain about
twenty miles in breadth along the foot of the lower
chain of the Himalayas, which we have left in the possession of the Hillmen. It is cultivated by Hindoos,
from whom their masters exact a swingeing tribute;
and as most of their revenue is drawn from this source,
the fear of losing it makes even Ghorkas shy of a
collision with the British Government. The soil is
fertile, and intersected by numerous streams, which, fed
by the eternal snows of the main chain, afford a more
certain supply of water than the great rivers that flow
into the Ganges from the South. The ground immediately under the hills is, however, wild and broken, and
covered with luxuriant jungles, which swarm with wild
animals of every species, from elephants to monkeys.
It is the custom of the magnates of Mofussilpore to
make an expedition thither in the spring of every year;
and Jung Bahadur, the mayor of the palace at the court
of Katamandoo, holds it in high repute as a shooting
ground. As the Nepaulese have no "modified resolu-
"tions concerning the sale of waste lands," it is probable
that this region will long provide abundant sport alike
for civil servants and native premiers. Last year the
party from the station had been a good deal annoyed by

the suspicion with which they had been regarded by the local officials; so Tom had obtained a permit from the great man himself, giving us leave to shoot for twenty days. It was attested by his seal, which gave his title at full length in English, "Jung Bahadur, G.C.B., Prime "Minister of Nepaul."

For months beforehand preparations had been on foot. The arrangements for a shooting party on a grand scale demand no scant amount of administrative capacity, and require all the personal influence of a man in authority to be successfully carried out. Three elephants must be borrowed from one zemindar, and four from another; and the brigadier at Dinapore must be requested to lend the services of a score of his hugest and most earth-shaking beasts, and his pluckiest mahouts. Then tents and howdahs must be looked up and repaired, and a small commissariat department organized for the provisioning of a little army of drivers, grass-cutters, and servants at a distance from the depôts. Then communications must be kept open between the station and the camp, and a daily dawk maintained on a system resembling as little as possible that of the General Post Office of India. Finally, the comfort of the Sahibs must be insured; bacon, cheese, flour, sheep, fowls, beer-shrub, brandy-shrub, sherry-shrub, Simkin-shrub, tea-shrub, belatte-pawnee, meta-pawnee,[1] penica-pawnee,[2] must be despatched on a-head, and a double set of horses laid down at six-mile stages along the whole line of road.

From the 16th to the 19th of February, elephants came to Mofussilpore in quick succession; and, as fast

[1] Lemonade. [2] Drinking-water.

as they arrived, we presented each mahout with a rupee and a bag of rice, and sent him on to camp. On the evening of the 20th, young Benson, the assistant-magistrate, treated his brother-hunters to a bachelor-dinner. We were four in number: our host, Tom, myself, and Mr. Mildred, an indigo planter who resided in the vicinity—a first-rate spear and rough rider, and a most keen sportsman, but unselfish enough to consider the sport of others as more important than his own. If ever I am sent to skirmish in open order, I should like to have Mildred for the front-rank man of my file. We got uncommonly jolly under the combined stimulus of Simkin and anticipation. After dessert was removed, we spent the evening in sewing up bullets in linen— a wise precaution, for it is poor work fumbling for a patch when, having just fired away all your ball at an antelope, you see a streak of yellow and black glancing through the grass twenty yards in front of your elephant.

The next morning we rose at half after three, and started off into the darkness in two tumtums, or dogcarts. Everybody in these parts keeps at least three horses: and no one who meditates a journey feels any delicacy about asking for the loan of as many as he requires, from the factories and stations bordering on his route. It soon grew light, and we bowled merrily along at the rate of eight miles an hour, including stoppages, and ferries, and shyings, and boltings, and rearings. The road, not having been constructed under the auspices of the Public Works Department, was in excellent order. A grass causeway ran along the centre, high and dry; while on either side was a sort of ditch sacred to bullock hackeries. Long before each set of nags had lost their freshness, we came in sight of another pair, standing sometimes beneath an ancient peepul-tree, sometimes under the walls of a ruined temple, sometimes in a grove of mangoes or palms. Mofussil horses behave in a most fiendish manner at starting; but, when once well off, they complete their stage with laudable zeal and propriety. Some are incorrigible planters, considering it essential to their dignity to stand perfectly still for ten minutes after they have been put between the shafts. Others jib violently and back into the cart-track beneath, while a cascade of gun-cases slides over the rear of the tum-tum, and a stream of Collectors pours out in front. In other cases, the owner holds the animal's head high in the air, to prevent him from kicking the vehicle to pieces; and, when the harness has been adjusted, sends him off at a gallop, and jumps up behind as best he may.

By eleven o'clock we had accomplished forty-seven miles in safety, and found ourselves at an old military station on the borders of Nepaul. During the war at the beginning of the century, a battalion had been quartered here, but the place had long been deserted. The bungalows were abandoned to the jackal and the cobra, the compounds were overgrown with brushwood, the wells choked with rubbish. One ancient lady, a Mrs. Grant—whose husband, the regimental surgeon, had died and been buried during the period of our occupation—lived on here for many years in perfect solitude, till she lapsed into semi-barbarism, quarrelling with her native servants, and keeping a number of deer and cats under her roof, from which she could not be persuaded to tear herself even after they had departed this life, and become too high to be agreeable pets. The aspect of the burial-ground was melancholy and singular. Amidst a group of trees enclosed within a ruined wall were scattered, fast crumbling to decay, those unsightly masses of brick-work which make hideous the last home of the stranger in India. Here, as elsewhere, most of the inscriptions had been removed by the rustics of the neighbourhood, to be used for grinding their curry; but some few remained, of which one, showing signs of comparatively recent repair, stated itself to be in " affectionate memory of Dr. Grant." Others recorded the names of officers hardly emerged from boyhood, whose pre-conceived hopes of the excitement of active service and the gaiety of country quarters were realized in ennui, brandy-pawnee, jungle-fever, and an early grave. One monument was erected to a Waterloo hero by " his friend, Lord Combermere," who has lived through another generation since his old comrade was buried in the wilds of Nepaul.

The last vestige of practicable road ceased at the frontier. So we alighted, unloaded the tumtums, and packed our guns and baggage on a couple of elephants. As the Happy Hunting Grounds were seven coss, or fourteen miles, within the Nepaulese territory, we took a few hours' rest and a hearty tiffin under the shade of a noble banyan tree—a tree that is to other trees as a patriarchal clan to a modern household. Just as, in primitive times, every community owned a common father, whose memory formed an indissoluble tie long after he was dead and gone, even when the family had increased into a mighty nation; so the banyan is a forest in itself, which, for centuries after every trace of the parent trunk has disappeared, grows outward and upward, till whole battalions might repose within the circuit of its boughs. Here we drank tea, and smoked, and did gymnastics on the branches, and read Tristram Shandy out loud, till three in the afternoon, when we saddled the horses, and re-commenced our march.

Before we had gone many yards, my horse, a fiery young Cabul stallion belonging to Mildred, said Ha, ha, and pitched me over his head; and then proceeded, after their manner, to eat me like a radish, from the feet upwards. He was not, however, destined to enjoy his unhallowed meal in peace; for his owner, who dismounted on the spot, and to my intense relief insisted on changing animals with me, speedily brought him to reason with a pair of heavy spurs and a cotton umbrella. We were conducted by a guide along a track, far more rugged than the fields on either side, through a rich country thickly studded with villages. Tom's eye, more practised or more partial than my own, detected numerous signs of mis-government. He bade us observe that the tillage had imperceptibly fallen off, and that the people lived in wretched wicker huts; while, on his side of the border, each man had his excellent mud cabin thatched with straw. The population was entirely Hindoo; but here and there we came across a Nepaulese official, clothed in skins, and invariably armed with the heavy curved knife which the native tribes far and near dread as the Tarentines and Etrurians dreaded the broadsword of old Rome. Our own sepoys, led by British officers, could not be brought to stand the charge of the Hillmen; and on more than one memorable occasion even the English bayonets gave way before the Ghorka blades. For a whole year, the regular army of Nepaul, a mere handful of some 12,000 warriors, defended their extensive frontier against tremendous odds. The earlier engagements in the war read like Prestonpans and Killiecrankie. At length, when Ochterlony, acting with great caution and skill, had out-manœuvred the chiefs of these Highlanders of the east, they avoided a Culloden, by signifying their agreement to an equitable peace, the terms of which have been faithfully observed by both parties—an instance of mutual respect rare in India. The specimens of the race whom we passed on the road, to judge by their appearance, would be awkward customers in a surprise or foray. Short, with thick firm limbs, light complexions, long matted hair, and an inexpressibly humorous cast of features, they looked us full in the face, and laughed and talked with a freedom and dignity which had quite a bracing effect on men accustomed to Bengalee servility and effeminacy. In fact, the Ghorkas are a military aristocracy, like the Spartans of blue blood; the other Nepaulese represent the Lakedæmonians or Pericœki, (in gratitude to dear Mr. Grote for that history which all scholars love and all pedants hate and envy, I make a point of spelling to his fancy,) while the Hindoos of the Terai are little better than Helots.

In a bold and singularly unsuccessful attempt to take a flying leap over a mud wall, Benson broke a stirrup-leather, and while he stopped to mend it with his boot-laces, Tom took occasion to question the villagers about the system adopted by the Nepaulese for getting in the revenue, expecting to obtain some information concerning the grades and duties of the collectors, the nature and amount of the assessment, the permanency of the settlement, &c. His audience burst out laughing, and replied that the received method of collecting consisted in placing a lattee, which is the name for the quarter-staff carried by all Indian peasants, under the defaulter's knee, and raising his leg till he became able to pay up. As to a Permanent Settlement, the Government officers sometimes brought a ryot's elbows behind his back, passed a lattee under them, hung him by his heels to a tree, and settled him there permanently, unless his quota was forthcoming; but they had never heard of any other. The amount of the assessment seemed to average about four times the sum that would be exacted for the same lands by the English Treasury, with as much more as could be squeezed out of the tenants by these legitimate means of coercion. In return for the tribute, the Imperial Government does not appear to have provided its subjects with cheap and speedy justice, or with facilities for the instruction of their children, or any of the other benefits by which we seek to compensate the natives for the loss of their independence, and salve our own consciences; while the state of the roads and of the irrigation went to show that the Khatmandoo Department of Public Works was hardly superior in efficiency to our own. The whole strength of the Ghorka administration seems to be concentrated on their War Office, and their Prime Ministers are better hands at shooting their uncles through the back with blunderbusses, than at compiling codes or devising sweeping measures of popular education.

A BLOODY FLUX.

As we went by a miserable hovel, a man ran out, and putting up his hands in the attitude of prayer, as is the universal custom among natives when addressing a superior, entreated Tom to cure him of a bloody flux, from which he had suffered for the space of two years. Tom said, kindly, that if he would come to Mofussilpore, every attention should be paid to his case; but this was not what the poor fellow wanted. He had fondly imagined that the Sahib would make him whole by a word or a touch. Europeans are rarer birds and more like black swans in these parts than in the British dominions, and very mysterious notions exist concerning their powers for good and evil. This was a fair instance of what the missionary tracts call "Illustrations of Scripture." How sick one got as a child of those little green books, which never tired of informing us that the Chinese rice-growers even now cast their bread on the waters and find it after many days; and that even now the Hindoos take up their beds and walk. The similes, drawn by our Saviour from the familiar scenes around him, come home to one with great force out here. Every week a magistrate, in Cutcherry, disposes of cases which forcibly remind one how little twenty centuries have modified the immutable ways of Oriental agricultural life. Still, when a farmer goes forth at dawn to find his boundary stone rolled inwards, or his crop choked with tares, he knows that "an enemy hath done this." Still the unjust Gomastah calls his lord's tenants unto him, and bids one who owes a hundred seers of indigo take his bill and write fifty, and another who owes a hundred maunds of grain take his bill and write fourscore, trusting wisely to the selfish gratitude of the mammon of unrighteousness. Still, when some strong man of doubtful loyalty has been deprived of his weapons under the Disarming Act, the dacoits dig through the wall, and first bind the strong man, and then spoil his house. The excessive aversion to pedestrian exercise that prevails among old residents, and the great difficulty which a fresh arrival experiences in obtaining a companion for a walk, frequently recalls the text which enjoins a special manifestation of unselfishness. More than once have I induced a good Christian to go with me a mile sorely against his will, who, when we have accomplished that distance, has freely offered to complete the twain.

As we approached the mountains the crops became poorer and fewer, and the patches of cultivation were surrounded with rude fences—a sure sign that we were come into the region of deer. At length we entered upon a grass plain sprinkled with brushwood, fringed on three sides with jungle. It was now the cool of the evening, and we put our horses into a gallop, which soon brought us to the border of a vast wood. After winding about through the trees for the better part of an hour, we hit upon the camp just before dark; and a very picturesque scene it was. The tents stood in an open space of an acre and a half or two acres, enclosed in the primæval forest. Along the west side of the encampment, at the foot of a bank that went sheer down to the depth of thirty feet, ran the river Bogmutty, babbling over the pebbles like a highland burn. To use the expression of old Pepys, it was pretty to see the excitement of my companions at the sound and aspect of a running brook. Men who, for a dozen years, had never known anything but stagnant tanks, or wide sluggish streams the colour of pea-soup, were beside themselves with delight at the tinkling of the water as it rippled over the shingle, the deep clear pools "with "here and there a lusty trout," the peewits calling to each other from the brink, the rocks which afforded so inviting a dressing-room to bathers who were sceptical on the subject of crocodiles and leeches. Some six miles to the northward the Himalayas sprang straight up from the plain to the height of five thousand feet; while, in the far distance, we could discern the white line of those mysterious hills beside which Monte Rosa and the Matterhorn are mere pigmies; from whose glaciers even Wills would turn away in despair; on whose summits not even a Tyndall could plant a thermometer.

If I live a hundred years (in which case the Government will have made an uncommonly bad bargain, as I shall have continued to draw my pension for half a century), I shall never forget that first morning in the wilderness. I sauntered out of the tent, after a long cool sleep, into an air as pure and fresh as the air of Malvern. All around the jungle-cocks were crowing and the sea-fowl hooting, while every now and then was heard the deep bellow of an elephant. In the space between the tents Tom was hard at work at a little table, signing, writing, and dictating to a native subordinate: while a sowar, or mounted policeman, blazing in scarlet and blue, stood bridle in hand waiting to escort the post into British territory. Mildred had got out his guns, and was examining them with that loving solicitude which a lady bestows on her gowns, jewels, and furniture, but which a man is too proud to show except in the case of a favourite fire-arm, or a decrepid salmon-rod which has seen tougher days. Benson was enjoying his coffee and toast, and between the sips read aloud an article in one of the Calcutta papers, proving from Scripture the Divine origin of the Contract Law, to which Mildred listened with an occasional grunt of satisfaction. In one corner of the camp lay the howdahs. In another, the cooks were making preparations for breakfast, which, as it was we who were going to eat it, we took good care not to observe too minutely. In the river below lay a dozen elephants; while others were cautiously descending the steep bank, or mounting it again after their bath. The huge animals wallowed patiently in the stream, while their mahouts scrambled over their bodies scraping them with a species of overgrown curry-comb. Those who had been half-washed presented a most droll contrast of colour between the white coating of dust and the natural black hue of their skin. We wandered forth into the wood, where the jungle-fowl—who are neither more nor less than cocks and hens in a wild state, with singularly beautiful plumage—ran and fluttered within a few yards of us. Every moment we came upon a group of two or three elephants, standing amidst a great heap of leaves and branches, which they consumed very leisurely and with an air of profound reflection. Meanwhile the drivers were grinding their curry under an extempore tent formed of pads propped up against each other, or saying the morning prayer with their faces turned towards far Mecca. Our horses were tethered in the centre of a lofty grove of ancient trees;

and near them stood the four howdah-elephants; noble beasts, who towered far above their fellows; their tusks ornamented with metal rings, and their broad foreheads painted in grotesque patterns. Elephants in good condition are very fat and full. Strange stories these old howdah-wallahs could tell us, if they had the gift of speech! They may have dragged a gun into action at Plassey, or groaned beneath the litter of the Grand Mogul when he was still sovereign of the continent from Nepaul to Travancore. Perhaps this sight of the wilderness reminds them, in a dreamy manner, of a Ceylonese forest, far back in the depths of time, where they wandered, and browzed, and bathed, and loved and were jilted, and fought, (for their small eyes get very green on provocation), until some white monkeys tied their legs together, and carried them off into a servitude which they have tolerated ever since with magnificent Oriental indifference. They have seen the empire of Delhi fade away, and John Company come and go. They have beheld the President of Council turn into Governor General, and the Governor General into Lieutenant of the Queen of India. They have witnessed a long succession of Deficits, and have attained to the days of a Surplus, palpable and tangible. They have lived to wonder at the roar and the rush of a steam-engine amidst regions where, with Scindia or Meer Jaffia on their backs, they have stood the roar and the rush of many a tiger and buffalo. I wonder whether they recollect their first mahout, and whether they think the rice now-a-days as good as it was in the heyday of youth, when they were still in their grand climacteric.

After breakfast we started for a point about a mile

distant, whence we were to begin shooting; and on the way we settled ourselves in our howdahs as agreeably as circumstances would allow. The howdah consists of a box of wood and wicker-work, open at top, with sides three and a half feet high. There is a tolerably comfortable seat in front for the Sahib, and a remarkably uncomfortable one behind for the attendant. On either side of the sportsman rest his firearms; a double-barrelled rifle and two smooth-bores loaded with ball, and one gun with a couple of charges of "number four," or "BB," shot for partridge and jungle-fowl. As most of the firing consists of snapshots within fifty yards, a good smooth-bore is every whit as effective as a grooved barrel. In a number of little partitions in the front of the howdah the ammunition lies ready to hand. Here are a couple of dozen of well-oiled bullets packed snugly in a tooth-powder box. There is the leather shot-belt which you have carried over Perthshire moor, and Galway bog, and Somersetshire stubble, till it has grown limp, and black, and greasy, and beloved. In this drawer roll too and fro, with every jolt of your animal the remnant of a batch of green cartridges, which the gamekeeper at your grandfather's gave you as a parting present at the end of your last day's shooting on English ground; the day you wiped the old gentleman's eye four several times, and were rewarded by a tip of a hundred pounds to buy hookahs, accompanied with an exhortation not to marry a Begum. Your Chuprassie sits behind with an umbrella covered with white linen, with which he contrives to come to the most frightful grief whenever you get among trees. In two holsters on either side of him swing a bottle of

HUNTING COSTUME.

lemonade and another of soda water, while your lunch is stowed away in the well beneath your seat. Your dress is simple; a flannel shirt; the trousers of your college boat-club, the wash-leather lining of which is very grateful towards the close of a hard day; a pair of canvas shoes, and an enormous pith hat with a thick pad hanging down your back, which, combined with the howdah, gives you the appearance of a sporting mushroom growing in a flower-pot. Your *tout ensemble* is not as elegant as that of a cockney on the twelfth of August; nor would it pass muster at a show meet in the grass-counties. But, as a dentist once said to me, " All is not stopping that glitters." I dare say Nimrod's leathers were of an archaic cut, and yet he rode to hounds as well as most antediluvians.

On arriving at the rendezvous we found the pad elephants, forty-four in number; which, with the howdah-wallahs, gave us a line of four dozen. Tom, whom we had elected captain, deployed them as well as the difficulties of the ground would admit. Then we advanced, Mildred on the right wing, Tom and myself in the centre, and Benson on the left. Oh, the wild romantic charm of that first day in the forest! The strange luxuriant vegetation. The parasites, hanging in festoons from tree to tree. The gaudy graceful birds, not now seated in uneasy attitudes under a glass case in a drawing-room, with a wire through their bodies, staring in ghastly fashion out of their bead eyes, but piping and darting about among their native foliage. The big baboons swinging from branch to branch, and the lesser monkeys scudding along the cordage of knotted creepers, unconscious of the existence of such beings as Savoyard organ-grinders, the curse alike of man and ape. The jungle-cock, cackling and running about among the fallen leaves, at which I take a deadly aim, when, as my finger already contracts on the trigger, a timely heave of my elephant flings the barrel ten degrees farther from the horizon. The cry on the far right of "Deer ahead! Look out!" And in and out of the trunks, comes dodging a bright red animal, which recalls in a second a flood of Zoological Garden associations. Trembling from head to foot, I drop the shot-gun, and put a rifle to my shoulder, which—"Con-" found it! It's on half cock!" At last I fire, and have the pleasure of seeing a white mark appear on the bark of a sycamore just above the deer's back. A fair shot enough; but, alas, a miss is as good as half a coss. And now my elephant is brushing through the brambles along the bottom of a nullah; and Benson has wandered in a vague manner away to the left, drawing a score of elephants after him; and Tom, in a state of white rage, has gone to bring him to book; and Mildred, who never does anything without an object, has gradually crept up towards me, and is marching on the bank above with his thumb on the hammer of his fowling-piece, and—whir-r-r-r, a vast bird rises before me, obscuring one whole quarter of the heaven with its wings and tail, and I give him both my barrels, and he reels and drops with a slow stately swoop, and lies amidst the tangled grass, gorgeous in death, the hundred-eyed favourite of the Queen of Olympus. Then, as the day draws on, we reach a part of the wood where the trees are young and the ground clear of undergrowth. Leaning back in the howdah, I fancy for the moment that I am passing through a plantation in an English county, and almost expect to see a board threatening to prosecute me with the utmost rigour, or an old keeper in a suit of fustian, with a bunch of vermin-traps hanging from his shoulder, or—What is that thing tumbling through the trees a-head? A cow? A big dog? Heavens and earth, a huge black bear! "Juldee, ma"hout! Juldee, budzart!"[1] We're gaining! we're "gaining! No, no! Yes, we are! He's gone. No; "there he is again. Will you look sharp, you beastly "old wallah?" Meanwhile, far behind, I hear Tom bawling to me to come back and be— No; the distance must have deceived me. After a fruitless chase of a mile, I obey, and, crestfallen and repentant, listen to a general lecture on my shortcomings, and a special order at sight of bear or tiger to call "Tallyho," and keep to the line. And, when no game is in view, I have the amusement of observing the almost human sagacity of my elephant; of watching him make his way, howdah and all, through thickets which a man on foot could not penetrate; breaking off great branches and tearing down creepers with his trunk, and pushing over small trees with his massive forehead. Then there are thoughts of tiffin, and occasional draughts of meta pawnee, and sweet anticipations of the lies I shall tell when I get back to Calcutta, and the flaming letter I shall write to the Scholar's table at Trinity. Oh! it is good to tear oneself for awhile from visiting cards, and white chokers, and swallowtail coats, to a life primitive and simple, without waistcoat or collar, care or dignity! It is good to tell the time by sunrise, and noon, and

[1] Quick, mahort! Quick, base-born man!

evening, instead of dividing the glorious day into periods nicknamed ten-fifteen and four-thirty; to eat when hungry, and sleep when weary, and meditate when you feel thoughtful, and talk when you feel gushing. It is good that your object for a time should be, not to send in a Report that shall touch a tender chord in the heart of your Chief Commissioner, but to keep your portion of the line in faultless order by a liberal use of all the powers of vituperation which Providence has allotted you; to shoot a pea-chick for soup, and a blue pigeon, whose feathers will complete the plume which you promised to that dear little girl with whom you danced the three last waltzes at the Bengal Club Ball.

During this expedition I began to realize the ruling principles of military operations. In order to appreciate the history of a campaign, the reader must constantly bear in mind that multitudes are always helpless and unwieldy. A single man, or a dozen or score of men, will carry their packs and rifles across a country for months together, at the rate of twenty miles a day, procuring food as they go along. But ten thousand men must be handled as if they were so many women. Good roads must be chosen, and plenty of them. The communications must be kept open, and provisions, clothes, and shoes stored at convenient points. The length of the day's march must be such as to allow the train of cannon, waggons, bullock-carts, and baggage mules to keep up with the fighting part of the force. I now began to understand the problems which have puzzled five hundred generations of schoolboys, with the exception possibly of the proverbial genius in the fourth form; why Epaminondas did not advance on Sparta from the battle-field of Leuctra; why Hannibal did not advance upon Rome from the slaughter of Cannæ. We never succeeded in moving our tents and furniture to a distance of more than four coss from the last encampment. The country being strange, there continually occurred some misunderstanding about the name and direction of places. Our guides lost their way, and our wheels came off, and our carters stopped to bathe in the nullahs. Sometimes there was no track, and the weakest and the most insane of the elephants had to be left behind to convey our heavy property. Then the rice fell short, and the oxen fell sick, and the mounted escort fell off, and our servants fell to loggerheads with the village people. Nothing but Tom's excellence as a quartermaster-general saved us from confusion a great deal worse confounded. He shone, not only as an administrator, but as a tactician. It is far easier work to manœuvre a battalion of volunteers, among whom every third man considers his claims to the colonelcy overwhelming, than to bring a line of half a hundred elephants through a thorn jungle without clubbing them hopelessly. As it is impossible to see more than ten yards to the right and left, a gap once made, there is every chance that the array will be split up into two fragments, marching towards opposite quarters. The mahouts are a lazy stupid lot, with none of the interest in the sport displayed by English beaters, and with a more than ordinary Hindoo faculty for going to sleep under circumstances the most unsuited for that pastime. They are very tender of their skins, and, when not strictly watched, are apt to follow the howdah elephant through the thicket in a long string, instead of beating the bushes on either side of him. Consequently every sportsman has to look very sharply after his section of the line. At first I expected to feel the want of an intimate acquaintance with the native terms of abuse; but a copious fount of vigorous English, assisted by the signs that are common to all time, was an excellent substitute for a full vocabulary of vernacular slang; the more so as I had provided myself with one disparaging epithet, which seldom came amiss, "Budzart," "base-born," which has the advantage, rare in Hindoo Billingsgate, of not embodying a painful and unscrupulous assertion regarding the female relatives of the person addressed. Probably the mahouts in the army of Hannibal were not over and above familiar with colloquial Punic, and yet that eminent general appears to have had no difficulty in explaining to them when their animals were to slide down a glacier on their hind quarters, and when they were to wait till the cruet-stand was brought up from the rear. I adopted a simple plan. Whenever a driver appeared incorrigibly sluggish or disobedient I made him take his place next me, within reach of my loading-rod. For instance, if a fellow in a turban loitered behind to steal sugar-canes, I would call out, "Hi, "pugree-wallah! Pugree-wallah, hi!" Hereupon was attracted the attention of all the men wearing pugrees, who were thus as a class interested in identifying the culprit; and, at a wave of my arm, they would shove him in front of the line, and pass him on till he came into the place of torment. One very drowsy old boy, with a long white beard, passed three-fourths of every

TRIALS OF TEMPER.

day in this unenviable post. The heat and the excitement of Indian shooting are a severe trial to the temper. It is especially necessary to be careful with your own mahout, as he sits immediately below, within the swing of your fist, and, as both his hands are occupied, the temptation to box his ears is, on provocation, fearfully strong. I should like to see Job himself at the moment when, as he is loading for dear life, with a leopard in the reeds before him, the mahout takes him under a branch which sweeps the top of the howdah, knocks him breathless on to the seat, scratches his pet rifle from muzzle to breach, and sends a charge of shot through the crown of his helmet. Unfortunately, your orders are liable to be mistaken on account of the similarity between the two words which are most often in your mouth, "left" and "right." Their sound is well enough represented by "binah" and "dinah;" though a young gentleman who has been pronounced "Satisfactory" in Oordoo will not be content with anything under "bahiná," and "dahiná."

At two o'clock we came to the skirts of a wide plain of turf, with here and there a patch of grass a foot or so in height, browned by the sun. To an English eye the nature of the ground showed poor promise of game. But my companions knew better, and agreed that the cream of the sport was still to come. We made a halt, and lunched on plum-cake and cold tea. No sensible hunter will touch alcohol in any shape till the day's work is over. Nothing but the strictest temperance can avert the dangers of the heat and glare. Indeed, total abstinence is the safest rule for the jungle. The first evening we indulged freely in ale and sherry; then we came down to claret, and from that to lemonade, and a mixture of beer and soda-water, which was very refreshing at the price. The charms of brandy and belattee pawnee, a beverage which goes by the name of a "peg" (according to the favourite derivation, because each draught is a "peg" in your coffin), are far too seductive and insidious for a climate which in itself finds more than sufficient work for the nerves.

After tiffin we advanced in a half-moon, so that the howdah elephants on the wings formed bastions, whence an enfilading fire might sweep from right to left. Our array presented a most impressive appearance as we moved over the plain in stately guise. No Eastern potentate marching to subdue an empire could present a more formidable front than this party of civilians beating for hare and partridge. The firing was incessant all along the line. Besides small game, the long grass swarmed with hog-deer and antelope, while now and then a majestic florican flapped away in the distance. Before we had gone very far, one of the pad elephants, who had throughout the day shown symptoms of mild frenzy, now threw aside every vestige of sanity, and knocked over three of his smaller comrades in succession, not being chivalrous enough to butt one of his own size. Tom, after a hurried investigation, declared him to be a criminal lunatic, ordered him to be put into a sort of straight pad, and told off two great tusk-wallahs to act as keepers, who beat him about with their trunks until he became tractable. Towards evening a spotted deer got up in front of Benson, who fired a shot which broke its leg. We started in pursuit, plying it with ball and slug, but for a long time it succeeded in keeping about eighty yards ahead, till it took sanctuary in a bush. When we came up we found ourselves in the most ridiculous plight, for every one of our thirty barrels had been discharged. At last Mildred loaded again, and shot the animal dead, while Benson and I gave it a parting salvo; and, finally, the Mahommedan mahouts jumped down and cut its throat, calling upon Allah, and pretending to imagine that it was still alive. By this piece of hypocrisy they comfort their consciences, for they profess to believe with the Jews that God "will set His face against that soul that eateth "blood, and will cut him off from among His people:" a doctrine which, since the manifesto of the bishops against the unfortunate man of Natal, I suppose we must all hold as necessary to salvation, in common with Hebrew and Mussulman. That night, when the game was laid in state at the tent-door, we counted fifteen holes in the body of the deer. You may be sure we did not dispute the possession of the skin.

And several days passed in like manner, as delightful as constant change of scene, the innumerable chances of the chase, and rare good fellowship could make them. We bathed, and hunted, and lunched, and hunted again. We had our fair share of incidents. Tom shot a peacock through the neck with a single ball, at a distance of two hundred yards, and I hit an old cow in the stomach at a distance of twenty, under the impression that she was a wild buffalo. A native thief, on being detected among the tent-ropes, ran a muck with a beer bottle, and created a panic among our servants, but was eventually knocked down by Mildred, who executed a rude justice on his person with a boot-jack, and then kicked him out of camp. We played whist, we skinned birds, we manufactured and wore to rags an endless supply of bad jokes, which, in after days, will be the shibboleth of the expedition. We disputed by the hour on neology, physiology, free-thought, free-trade, free-will, the respective merits of light and heavy charges of powder, and the virtues of tobacco as a soporific. On the Saturday night we held a general council, to consider the propriety of shooting on the morrow, since there were no ladies or clergymen to scandalize, no church to attend, and nothing to do but to read "Tris-"tram Shandy," which can hardly be said to come under the category of Sunday books. Old associations prevailed, and we resolved not to have out the pad elephants, but to make a *détour* to the next camping-ground, and "shoot anything we came across," which comprised five pigeons, three hares, a jackal, a wild cat, and a cobra-capella. At length, during dinner, one evening, a cowherd came with information, or kubbur, concerning a tiger, which had carried off a bullock at a place some six miles to the eastward. Now here was kubbur, but the momentous question was, "is it "pucka?" Tom thought it looked well, and, if the man's story was true, our chances seemed very good; for a tiger invariably lurks three days in the neighbourhood of his prey.

We went to bed in high expectation, and the next morning Benson called up the whole party four several times before six o'clock, our usual hour for rising. "You have waked me too soon," as the Irishman said when suspended animation was restored during his premature funeral rites. Tom's native official was very

TANTALIZATION.

anxious to be allowed to see the sport, but refused an offer of one of the pad elephants, on the ground that he entertained "apprehensions that inconvenience would "result from the friction;" so I took him up in my back seat, while the man who had lost the bullock stood behind Tom's howdah. The forest in which the tiger was supposed to be lying was very extensive, which considerably decreased our hopes. Our captain gave strict orders to fire at nothing except tiger and sambhur, a gigantic deer of the elk species. As invariably happens in such a case, the less noble game seemed to find pleasure in tantalizing us. Antelopes stood gazing upon us out of their large eyes for minutes together. Great hogs trotted gravely away within pistol-shot. Pea-fowl and jungle-hens scuttled about till the ground beneath looked like a poultry-yard. At last a very small fawn proved too much for my forbearance. But the consciousness of guilt unnerved my arm. I missed, and Tom's voice pealed down the line—

"Is that a tiger?"

"No; a deer."

"What? A sambhur?"

"I—I—I'm not quite certain. I think it was."

Soon after, a peacock, which had strutted before my nose for a quarter of a mile, became irresistible. I fired, and, being now hardened in crime, not unsuccessfully. Then came the question—

"Hallo! What's that?"

"H'm. My gun went off."

"I know that. What did it go off at?"

This time I judiciously pretended to be out of ear-shot.

M

After struggling through two miles of frightful thicket we came to a dry nullah, along which we marched, feeling the bank with our right. A conviction seemed to prevail that a crisis was approaching. "Confound "those mahouts," I said, "they're trying to sneak off." My companion replied, "Sire, they seem bent upon "absconding." And now we reached a spot that to a novice had much of horror and mystery. On the brink of the ravine lay a tract overgrown with rank coarse grass, which overtopped the shoulder of the tallest elephant. Every tree in the neighbourhood was covered with a swarm of foul vultures, who filled the air with discordant ill-omened cries. We began to perceive a strong smell of putrid flesh, which became more oppressive as we drew on. Here, or nowhere, was the tiger's lair. The contrast which our array now presented to its ordinary appearance was as marked as that between a battalion on parade and in action. The drivers of the smaller beasts hung back, and one by one left their places in the line, while the howdah-bearers gradually converged towards the point where the stench and the cloud of flies told us that the tyrant of the jungle could not be far distant. Silent as death, with finger on trigger, every nerve quivering with excitement, straining our eyes downwards to left and right, we advanced in a cluster, step by step, through the tangled vegetation. To my dying day I shall never forget the look on Mildred's face as he peered into the ground below. Ten yards from the brink of the gully we came upon the mangled remnant of the bullock, and then the grass was agitated as with the motion of some large animal, and, casting back a glance of scorn, at the throng of

THE DEATH STRUGGLE. 163

men and brutes, forth he stalked from his covert, the Royal Nepaul Tiger. Quick as thought came the report of all our rifles, and more than one red spot appeared on his tawny flank. With a roar, a flash of his tail, and one tremendous bound, he was among us. I have a very dim recollection of what followed. Bullets were whizzing all around, Tom firing over my shoulder, and Benson into my howdah; the tiger at one time on the head of Mildred's elephant, at another between the legs of mine ; our beasts trumpeting, and plunging, and rolling; the rank and file scampering away in ungovernable terror. At the end of what seemed ten minutes, and was perhaps ninety seconds, the tiger lay dead amidst the trampled grass, with six balls in his body, one in the foreleg, and another through the brain.

We returned in triumph, shooting at everything that presented itself. I achieved a conquest over an ancient swine, which I brought down as it careered past at a distance of at least fifteen feet from the muzzle of my gun, at the rate of two miles an hour, including stoppages. As our Mahommedan followers refused to have anything to do with the unutterable flesh, we forced some Hindoos to alight and hoist the boar on to an elephant as it knelt on the ground. It is hard to say whether the men or the animal evinced most disgust. For a long time the mahouts pretended that the weight was more than they could manage; but at last they heaved the pig up, upon which the elephant raised itself on its forelegs, shot off its burden behind, and scrambled away in this absurd attitude, roaring horribly. After a quarter of an hour of this nonsense, during which I endeavoured in vain to quicken the movements of the group by pelting them with custard-apples from an overhanging bough, I appeared among them with my loading-rod, as a *diabolus ex machinâ*, and the job was done in fifty seconds. Tom offered to prepare the boar's skull to be preserved as a trophy, which excited the most supreme contempt in the breast of Mildred, who remarked, " Some time hence, when the whole thing " has been forgotten, you can say you *speared* him."

We agreed to drink our last two bottles of Simkin in honour of our signal victory. After dinner the fun became uproarious. Every glass added an inch to the length and height of the tiger, till at last he assumed such monstrous proportions in Benson's mouth that Mildred jotted down the items, and chalked a rude sketch of the animal on the table. The result was certainly startling. "Gad, sir," said the artist, "a " young elephant is nothing to him." At last Tom knocked down Mildred for a song, who gave us the following plaintive ditty, replete with touching allusion to Government paper, in which he had lately taken a deep interest, with a view to future investment.

> " John Company, my Jo, John,
>   When we were first acquent
> You borrowed, like the Yankees,
>   At eight or ten per cent.
> Our Fours are now at par, John ;
>   Our Cash Requirements low.
> Yet honour to your old good name,
>   John Company, my Jo.
>
> " John Company, my Jo, John,
>   Those tight tight days are past,
> The English budget system
>   A surplus shows at last.

> In eighteen seventy-three, John,
>   To limbo you must go,
> And all your stock will be redeemed,
>   John Company, my Jo."

Tom followed with a chanson a thought too local for English taste. Still, if Longfellow considers himself justified in borrowing the burden of a song from the dead languages, a Mofussil collector has surely a right to pay the same compliment to Oordoo, the current dialect in the north of India. " Juldee jao " really does mean "go quickly;" whereas "excelsior" is not "higher," but simply "taller," a horrid bit of Americanism. Pray observe that " lao," which is pronounced like the first three letters in "lout," is the Hindoostanee for " bring ; " that " qui hye " is the ordinary summons to a servant ; that a mookhtar is a native attorney and a omedwan a native petitioner; and that Mahommed is a name as universal among kitmutgars as John among London footmen.

> " When from the palkee I descend,
>   Too weary to rejoice
> At sight of my Mofussil friend,
>   I cry with feeble voice,
> Ere yet within the genial tub
>   I plunge my clammy brow ;
> ' Qui hye, Mahommed, brandy shrub,
>   ' Belattee pawnee lao ! '

> " As from Cutcherry home I spin,
>   Worn with the ceaseless rout
> Of mookhtars quarrelling within
>   And omedwans without,
> My servant catches from afar
>   The mandate, 'Juldee jao !
> ' Hullo, there ! Brandy, kitmutgar
>   ' Belattee pawnee lao ! '

" When I, a poor forsaken brute,
 On fevered couch repose ;
No man of medical repute
 Within a hundred coss ;
One sovereign remedy I know,
 Whose virtues all allow ;
' Qui hye, Mahommed, Brandy do !
 ' Belattee pawnee lao ! ' "

Yours truly,

H. BROUGHTON.

LETTER VII.

ABOUT CALCUTTA AND ITS CLIMATE; WITH SERIOUS INFERENCES.

CALCUTTA, *April* 12, 1863.

DEAR SIMKINS,—The hot weather has set in. These words may convey to you no very definite idea, beyond the general one, of punkahs and iced champagne; but to us they are the earnest of miseries which are unutterable. The amenities of life are over for the year. The last waltz has been danced in the assembly-rooms; the last wicket has been pitched on the cricket ground; the last tiffin eaten in the Botanical gardens; the last couple married in the cathedral, at the very sensible and uncanonical hour of half-past five in the afternoon. People have settled themselves down to be clammy, and gloomy, and hepatic for six grilling months. The younger and more vigorous effloresce with a singularly unpleasant eruption, known as "prickly heat"—a condition which is supposed to be a sort of safety-valve for feverish tendencies, and which, therefore, excites the envy of all who are not so blessed. Conceive a climate such that an exquisitely painful cutaneous disorder is allowed to be a fair subject of congratulation! And in such a plight, amidst a temperature of 97° in the shade and anything from headache to apoplexy in the sun, men are supposed to transact official work from morn till stewy eve. Is it fair to expect high efficiency under such circumstances? Are enlarged views compatible with enlarged livers? No strain is put upon the reflective powers of Strasbourg geese. Their most active mental exercise is a vague consciousness of an increasing weight under the right wing. And why should English gentlemen be debarred from a privilege extended to Alsatian fowls? It required the transcendent genius of Milton to imagine for the lost angels this aggravation of their punishment, that they should carry on public business amidst the burning marle, and beneath the torrid clime vaulted with fire. The second book of "Paradise Lost" reads like the proceedings during the meeting of a Supreme Council to decide on the question of peace and war with Burmah or Nepaul, in which the aggressive schemes of Moloch, the first ordinary member, are opposed by Mammon, the financial member, who is nervous about his surplus, and who thinks that the country needs "repose" in order that her resources may be developed by judicious, but hearty aid from Government.

> " This desert soil
> Wants not her hidden lustre, gems and gold;
> Nor want we skill or art, from whence to raise
> Magnificence. And what can Heaven show more?"

There can be no doubt that Mammon was adverse to an annexation policy. And yet the poet does not inflict upon the fallen cherubim any heavier task than that of making and listening to speeches, a labour which he justly considered to be severe enough for such an atmosphere. There were no reports to be written, no accounts to be kept, no boxes to be worked off and passed

CALCUTTA.

on. Thammuz would find his annual wound a very different thing from an annual estimate of the net produce of the sales when opium was at 1423 rupees a chest; and Astoreth would soon have worried herself into an attack of dysentery, if the Sidonians, instead of paying her "their vows and songs," had paid five per cent. on Madapollams tariffed at ninepence, and disposed of in the market at one-and-fourpence the pound. Why, I ask, should the condition of enlightened public-spirited civilians be worse than that of Rimmon and Beelzebub?

Take your map of India, and find, if you can, a more uninviting spot than the town whose name stands at the head of this letter. Placed in the burning plain of Bengal, on the largest delta in the world, amidst a network of sluggish, muddy streams, in the neighbourhood of the jungles and marshes of the Sunderbunds, and yet so distant from the open sea as to miss the benefits of the breeze which consoles Madras for the want of a cold season and a Permanent Settlement—it unites every condition of a perfectly unhealthy situation. If the Government were in want of a site for a convalescent hospital, they could not pray for one more to their taste. The place is so bad by nature that human efforts could do little to make it worse; but that little has been done faithfully and assiduously. "God made the country," evidently without a view to its becoming a European colony; and "man made the town," and the municipal council made the drains. The combined effect is overwhelming. Statistics cannot express the state of the native streets. The unassisted genius for manufacturing smells displayed by the Hindoo becomes stupendous when aided by the sanitary measures of the local authorities. A walk in Dhurrumtollah Lane would prove too much for a City Missionary, and would try the stomach of a costermonger. During the hot months, the English aristocracy live entirely among the lofty mansions fringing the Maidan, the vast plain of turf which forms the Hyde Park of Calcutta. Here they lead an artificial life amidst gardens, and verandahs, and spacious saloons alive with punkahs, and would as soon think of walking as of taking their carriages fifty yards within the limits of the Black Town. In fact, we have at our doors a region which we dare not enter under penalty of a headache, or of feeling like a French juryman returning from the Exhibition *viâ* Folkestone and Dieppe. It is only necessary to make an hour's journey up or down the river in order to appreciate the atmosphere of Calcutta. At Barrackpore, where the average rate of mortality does not much exceed that in the Irish quarter of Liverpool during a typhus fever in the haymaking season, the air appears balmy and genial to a visitor from the capital.

A soldier might go through three battles of Waterloo with no greater risk of life than he incurs during a residence of a year in Fort William. Out of every thousand soldiers quartered in Bengal, sixty-five die in the course of every twelvemonth. And these not old Quihyes, with clogged livers and shattered nerves, but picked men in the very spring and prime of life, sent forth from home sound in wind and limb, with open chests, and arched feet, and broad straight backs. Of soldiers' wives forty-four die yearly in the thousand; and, of their children, eighty-eight in the thousand. As an old surgeon said, in 1672, of the Europeans in Bombay, "They reckon that they walk in charnel-houses. "In five hundred one hundred survive not." The European army in Bengal has, hitherto, disappeared in every ten and a-half years. This computation of course includes the men who have been invalided. The yearly mortality among the officers rises from nine to the thousand in London to twenty-four to the thousand in Bengal. The civilians, by dint of horse-exercise, and ice, and cool rooms, and trips to Simla, and furloughs to Europe, and (a better medicine than any) constant and interesting occupation, keep down their average to something over seventeen in the thousand. But a hard-worked official finds no lack of indications that he is not at Malvern or Torquay. After his first year in Calcutta, an Englishman can no longer sleep as he once slept, or eat as he once ate, and it is lucky if he drinks no more than he once drank. If you asked him to run, he would laugh in your face. I sometimes think that our uniform success in Indian warfare may be partially due to the fact that our countrymen, by long disuse, lose the power of running away. Above all, the mental faculties deteriorate surely and rapidly in this hateful climate. The mind, like the body, becomes languid and flabby and nerveless. Men live upon the capital of their energy and intellect, backed by occasional remittances from home, or from the hills. While this sudarium continues to be the seat of government, the public interests do not suffer only under the head of sick allowances and pensions; the work done here by the servants of the Crown, is far inferior in quality and quantity to what it would be in a more congenial air.

This may be clearly seen in the case of literary composition, which I take to be the most thorough strain on the mind—a sort of moral gymnastics, the greatest exercise for the greatest number of intellectual powers. At home, on a pinch, a man may write his very best for five hours in the day, and four months on end. Perhaps " Ask Mamma" might be produced at the rate of eight hours a day, and " Aurora Floyd" at the rate of twelve, while the accomplished author of " Proverbial Philosophy " may have spent weeks together in the sweet throes of creative travail. Poor old Tupper! thou art, as it were, the village donkey, at whom every one has a shy as he passes onward to his daily work. Blessed for thee will be the hour, in which a new Montgomery may take his place beside thee on the green, at whom wayward youth may discharge the potato of satire ; to whose tail fastidious middle life may attach the tin kettle of hostile criticism. Sweet it is to lie on the rosewood tables in a Clapham drawing-room ! Sweet to be quoted in households where even Cowper may not penetrate, where even Pollok is held to be profane and worldly ! But these joys may be too dearly purchased. Do they compensate thee for the ruthless raillery of the *Saturday Review?* For the clumsy mockery of the *Press*, kicking, not a sick lion, but a prostrate brother ? Do they repay thee for the misery of seeing thy divine name popularly quoted at the opposite end of the poetic scale from that of the Swan of Avon ? What Review, weekly or quarterly, metropolitan or provincial, canst thou open without lighting upon that baleful, but familiar phrase, " all bards from Shakespeare to Tupper ? " Or that sentence, which thou believest to be a translation from Sophocles, which speaks of thee in connexion with gods, and men, and columns?

But to return. Three consecutive hours of original composition on a summer-day in Calcutta, is a sufficient task for the strongest brain. Woe to him who ventures to court the muse in the first watch of the night, the hour when she lends the kindest ear to her votaries. When he tears himself from the pleasing labour, it is with nerves in high excitement, and a sensation in his head as if all the vessels and cellules in which thought lies were in a state of rabid red inflammation. A sleepless couch is the certain penalty for his presumption; and sleep is even more a necessary of life here than in England. So that, after fancying that he has wrested some hours of study from the unwilling night, he finds himself in the position of the Emperor Titus. I sometimes think that the classical idea of departed spirits' shadows pursuing shadowy occupations, hunting incorporeal game, mining for immaterial treasures, tending visionary sheep, must have been suggested by the experiences of the day that succeeds a sleepless night. You go about your ordinary cares without interest; you eat and drink without gratification; venison seems tasteless, and champagne insipid; you read without reflection, and talk without animation; your actions are prompted by habit, not by choice; you seem to live, but life is neither painful nor pleasant. I cannot conceive a man, who knows in what the value of writing consists, after having completed one book while resident in this climate, deliberately and in cold blood commencing another; and I believe that no one, who had lived and toiled here for ten years, would be capable of producing a first-class work. Even Anthony Trollope would succumb to the exhalations of the Lal Bazaar. Even Dr. Stanley would become as Cumming, and Tennyson as— no, *requiescat*.

> "Allusions sore unmoved he bore,
> And watched his books attain,
> By his foes' admission,
> The seventieth edition,
> Like 'The Rights of Man,' by Paine."

Surely this simple epitaph would well suit one who fondly imagined that he was writing poetry when he addressed the Princess Alexandra thus—

> 10,000,000 welcomes!
> 100,000,000 welcomes!
> 1,000,000,000 welcomes!

Farewell, my Tupper!
1,000,000,000,000,000,000 farewells!

Hear Dr. Moore, of the Bombay Medical Service, a most able and observant officer—

"In Indian hill ranges it is not the terrestrio-miasmatic causes of disease alone which are partially escaped; it is the absence of intense heat, the lowering of the temperature some ten or fifteen degrees, which allows the European to recover his elasticity of vital and physical powers—which the fervid heat of the plains depresses to the lowest existing point —which allows him to obtain a moderate quantity of exercise, without undue fatigue and exhaustion, and which conduces to his obtaining rest and sleep by night, free from the forbidding causes of the plain— heat and mosquitoes.

"As a natural consequence, the body not only be-

" comes invigorated and inspirited, but the mind also
" more active, and capable of greater and sustained
" action.

" A clear intellect, and a temperature of 88° Fah-
" renheit, are almost incompatibilities, when long and
" continued intellectual exertions are required; and it
" may be stated, that the capabilities of any individual
" as regards the latter vary inversely as the heat of the
" climate. Intense application and deep thought never
" prospered long together where the body is always on
" the *qui vive* to keep itself cool. The hands, perhaps,
" may be taxed, but not the head. The latter, after a
" certain time, either fails or performs its work unsatis-
" factorily.

" Hence, in hill stations, whether for good or evil,
" there is generally a fresher, more energetic, and, it
" perhaps may be added, more intellectual tone than is
" met with among the dwellers on the plains. There
" is not the heat to feel and talk about, and the climate
" seems to instil a new life into both mind and body.
" It gives a greater elasticity, and enables Europeans
" to undergo more than they could possibly endure
" under the 'punkah' and 'tatties,' or exposed to the
" heat without those necessaries. It is the circum-
" stance of a hill climate being a sanatarium *for the
" mind* as well as the body which adds so immensely
" to its value."

But, besides sanitary defects, there are other objections to Calcutta as the seat of the Central Government; for, as long as that Government remains here, it can be central only in name. At present the chief city is poked up in an angle of the empire, with nothing to the east of it except part of our Burmese dominions. It lies at a distance of nearly five hundred miles (as the crow and General Pope fly) from Allahabad, the capital of the North-West; six hundred miles from Lucknow, the capital of the Chief Commissionership of Oude, and from Nagpore, the capital of the Chief Commissionership of that ilk; more than eight hundred miles from Delhi, the focus of native interests; nine hundred from Madras; more than one thousand from Bombay; and between eleven and twelve hundred miles from Lahore. During the crisis of the Mutiny the people on the scene of action were left to manage as they best might, without orders from head-quarters, and with small chance of making their position known to the supreme authorities. Sir John Lawrence fought his province as a brave captain fights his vessel when he finds himself surrounded by the hostile fleet in a fog which prevents him from discerning his admiral's signals. It is fortunate for England that our officers acted in the spirit of Nelson's golden rule—" when a " commander is in doubt what to do, he cannot be in " the wrong if he lays his ship alongside the nearest " enemy." But it is not only while great events are in progress that the inconveniences of the hole-and-corner situation of Calcutta are severely felt. In the most piping times of peace (why are times of peace piping?) the expense and delay in the transmission of despatches constitute a very serious public evil. When instructions from the India Office at Home, relating to the Punjab, arrive at Bombay, they are within nine hundred miles of the Government to which they refer; but, as they must be submitted to the Supreme Authorities, before they reach their destination they will have made a journey of two thousand two hundred miles in a direct line: and a journey of two thousand two hundred miles in India is no joke.

But the Imperial Government should not only be locally central. It must likewise be morally central. As long as the Viceroy, the Council, and the Secretariat are settled in the capital of a Presidency, that Presidency will always rule the rest of India. To this day Bombay and Madras are familiarly spoken of as "the "Minor Presidencies;" while the north-west provinces, with their thirty millions of inhabitants, and the Punjab, with its sixteen millions, are regarded as mere dependencies of Bengal. And how should it be otherwise? From the time that our Eastern dominions were united under the superintendence of one supreme authority, that authority has been located at Calcutta. As long as this state of things lasts, Bengal influences and Bengal habits of thought will direct or modify every measure of the Supreme Government. There is no danger lest the servants of the favoured Presidency should use their power for their own selfish advantage. But it is not good that the officials of Bombay and the Punjab should have no voice in matters which are of special moment to themselves, or which concern the general interests of the empire. It may be said, without exaggeration, that a young fellow who begins his career in the Southern Presidencies has no hope of ever taking part in the general administration of the country. A man might count the Madras and Bombay officers who are employed in the Supreme Administration on the fingers of one hand, even if he had passed some time in the establishment of Adoni-bezek, in company with the threescore and ten unfortunate royal personages who gathered their meat under the table of that remarkably unpleasant monarch. The knowledge of this has the most depressing effect on the *morale* of the services which are thus virtually excluded from high and honourable office. This objection to Calcutta as the official capital is so strong as to outweigh all others. It is absolutely essential that the Supreme Government should be impartial, unbiassed by local prejudices or associations,—in a word, imperial; and, while India is, to a certain extent, misgoverned from this cause, Bengal is over-governed. Zealous and able Councillors and Secretaries of State, who watch things going wrong under their nose, would be more than official if the temptation to direct interference did not sometimes prove too strong for their forbearance. The local powers are hampered, and trammelled, and fretted by the constant presence of a superior authority. No one would be more heartily glad to see the backs of the members of the Supreme Government than the magnates of the Presidency of Bengal.

The expense of changing house is, of course, the strongest argument against moving the seat of Government from Calcutta to some less enervating and pestilential climate; and undoubtedly it would cost no trifle to found a new official metropolis for a country of more than four times the area of Great Britain and France together. But, when we look the matter in the face, many of the difficulties vanish. From the circumstances under which our Eastern empire came into existence, a large share of power remained in the hands of the provincial authorities. It was long before the Southern Presidencies could be brought to acknowledge what Mr. Grote would call the Hegemony of Bengal; and even now the idea of centralization is repugnant to the Indian official mind. At Madras and Bombay, Allahabad and Lahore, Nagpore, Lucknow, and Rangoon, much public business is carried on which in a European State would be transacted at the capital city. Consequently, the staff of public servants stationed at Calcutta, and attached to the Supreme Government, is not so large as to render the removal of that Government a work of extraordinary labour and cost. A very large proportion of the *employés* resident in the capital belong to the Government of Bengal, and would therefore stay where they are. It must not be forgotten that the whole legal staff come under this head—judges, barristers, attorneys, clerks, registrars, and false witnesses. Even the High Court is a Bengal tribunal.

In the case of an empire which can trace the history of its growth through long centuries, the associations which gather round the chief city form a tie which few Utilitarians could find it in their heart to break. Even in that fearful year when the Thames gave up his dead cats, when volumes of foul vapours rolled in at every one of Barry's mullioned windows; when honourable members sat gloomy and silent in the smoking-room, or lay on their backs on the floor of the dressing-closets in the agonies of nausea; when Pam became sobered and Bright pale and pensive; when there was only a basin between Spooner and Eternity;—not then did it cross the mind of the most qualmish legislator to suggest that the English Curia should be transferred from the sacred soil of Westminster. That august ally of ours, though he carefully demolishes every relic of the old *régime*, and of the great events which have placed a gulph between the eighteenth and nineteenth centuries, aims only at adorning the ancient site, and has no thought of creating a new Paris in a distant department. Such, at least, I presume to be his intentions; for the Imperial secrets, if Mr. Tennyson is to be believed, are entrusted only to a single confidant of very questionable reputation. Even the Yankees seem unwilling to abandon those sacred walls within whose precinct they and their fathers have talked bunkum for a couple of generations; those classic haunts, hallowed by the recollections of Daniel Webster, and the bodily presence of Mister Chase; that sublime Capitol, towards which their legions have fled in dire confusion from many a field of victory —which not even the cackling of Cassius Clay, nor the Camillus who found a Veii in Richmond, will save from the clutches of the barbarians from the South; that rostrum on which, in years to come, the heroes who solicit the suffrages of their countrymen will bare their backs and display the scars which testify to their prowess on more than one hard-run day of battle.[1]

In the case of Calcutta there is no reason to entertain scruples on this score. As I am curious about the scenes and circumstances of notable events, immediately on my arrival I instituted an inquiry into the existing associations of the place, and got together

[1] The foregoing passage is retained as a proof of the decency and discrimination with which a young Englishman, in 1863, thought fit to discuss the greatest events of his time. I sinned with my elders, and repented with my betters.—Sept. 1865.

the following collection, which is not so rich that it deserves to have much weight when the expediency of changing the seat of Government comes to be considered.

1. A Baboo was alive some years ago, who stated himself to have been the native secretary of Warren Hastings, and who pointed out the tree under which the duel took place. According to his own account, he was at hand when that Sahib of chequered fame fought with Francis Sahib, "to decide which should be Governor-"General"—a theory not wholly devoid of truth; for, if Hastings had been killed, his adversary would assuredly have seized the reins. The value of this old gentleman's testimony was somewhat impaired by the fact that his presence, on the occasion in question, did not form a feature in the earlier editions of the story, and is strongly suspected to have been an afterthought.

2. There are those still living who have often talked with an ancient lady who remembered, as a very young girl, during an early ride on the Maidan, seeing a gentleman carried across the grass. On asking his name, she was informed that he was Mr. Francis, supposed by Mr. Macaulay and Lord Stanhope to be the author of the letters of Junius, and that he was returning with a bullet through his body, from an interview with the Governor-General.

3. The Black Hole was somewhere in Tank Square, though some think that it is a certain room at the office of the Board of Examiners.

4. Enthusiastic antiquarians profess to find traces of the Mahratta Ditch in the neighbourhood of Ballygunge. Others are of opinion that these faint indentations in

the soil are an early effort of the Public Works Department in the canal-making line.

Wherever a great mass of public buildings and private residences has been accumulated in a long course of time, the removal of the *personnel* and paraphernalia of Government would occasion much individual distress and a considerable loss to the State. When Constantine resolved on founding a new Imperial capital on the shore of the Bosphorus, it must have caused a bitter pang to many an old official when he was bidden to surrender "the smoke, the pomp, the din of favoured Rome;" to turn his back for ever on the temples, and arches, and theatres of the glorious city; the long succession of echoing squares, fringed with stately colonnades; the colossal baths where he had perspired, and sipped negus, and betted, and talked scandal ever since he came to man's estate; the Mint, under the Capitol, where he sat as quæstor during his first and proudest year of public life; the causeway of Appius, along which he drove, through the tombs of his ancestors, to take possession of his province; and the portico under which, after his return, he stood to be congratulated on his acquittal from the charge of extortion and oppression, on the day when he so triumphantly established his innocence at the rate of a hundred thousand sesterces to each judge, and a Venus Victrix, by Scopas, to the Prætor. It must have been a terrible blow to him when the gorgeous Basilica, where he had listened to the eloquence of the great pleaders of the day, was turned into a little Bethel for Christians, and when his pretty house-property on the edge of the Esquiline Hill, where two Augurs and the Emperor's barber lived within four doors, went down fifty per cent. in value on the publication of the fatal edict which announced that Byzantium was henceforward to be the mistress of the world.

Calcutta, however, is not Rome; though old Job Charnock, the Quirinus of the town, when he pitched his tent under a fine banyan-tree that grew where Fort William now stands, would probably have been considerably astonished had he been told that he was the nucleus of a population that would one day exceed four hundred thousand souls. Still, the servants of the Indian Government will, on their departure, have but little reason to regret the board-rooms they leave behind them. It is not too much to say that there is nothing here which answers to a public office in London. The business of the State is transacted in private houses hired or bought for the purpose. The lobby of the Treasury is a dirty closet with a whitewashed wall, daubed with specimens of native art, and opening into an untidy back-yard. Out here the Horse Guards would be regarded as an elegant and commodious pile of architecture, and the National Gallery as the model of a chaste and classic style. The only building which can properly be said to belong to the Supreme Government is the palace of the Viceroy; and this would not be wasted, as the want of accommodation for the Courts of Law is a crying evil, and Government House, from the peculiarity of its form, is admirably suited for judicial purposes. Twelve halls of justice might be provided—for the worst of which the judges at Westminster would pull wigs—with ventilation that would win a smile of approval from Baron Bramwell, or, as I suppose I ought to say, the late Baron Bramwell, since long before this reaches you he will probably have fallen a victim to the outraged relatives of expatriated garotters. The result of the proposed change would be that a couple of dozen of the finest mansions in Calcutta would be thrown into the market—a most timely supply, as the scarcity of house-room is already painfully felt. They would be immediately snatched at by the families who are now living in discomfort and publicity at hotels and boarding-establishments, because respectable and convenient dwellings are not to be had at any price. No perceptible effect would be produced upon society by the departure of the Viceroy; for it may be confidently asserted that no one resides at Calcutta because it is fashionable. In India everybody lives within reach of his business; and, when he has got money, he goes to spend it in England.

Some hold that there is danger in removing the Government from a bustling populous city, where the healthy breezes of public opinion circulate freely, to a solitude where it will be surrounded by an impenetrable official atmosphere. But on this point men are misled by European analogies. It is idle to endeavour to find a counterpart out here for every English institution, from Magna Charta down to the skating club. If I dared, I would say that the state of feeling on Indian matters that prevails among the great majority of our countrymen at home has far more in common with the public opinion of the Civil Service than with that of our small and peculiarly constituted non-official society :—

ἀλλὰ μάλ' αἰνῶς
αἰδέομαι Τρῶας καὶ Τρῳάδας ἑλκεσιπέπλους.

JUBBULPORE.

I am in a mortal fright of the Calcutta gentlemen, and the very pretty Calcutta ladies with wide crinolines.

Next comes the choice of a permanent site; for the Supreme Government must not go cruising about like a returned Indian, who cannot make up his mind whether to settle in a Cheltenham villa, or a Brighton Crescent, or at Rugby to educate his sons, or in London to dispose of his daughters. For some time subsequently to the Mutiny, Delhi was generally talked of. There was much of the romantic in the notion of enthroning the Lieutenant of the Crown in the palace of the Mogul. It was supposed that the native mind would transfer to the representative of the Empress of India the prestige attached to the line of Baber and Aurengzebe. But Delhi is neither much more central nor much more healthy than the present capital. It lies almost as far to the North as Calcutta to the East. The air, taking the whole year round, is as hot; and the drainage would, doubtless, very soon be as bad. It is worth while to incur expense and trouble for the sake of a change to a hill climate, and to a hill climate only.

Fortunately, a region exists which unites all the conditions desirable for the official capital of a great empire. On the new line of railway from Allahabad to Bombay, in latitude 23° 7′ N. and longitude 79° 57′ E. stands Jubbulpore, at an elevation above the sea of near fifteen hundred feet. The Washington of the East might spring up on these high table-lands, amidst the park-like undulating scenery in the vicinity of the town—and in India vicinity means anything within fifty miles. A branch line from Jubbulpore would bring despatches to hand twenty-four hours subsequent to their arrival at

Bombay, and in twenty-two days after their departure from England. The spot is the very centre and ὀμφαλὸς of the continent. It lies a hundred and fifty miles from Nagpore, two hundred from Allahabad, three hundred from Lucknow, something over five hundred from Calcutta, something under six hundred from Bombay, and about seven hundred miles from Madras in the far south and Lahore in the extreme north. The public opinion of the whole of India would be applied equably and in due proportion to all the measures of the Supreme Government, which would no longer be swayed by the influences of a single Presidency. The high officials would be drawn from all quarters, would reflect the feelings and interests of many different provinces, and would bring to the service of the Crown a great variety of ideas and experiences. A representative element would thus be introduced into the constitution.

One most beneficial result would ensue, which is not evident at first sight. The removal of the seat of Government to the table-lands of the Central Provinces would have the effect of a gigantic scheme of colonization, as far as colonization is practicable in India. With reference to this question, much has of late been talked and written. Most people who know anything about the country have a pretty decided opinion on the subject. It is impossible to induce men to work in a climate worse than that of Jamaica, for less than half the wages earned by a Dorsetshire peasant. Skilled labour of the highest class will always find its price out here. Clerks, and factors, and engineers will never have any difficulty in earning a livelihood ; but poor people, without capital or education, could not find employment in any considerable number. Besides, colonization is hopeless unless the colonist can manage to live himself, and rear his children and grandchildren. On this point Dr. Moore speaks very positively:

"It is the fashion now, in some quarters, to declare "that the dangers of Indian residence and service have "been deeply overrated, and that there is little or "nothing in the exceptional character of the climate of "India to render it necessary that special inducements "should be held out to persuade people to reside therein, "and this, too, in the face of so many stern facts which "have confronted us within the last few years. How "many more victims must be added to the list of those "killed by climate, before the dangers of a tropical resi- "dence become appreciated?

"If colonization, as America and Australia have been "colonized, were possible in this country, some instances "of the kind would already have occurred. But the "melancholy truth is, that the European race dies out. "Of the numerous pensioners who have settled at our "principal military stations, how many have been "colonists? There is not one single instance. There is "not a great-grandchild, or grandchild of these pensioners "retaining their European characteristics. An infusion "of native blood is *essential to the continuance of the* "*race.*

"*The fact is, for the white man or his offspring, there is* "*no such thing as acclimatisation in India.* As a rule, "Europeans enjoy the best health, and suffer less from "heat, during their first years of residence in this country. "Acclimatisation, as regards an Indian sun, is simply "impossible. Exposure, instead of 'hardening' the "system, actually has the contrary effect, *and, the longer Europeans remain in this country, the more they feel the effects of the vertical sun.* When Europeans urge that "they have exposed themselves to the sun for years, and "have never felt any evil effects, it is only saying that " the losing battle between the sun and their constitu- " tion is not yet over; but every day's exposure brings "them nearer to the final triumph of their solar ad- " versary. The lamented fate of that gallant sun-defier, " Colonel Jacob, who advised young officers not to mind "the sun, as it 'would only tan their cheeks,' is an " *apropos* example of the foregoing."

Colonization, in the usual sense of the word, is, therefore, impracticable. But, if a modified system can succeed anywhere, or under any circumstances, it will be in the event of the settlement of the Supreme Government on a new and salubrious site. At present, all our large European communities are planted in and about ancient and important native towns, already civilized up to a certain point. Our example has produced no perceptible change in the manners, ways of thought, and religion of the bulk of the inhabitants of Calcutta, Madras, or Delhi. But, when the Governor-General, in all his glory, with a couple of European regiments and a great staff of officials, comes down like a god from Olympus, among a sparse and wild population, there is every hope that a Christian and Anglified colony will gradually be formed in the very heart of India.

One objection remains to be answered. It is maintained that, in case of another mutiny, the position of the Government, many hundred miles from the sea, and in the midst of hardy, warlike tribes, will be alarming in the extreme. To this I answer, that our power is now, humanly speaking, absolutely secure from an internal shock. In the fatal spring of 1857, the European force in India was barely twenty thousand strong. Vile roads, and treacherous rivers, were the only channels of communication. The artillerymen, the skilled labourers of the army, whose training is a work of much time and expense, and whose services are absolutely essential to the success of military operations, were for the most part natives, and sworn foes to our rule. At present seventy thousand English soldiers are distributed over the three Presidencies. The whole continent is covered with a network of telegraph wires. Railways already completed, or in rapid process of construction, connect all the chief cities; and light tramways are being pushed out in every direction from the grand trunk lines. Excepting one or two local corps, posted in savage and unhealthy districts, there is not a black gunner or driver within the borders of the empire. Every battery is worked exclusively by Europeans. Forewarned, forearmed, fifty General Lloyds would find it difficult to bungle us into another crisis. The condition of the Punjab is undoubtedly critical, but the distance between that province and Jubbulpore is greater than that between Paris and Vienna.

Something must be done, and that soon. At home, Calcutta is regarded as a city of the plague. When a man sails from Southampton, his friends bid him farewell, with the same look on their faces as the secretary of the Church Missionary Society wears when he sends out a supplementary batch of African bishops, of whom not one in six is destined to return to convulse the episcopal bench with problems propounded by sceptical Zulus and latitudinarian Bosjesmen. And no wonder; for, of the distinguished Englishmen who for many years have gone forth in mature life to bear high office in Bengal, most have found their graves on the banks of the Hooghly, or, with shattered health and blighted hopes, have returned to die. Splendid, indeed, were the prospects which induced Lord Dalhousie and Lord Canning to surrender the joys, the comforts, the manifold interests of English life. It was a noble position which tempted them to these shores; but the conditions of the tenure of that position were hard indeed, for it was written on their lease that they were never to hold another. But, sadder still, the Nemesis, which, if the old Greek poets are to be believed, attends upon high fortune, was not to be contented with one sacrifice. Lady Dalhousie, prostrated by the effects of the deadly atmosphere of the capital, sank and died during the homeward voyage; and an exquisitely simple and beautiful monument, strewn daily with fresh flowers, in the sweetest nook of the viceregal gardens at Barrackpore, marks the spot where Lady Canning best loved to linger away the evening hours during her splendid exile. Poor Mr. Wilson, who came out in the cold season full of vigour of mind, but at an age when a man cannot with impunity begin taking a vapour-bath daily and all day long, at first used to talk of the climate with good-humoured approbation; but, when the terrible summer came upon him during the severe labours of the first Indian budget, he ceased to joke, though he stood to his post to the death with truly admirable courage and devotion.

This view of the subject deserves most serious consideration, for it is impossible to over-estimate the benefit to India that is derived from the influence and labours of statesmen and jurists who are already famous at home. The advantage does not end here; for, on his return, a man of established English reputation can do much to excite the interest of the public in the affairs of our eastern empire. We venture to say that three-fourths of the knowledge of Indian matters possessed by a young fellow at Oxford or Cambridge is derived from Lord Macaulay's Essays on Clive and Warren Hastings. The service, and the nation at large, owe much to the efforts and example of such a man as Macaulay, fresh from the lobby of the Commons and the drawing-room of Holland House ; of such men as Mr. Wilson, Mr. Laing, the present financial minister, and the accomplished scholar and jurisconsult, who now holds the office of Legal Member of Council. The introduction of the English budget, with all Mr. Gladstone's recent improvements, is alone an incalculable blessing. Measures are being taken for the despatch of subordinate officials trained in the Home Treasury and Audit office— a step that promises to be of great advantage to the administration of the public departments in this country. But the evil repute which is attached to the air of Calcutta will be fatal to any extensive system of mutual accommodation in intellect and experience between the mother-country and her greatest dependency.

There are few public men who would not be pleased with the idea of spending two or three years in a most interesting land, amidst an ancient and peculiar society, and a mysterious wide-spread system of idolatry, with unbounded powers of effecting good in his generation, a noble income, an eminent position, and every opportunity for keeping his name in the mouths of his countrymen. It is exactly what would, at one time, have appeared most fascinating to the late Sir George Cornewall Lewis. Such would be the case if the seat of Government were planted amidst high table-lands, and in a bracing air, where an Englishman would miss nothing except the east winds in March and the fogs in November. As it is, he exchanges the excitements and amenities of London and country-house life ; the long cool sleep ; the breakfast seasoned by a fresh appetite and the *Times* newspaper ; the afternoon ride in the park ; the chat in the smoking-room at his club, cut short by a telegraphic summons to a division on the Irish Drainage Bill ; the speech-day at Harrow, where he sees his firstborn quarrel with Cassius and cringe before Sir Anthony Absolute as *he* quarrelled and cringed a quarter of a century before ; the heather in August ; the run with Lord Fitzwilliam purchased at the price of a wigging from the Treasury whip, a night in the train, and a breakfast in the refreshment-room at the Shoreditch Station—he exchanges all this, for what? For the privilege, at forty or fifty years of age, of entering upon a life of compulsory hypochondria and inevitable valetudinarianism ; measuring his food by ounces, and his drink by gills ; abstaining from fruit by the advice of one old Indian, and from ice-pudding at the warning of another ; rising six times in the night to kick his punkah-bearer awake; issuing forth, after fevered broken slumbers, for a dreary objectless constitutional ; growing weak, thin, languid, and still slaving on till a definite

A CALCUTTA BALL.

malady overtakes him; then, tossing outside the Sandhead in a dirty, comfortless pilot-brig, in the vain hope of staving off the inevitable; returning to the hateful city to work again, to droop, to despair, to rally once during the short winter months, and then to sicken for the last time. Eight thousand a year and the title of Honourable are dear indeed at such a price.

The other day we made up a party to go to a ball at the town-hall, the last of the rapid succession of brilliant entertainments which have enlivened our short and cherished winter. During the past cold season fancy-balls were the rage. This ball, however, was no fancy, but the sternest reality. You probably never waltzed in full evening dress round the inner chamber of a Turkish bath, and therefore can have no conception of the peculiar charms of the dance in this climate. Terpsichore is a muse who loves shade, and zephyrs, and running streams; but not shade in which the thermometer stands at 93°, where the zephyrs are artificial, and the only running streams those on the faces of her votaries. The waste of tissue during a galloppe, with a partner in high training just landed from England, is truly frightful. The natives understand these things better. They let the ladies do their dancing for them, and content themselves with looking on. I sometimes think that Orientals agree to consider women as chattels, in order to avoid the trouble of paying attentions to the sex. It cannot be denied, however, that this is very hard upon the women. Making love is no joke out here; though, in one sense, Indian lovers may all be said to be ardent. It is all very well in a humid northern atmosphere to talk of the torch of Cupid, and the flames which dart from the eyes of your mistress, and the genial glow of mutual affection; but in the Tropic of Cancer these images acquire a horrible significance. Talk of dying for your sweetheart! But what if you were comfortably ensconced on the breezy side of the punkah, within reach of an ice-pudding—would you cross over to where she sits panting between a fat brigadier and a fatter chaplain? If after supper you were to swear to her that you had looked for her in vain, it would surely be one of those

> "Lover's perjuries,
> At which they say Jove laughs."

There is no fear of her testing your devotion like the lady at the court of King Francis, who flung her glove into the arena among fighting lions, for here it is no easy matter to doff a glove on the spur of the moment, from causes that do not require explanation. Perhaps a little quiet dalliance inside a retired tatty[1] is the most tolerable form of flirtation; though even in this case you are liable to interruption by stepping upon a plateful of mangoes, or a bottle of claret, which the kitmutgar has deposited there to be cooled.

Sweet Emily R——, most piquante and wayward of all step-daughters of Deputy-Assistant-Income-Tax-Commissioners, hast thou yet forgotten thy favourite Competition Wallah? Didst thou ever deign to wonder what secret cause estranged that much-enduring snub-

---

[1] A tatty is a framework placed over the window, stuffed with scented grass, which is kept constantly wet. The air from the outside, after passing through this erection, is supposed to give coolness to the room, and undoubtedly does give lumbago to the people who sit in it.

nosed youth, who once was the most submissive of the captives who were dragged at the wheels of thy buggy? Perchance, in thy vexation, thou didst accuse the wiles of the black-eyed sister of the Joint Magistrate of Bogglegunge. Perchance thou didst imagine that the approaching examination in Persian allowed thy swain no leisure for the more grateful but not less perilous ordeal of courtship. Yet my heart owned not the sway of any other dame. The snare of the Siren of Bogglegunge was in vain spread in the sight of at least one civilian. I should not have been deterred from plucking a feather for my cap out of the wing of Cupid by any fear of being plucked in the tongue of the children of Cyrus. The motive for my coldness was far other. Dost thou remember how, at the United Service Club, we pulled a cracker which contained a scroll bearing these tender lines :—

> "As when a roaming busy bee
> Inflicts its sting upon my knee,
> So thou, O fair, within my heart
> Hast caused a wound that makes me smart."

Next morning I awoke from a late sleep, during which I dreamed alternately that I had been appointed Secretary of State for India on condition of taking you to wife, and that I was being kicked by the aide-de-camp from Government House, to whom thou didst give all the round dances after supper. I found on my dressing-table that hallowed slip of paper, sticky and sweet with the remains of the bonbon which it had enveloped. Dreadful to relate, it now formed the rendezvous for two long armies of white ants, which ascended and descended the opposite legs of the article of furniture in question. One string passed across the carpet into the cupboard where I kept my pickles and soda-water, while the other filed in unbroken order over the matting, up the bed-post, round the edge of my mattress, and thence on to the shelves where my Radley and Cambridge prize-books stand, a glittering row. Thenceforward those two colonies have planted themselves, the one among my literature, and the other amidst my condiments, being apparently desirous of settling the problem of white colonisation in India. From that fatal morn I have never seen thee without thinking of white ants; never listened to the accents of thy voice without feeling a tickling as of an insect meditating a bite; never heard thy once-adored name without experiencing an irresistible inclination to scratch the calf of my leg. What love could hold out against such a connexion of ideas? Certainly not that of a young civilian in his first year of residence.

A serious drawback to the enjoyment of an English ball is the impossibility of getting at any accurate information concerning your partners or your rivals. If your attention is attracted to any stranger by his taste in dress or style of dancing, or his ugliness, or his equanimity and self-reliance when his quadrille has fallen into inextricable confusion, your inquiries about him will probably be answered by the assurance that he seems "a dellish cool fler," or that he is "a fler "with lots of money;" or you will be told something about his father, or his elder brother, who meets with the qualified approbation of being "not a bad sort of "fler." You are struck by the appearance of some *débutante*, and request an introduction. Your good-natured hostess presents you to each other with some cabalistic words, amidst which you distinguish your own titles clearly enough, but can catch no part of the lady's name except the last syllable, which sounds like ——son. " The next lancers? Can she favour you? Well, then " the galoppe? Number six, you believe." The first round proves to you that she dances very prettily; and during the last quadrille before supper you learn that she talks and listens nicely, and that she can preserve an equal mind in the awful crisis when one couple is dancing " Trélise," and another " Pastorale," and the rest are standing still in despair, or vaguely dodging about in a sort of spontaneous " Chaine Anglaise." A very minute allowance of champagne has the most genial effect. Having discovered that she has been on the Continent, you make the remark which never fails to elicit a symptom of interest from the haughtiest or stupidest of belles, " What very objectionable persons ' one does meet abroad." From this common ground you gradually approach the subject which forms the staple of ball-room conversation, the extreme shyness of ordinary people. If you stand within ear-shot of a couple talking behind a curtain, or on the landing-place, it is ten to one that you will find them discussing this mental phenomenon—the gentleman indulging in a mild imitation of the ethical small-print articles in the *Saturday Review*, firing off, from time to time, the epithet " self-conscious; " while the lady draws her illustrations from individuals among the company then present. After supper, you induce your partner to coax her chaperone to stay out one more waltz; and then, as you re-ascend the stairs, after having paid her the last offices, you resolve to call next day and show her that passage of Robert Browning, whom she owned never to have read, and of whom you strongly suspect that she has never heard. But on reflection you begin to be aware that you have no conception who she is or where she lives. All you know about her is, that she has black eyes, that her aunt disapproves of theatres, but that she has witnessed the moving panorama of the Mississippi, that she has a brother in the 49th, and that she hates men who hop in the polka. You apply to your hostess, who, inasmuch as she has brought together nearly five hundred pairs in the course of one evening, naturally wonders what young lady you can possibly refer to, but thinks she may have been a distant relation whom Mrs. —— asked leave to bring. Now, there is nothing of this sort in India. Your curiosity regarding a cavalier will not be satisfied with a statement concerning his dress or manners, or his merits and demerits as a " fler," but by the solid palpable fact of his being the acting Sub-Inspector-General of Opium Godowns :[1] for everybody here is something as well as somebody. If you want to know the name of the brunette who is standing up with the man in Windsor uniform, the reply will be, " Brunette ! I should rather think she " is ! There's a strong touch of the tar-brush in that " quarter. Why, her father was old Joe Collins, once " Commissioner of Pollyghaut, who went out the other " day after being eight-and-forty years in the service. " For the last part of his life he gave into native ways. " He married her a few years before his death. The " mother, I mean. She's alive now, somewhere up in

[1] Storehouses.

"Oude, and is supposed to have made away with a "deal of Joe's property. His grandson is coming out "by the next boat to look into the matter. The girl "is a good girl, and lives with her uncle, the Sudder "Judge."

Besides the facility of identifying everybody one meets, there are other signs of the strong official element in the composition of Society. Nowhere are the rules of precedence so rigorously observed as in Calcutta. I have heard a Member of Council complain that for a whole fortnight he always took the same lady in to dinner; and, inasmuch as I am a very minor Sahib, I have never had the pleasure of descending the stairs in other company than that of a male personage of my own calibre. Fortunately, the English character is entirely free from any bias toward bureaucratic exclusiveness or conceit. Civilians who draw salaries as large as twenty insolent Prussian Directors-General or pompous French Sub-prefects, always bear in mind that they or their companions are English gentlemen. It is impossible, however, long to forget that you are in the midst of a community of public servants. For instance, a person in ill health is always spoken of as being "sick"—a term which has a curious effect till it becomes familiar to the ear. The employment of it arises from the peculiar constitution of society. When a member of the service hears that another member has been taken ill, his first ideas are not those of doctors, or nurses, or lawyers, or clergymen, or undertakers. They run in the line of sick-leave and sick-allowances. Some time ago I was much puzzled at hearing nothing talked of except the probability of a gentleman in mature life being "confirmed." Everybody took the deepest interest in his approaching confirmation. The conversation of Calcutta was so full of the rite in question that it sounded like one of Miss Sewell's novels. To add to my bewilderment, our excellent bishop was on a pastoral tour, and was not expected back for some weeks to come. Having a dim notion that Anglo-Indian society was somewhat Pagan, I presumed that the religious education of this person had been lamentably neglected. It turned out that he performed temporary duty in the place of an *employé* who was absent on sick-leave, and whose recovery was so doubtful that there was every prospect of his substitute being permanently "confirmed" in the office. The gentle sex take a deep interest in this branch of public affairs. I love to hear a pair of pretty lips pronounce on the chance of the Acting Appointment held by Miss Meta Pornideau's betrothed becoming "pucka," or declaiming against the iniquity of the authorities in having banished into the Mofussil young Sir Henry Currey, Bart., whose family have enjoyed the loaves and mango-fishes of Calcutta ever since his great-grandfather was chairman of the Board of Directors during the trial of Warren Hastings. The ladies manage the affairs of the charities of the town with a knowledge of the forms of official business which would delight the heart of Sir Gregory Hardlines. They form committees, and distribute the superintendence of the various departments, and send round reports—which the older hands supplement with copious minutes, while the less experienced content themselves with a bare expression of approbation or disapproval ; just as a new Member of Council "concurs in the compromise sanctioned by his colleagues."

You may remember that in an early letter I remarked upon the absence of "Dundreary." At first there was relief in the thought that so many thousand miles of sea foamed between myself and that polished but simple nobleman. Time, however, has led me to think otherwise. The great want in India is a diversity of minor subjects of conversation—novels, plays, reviews, heretical books, sensation-histories of the Crimean War, Leotards, Blondins, trials de Lunatico Inquirendo costing five hundred pounds a day, international prize fights— in short, all those petty interests which may be summed up under the generic head "Lord Dundreary." We sadly need some yeast to keep society from becoming doughy. As an education, nothing can be better than the early years of a civilian's career. It is a great thing to live in a community where every one has work to do, and where almost every one does it with a will; where intolerance and bigotry are at a ruinous discount; where broad liberal unselfish views are as plentiful as blackberries at the bottom of a Surrey valley. But, after a time, symptoms appear which show that the mind needs the stimulus of variety. You begin to perceive that the drones of this world have their use as well as the bees. However much mischief Satan may find still for idle hands to do, those idle hands certainly provide a great deal for busy people to talk about. This state of things is painfully felt—as is proved by the avidity with which we seize on any scandal from Simla, any trumpery squib in the daily journals, any question about the desirability of excluding pigs from the agricultural show in deference to native prejudices. But all this is very poor mental food for men who have received a first-rate home education. A civil servant who neglects to keep up a lively interest in general subjects by a conscientious perusal of the English newspapers and periodicals, by a certain modicum of standard reading, and by a furlough judiciously spent in London society and Continental travel, is in danger of lapsing into an honourable and public-spirited bore. Unless he takes unremitting care of his intellectual health, he can no more expect, on his return, to enter kindly into English interests and English conversation, than he can hope to enjoy roast-beef and plum-pudding with his digestion impaired by hot curries and Manilla cheroots.

Happily, it is no uncommon thing for men to bring home at the end of their term of service a vigorous constitution both of mind and body. The habits of our countrymen in India have long been in steady course of improvement. It has generally been found that a manly valiant race, which has imposed its yoke upon an effeminate and unwarlike people, in course of time, degenerates and becomes slothful and luxurious. Thus the Persians adopted the manners of Medes, and the Macedonians the manners of Persians. Thus Marc Antony—or, as some people spell him, Mark Anthony—and his followers became half Egyptians under the influence of the lovely Begum of Alexandria; and the sun was reduced to the painful predicament of beholding, among the military standards a base canopy; while the Roman soldier, alas! (O posterity, you will deny it) was bound to the service of a woman. With the English in the East precisely the opposite result has taken place. The earliest settlers were indolent, dissipated, grasping, almost Orientals in their way of life, and almost heathens in the matter of religion. But each generation of their successors is more simple, more hardy, more Christian than the last.

Mrs. Sherwood's pictures of a Mofussil station, of a merchant's household in Calcutta, of an indigo factory among the jungles in the days when Lord Wellesley was Governor-General, are well worthy of careful study. Our knowledge, derived from other sources, fully bears out her vivid descriptions of the splendid sloth and the languid debauchery of European society in those days— English gentlemen, overwhelmed with the consequences of extravagance, hampered by liaisons with Hindoo women and by crowds of olive-coloured children, without either the will or the power to leave the shores of India; English ladies living in a separate establishment from their husbands, in semi-oriental retirement, drinking largely of beer and claret, smoking hookahs, abandoning their little ones to the fatal blighting bestial influence of native conversation and example, maintaining not even the pretence of religious belief or practice, having no hope, and without God in the world. Great men rode about in state-coaches, with a dozen servants running before and behind to bawl out their titles : and little men lounged in palanquins, or drove a chariot for which they never intended to pay, drawn by horses which they had bullied or cajoled out of the stables of wealthy Baboos. Writers not yet within years of man's estate gave champagne dinners, ran racehorses, and put together a pretty nest-egg of debt before they had passed the examination which qualified them for public employ. As a natural result, there were at one time near a hundred civilians of more than thirty-five years' standing who remained out here in pledge to their creditors, poisoning the principles of the younger men, and blocking out their betters from places of eminence and responsibility. The amount of bribery and extortion was something stupendous. A worthy of the name of Paul Benfield,[1] at a time when he was drawing a few hundred rupees a month as a junior servant of the Company, petitioned the Madras Council to assist him in getting a sum of two hundred and fifty thousand pounds owed to him by a single native prince. From this chaos of profligacy and corruption emerged, from time to time, that jaundiced purse-proud Nabob, who roused the indignation of our forefathers by his insolence, his ignorance of everything English, his effeminate habits transplanted to a clime where men lead a manly life, his curries and spices, his fans and cushions, the crowd of shivering helpless dark-faced beings who hung about the corridors of the hotel in which he occupied the choicest suite of rooms.

Things are changed now, thank God! Many stations boast a chaplain and a pretty little parish church, where the punkahs surging to and fro recall the swing of the

[1] When Cicero was chief-commissioner of the non-regulation province of Cilicia, he complained bitterly in his private letters of the rapacity of the celebrated Brutus, who plundered the wretched Baboos of Cyprus through the agency of one Scaptius. Brutus was very importunate with Cicero to make Scaptius a collector, with full powers of a magistrate. Lord Macaulay, who had no love for the oligarchical party of those days, says in a marginal note in his favourite well-thumbed copy of the Letters to Atticus: "This patriot seems to have been little "better than a Paul Benfield."

censers in a Catholic temple. In other places the coolest room in the cutcherry or the Government school is swept and garnished every Sunday morning, and the collector, assisted by his joint magistrate, performs the service, with now and then a sermon from the works of his favourite standard divine; while the superintendent of police, who has an ear for music, plays the harmonium and leads the choir. It is a question whether the congregation do not benefit by the substitution of the official for the clerical element, since the clergymen who can be induced to take duty in India, are, as a rule, no cleverer than they should be. One Sunday, at Mofussilpore, the chaplain of a neighbouring cantonment offered to drive over and officiate. We were disappointed, since Tom and his colleagues chant Gregorians in a style which excites the admiring envy of the whole division, and the reverend gentleman was known to disapprove of this interference of the laity. He gave us, according to his usual custom, a sermon which he had written for a military audience. In this particular discourse he addressed himself to wives. He exhorted them to endure ill-treatment with meekness, even if their husbands should beat and starve them. Above all, he warned them against betaking themselves, in despair, to drink, or evil courses. He then drew a pathetic picture of the horrors of *delirium tremens,* and the other temporal consequences of gross sin: an admonition which was all very well when directed to soldiers' wives, whose lot is as hard and perilous as that of any class of women, but which savoured of the absurd when addressed to a congregation among whom the only matrons present were the ladies of the judge and the collector. Nowadays, at any rate, the natives cannot taunt us with being ashamed of our religion. In fact, the English societies here are so small, and the goings out and comings in of every one so well known to his neighbours, that men attend public worship more regularly here than at home, if it were only to avoid giving offence to their weaker official brethren.

The days of corruption have long passed away. The hands of a civil servant are as pure and white as his summer trousers. Men have learned to resist the temptations to indolence and dissipation. They drive dog-carts instead of being driven in coaches, and very much prefer a gallop across country to snoozing about in a palanquin. They walk up partridges, and ride down hogs, and no longer relax their minds with hazard and cock-fighting. Honest dancing has driven out the vicarious nautch, an amusement the moral tendency of which might be called in question. A quiet pipe in the verandah after dinner has succeeded to the eternal omnipresent hookah, and habitual indulgence in brandy-pawnee is no longer allowed to be respectable. Did you not always imagine brandy-pawnee to be a drink compounded of many ingredients, a sort of tropical dog's nose, like sangaree, or those abominations in the American refreshment-room at the Great Exhibition, which sapped the health of the more curious and foolhardy among the visitors? It is merely brandy-and-water, the most simple and handy agent for any one who has a mind to derange his liver and destroy the coats of his stomach in the shortest possible time. Sobriety and decency have had their ordinary effect upon the intellect of society. Book-clubs have been established all over the continent, which are well supplied from home with all the new publications, including the chief reviews and magazines. The *Evening Mail*, each copy containing the pith of two numbers of the *Times*, is taken in at many stations. A man finds it uphill work still to keep himself *au courant* with European matters; but it is no longer a struggle in which success is hopeless. The time has already gone by when returned Indians could talk of nothing else but lacs and jaghires, (which people at home took to be a sort of leopard,) and the time is fast going by when they can talk of nothing but the Amalgamation Act and the Ryotwar Settlement.

With reference to the subject treated of at the commencement of this letter, I venture to insert a song, composed by a friend who is passionately devoted to the study of the laws of sanitation and mortality. He carries his enthusiasm on the subject so far as to tinge with it his view of every conceivable matter, religious, political, and literary. He once wrote an anonymous letter to the Laureate, commenting on the lines in the " Vision of Sin "—

> " Every moment dies a man—
> Every moment one is born."

He observed, with great truth, that if this statement were correct the population of the world would remain stationary, and urged the poet to alter the lines thus—

> " Every moment dies a man,
> And one and one-sixteenth is born."

He owned that the exact figure was one, decimal point, ought, six, four, seven; but (as he said) some allowance must be made for metre.

ODE TO CALCUTTA.

I.

Fair city, India's crown and pride,
Long may'st thou tower o'er Hooghley's tide,
Whose hallowed, but malarious stream,
The peasant's god, the poet's theme,
      Rolls down the dead Hindoo ;
And from whose wave, a stagnant mass
Replete with sulphuretted gas,
      Our country beer we brew !
As o'er a pulse physicians stand,
Intent upon the second-hand,
      Determined not to miss ticks,
I watch thy sanitary state,
Jot down of deaths the annual rate,
And each new epidemic greet,
Until my system I complete
      Of tropical statistics.

II.

Of those with whom I laughed away
On Lea's[1] fair banks the idle day,
Whose love would ne'er my breast allow
To hold concealed the thoughts that now
      Within my heart are pent,
Who hung upon my every breath,
Of those dear friends I mourn the death
      Of forty-five per cent. :
And Harry Gray, my soul's delight,
The brave, the eloquent, the bright,
      The versatile, the shifty,
Stretched hopeless on his dying bed,
With failing strength and aching head,
In cholera's malignant phase,
Ah ! woe is me, will shortly raise
      The average to fifty.

---

[1] The old East Indian College stood within a mile and a half of this river.

HEPATITIS.

III.

And when, before the rains in June,
The mercury went up at noon
To nine-and-ninety in the shade,
I every hour grew more afraid
    That doctor Fayrer right is
In hinting to my wife that those
Inflammatory symptoms rose
    From latent hepatitis.
I'll, 'ere another week goes by,
For my certificate apply,
    And sail home invalided :
Since, if I press an early bier,
The deaths from Liver in the year,
Compared with those produced by Sun,
Will (fearful thought!) have then by one
    Their ratio exceeded!

        Yours truly,
            H. BROUGHTON.

LETTER VIII.

ABOUT THE HINDOO CHARACTER; WITH DIGRESSIONS HOME.

CALCUTTA, *April* 17, 1863.

DEAR SIMKINS,—One morning, at the beginning of this month, as I lay between sleeping and waking, near the open window, I began to be aware of a hideous din in an adjacent street. At first the sound of discordant music, and a confused multitude of voices, impressed me with a vague idea that a battalion of volunteers were passing by in marching order, headed by their band. This notion, however, was dispelled by the appearance of my bearer with the tea-tray, who informed me that this was the festival of Cali, the goddess of destruction, and that all the Hindoo people had turned out to make holiday. I immediately sallied forth in the direction of the noise, and soon found myself amidst a dense crowd in the principal thoroughfare leading to the shrine of the deity. During a few minutes I could not believe my eyes; for I seemed to have been transported in a moment over more than twenty centuries, to the Athens of Cratinus and Aristophanes. If it had not been for the colour of the faces around, I should have believed myself to be on the main road to Eleusis in the full tide of one of the Dionysiac festivals. The spirit of the scene was the same, and at each step some well-known feature reminded one irresistibly that the Bacchic orgies sprung from the mysterious fanaticism of the far East. It was no unfounded tradition that pictured Dionysus returning from conquered India, leopards and tigers chained to his triumphal car, escorted from the Hyphasis to the Asopus by bands of votaries dancing in fantastic measure to the clang of cymbals. It was no chance resemblance this, between an Hindoo rite in the middle of the nineteenth century, and those wild revels that stream along many a Grecian bas-relief, and wind round many an ancient Italian vase; for every detail portrayed in these marvellous works of art was faithfully represented here. If one of the life-like black figures in the Etruscan chamber of the British Museum could have walked down off the back-ground of red pottery into the midst of the road conducting to Cali Ghaut, he would not have attracted the notice of the closest observer. Every half-minute poured by a troop of worshippers. First came boys, stark naked, and painted from head to foot in imitation of leopards and tigers, while others guided them with reins of thin cord. Then followed three or four strange classic figures, wearing the head-dress which is familiar to us from the existing representations of bacchanalian processions, dancing in an attitude which recalled, spontaneously and instantly, the associations of Smith's "Dictionary of Antiquities." The only circumstance which was not in common between "Tolly's "Nullah" and the Cephisus, was the censer of live charcoal which these men carried before them, supported by wires passed through the flesh under their armpits.

Into this, from time to time, they threw a powder, which produced a sudden flash and a most infernal smell. Behind them, his brows crowned profusely with foliage, was led in mimic bonds the chief personage of the company, who was supposed to be under the direct influence of the god. All around him, musicians were beating tomtoms and clashing tambourines, like the satellites of Evius, on the day when he leapt from his car into the arms of the forsaken Ariadne: as he still leaps on the glowing canvas of Titian. All was headlong licence and drunken frenzy. After struggling through the throng for a mile and a half of dusty street, I came to a narrow slum which descended to the Ghaut, or landing-place, of Cali, which lies on the nullah of the mythical hero Tolly, who, perhaps, was the Atys of this Oriental Cybele. From this lane, a passage a yard or two in breadth opened on to a dirty court, in which stood the sanctuary, whence Calcutta derives its name; which was an object of awe and reverence to the surrounding population for ages before the first ship, laden with Feringhee wares, was warped up the neighbouring river. It seemed impossible to pierce the mob of devotees, and penetrate to the holy place; but not even religious madness, not even the inspiration of bang and toddy, could overcome the habitual respect paid to a white face and a pith helmet. A couple of policemen cleared a passage for me to within a few feet of the sacred image. It appeared to be a rude block, ornamented with huge glass beads; but I dare say the Palladium, which fell from heaven, was not a very elaborate device; and yet it saved the reputation of a young Roman lady, and gave a synonym to an English

A DRAWBACK OF IDOLATRY. 213

jury. Before I reached home, what with the jostling, and hubbub, and stench, I was very glad to get back to the society of clean, fragrant Christians. As I grew every moment more tired and hot, the exhibition seemed to savour less of the classical and more of the diabolical. At last, I came to the ill-natured conclusion, that Satan was at the bottom of the whole business, and not the golden-haired Dionysus. The remarkably unpleasant Mœnads around me suggested the idea of perspiration rather than inspiration; and I felt inclined to exclaim—

> Dea, magna domina Tolli, Calië dea domina,
> Procul a meo sit omnis tuus ore, precor, odor!
> Alios age hinc olentes. Alios age putridos.

This singular system of idolatry, so perfect in organization, so venerable in its extreme antiquity, already shows evident marks of decay. The study of the history of creeds teaches us, that the laws which govern the religious opinions of mankind may be ascertained as surely as the laws which govern their political and social opinions. A rude nation is content with an absurd, irrational superstition; while a highly civilized community requires a logical and consistent faith. You might as soon expect, in the England of the nineteenth century, to find Ptolemy the great astronomical authority, and Galen the great medical authority, as to meet with tenets such as those of the Church in the dark ages. Men who are accustomed to examine with care the principles of constitutional government, of commercial policy, of international law, of personal rights;—men who will not admit the existence of the most insignificant fact in geology or physiology, without a rigorous investigation,—are not likely to be indifferent concerning truth or error in matters to which the interests of this world are as nothing in the balance. The same causes that set John Stuart Mill at work upon the questions of small holdings and limited liability, which led Maclure in quest of the North-West Passage, and Sir Charles Lyell in search of flint knives and pre-historic men—these very causes incite adventurers of another class to seek a reason for the faith that is in them, amidst perils, to which polar bears and icebergs are a trifle. Yet, incredible as it may seem, instead of bidding them God-speed, we prosecute them, and sequester them, and backbite them, and take away their good name and their fellowships. When a *savant*, after a faithful and diligent inquiry, arrives at a conclusion with which we disagree, we are none the less pleased that the subject has been sifted, and we buy his book, and tack some mystical letters to the end of his name. When a theological writer follows this example, we say that his number is six hundred threescore and six, and trounce him of about as many pounds a year.

But I have wandered far enough from Cali Ghaut. You may well imagine that such a scene of idolatrous barbarism as I have described must seem shocking and absurd to natives educated in European literature, and versed in European habits of thought and business. The schoolmaster has long been abroad, and the rationalist generally treads on the heels of that functionary: for the earliest and most natural heresy is an attempt to rationalise the irrational, and extract from the follies of the old faith a consistent system of morality and divinity. Towards the beginning of the present century, Ram Mohun Roy, struck with the idea of divine unity, which he had learnt from the Bible and the Koran, with much audacity and ingenuity undertook to trace out an underlying current of Monotheism in the four books of the Vedas, the most sacred of the Hindoo Scriptures. During a residence in England, he regularly attended a Unitarian place of Worship. His sect went by the name of "Vedantists;" in fact, the "Evangelicals" of the East. The orthodox Pundits took alarm, and declared him a heretic, but not before they had most clearly shown that he had entirely failed to explain away the polytheist character of the Hindoo theology. It never occurred to them to assert that this pretended new idea had been exploded as far back as the reign of Shah Jehan.

When, however, European principles of criticism were applied to the Vedas, grave doubts began to spring up concerning their divine origin. One book was evidently the primary basis of the other three, which were little more than a confused liturgy. The Vedantists now began to talk about "natural religion." They refused any longer to acknowledge the high authority of the writings from which their sect received its first name, and professed to believe only in the pure and eternal God, or Brahma. By a strange inconsistency, they still use the old Vedic ritual, the hymns of which they sing to the best music that can be procured in Calcutta; which is not saying very much for it.

You urge me, in all your letters, to tell you something about the aborigines of India. You write as if you were making inquiries about a set of savages, their bread-fruit, their canoes, and their clubs. I have not hitherto gratified your wish, because I am one of those who think that the people of India deserve more than cursory observation, inasmuch as they are the most important class in India;—for whose benefit we hold the country, and to whom we shall have one day to account for the manner in which we govern it. Extraordinary as this opinion may seem to some people, it is backed by the high authority of Sir Charles Wood and Lord Stanley, Sir John Peter Grant, and the vast majority of the Civil Service. I hate the "damned nigger" style. One requires more than a few months to form a correct set of opinions and impressions concerning an ancient and wealthy society, with a singular and complicated organization; whose habits, instincts, and ways of thought, to a European eye, form "a mighty maze," which, nevertheless, if it be closely examined, will be found to be "not without a plan."

In order to lay a foundation for a conception of the native character, it is essential first to clear away all our preconceived notions of what that character ought to be. It is impossible to judge a Hindoo by any other known standard. He is not, like the North American Indian, a barbarian with a few sound ideas about the bearings of the stars and the habits of deer, and a few crude ideas about the Great Spirit and the future condition of his faithful dog. He is not, like the European of the middle ages, the member of a community, rude indeed as yet, and undeveloped, but replete with the germs of a vigorous civilization. The institutions of his country, though grotesque enough in our point of view, are as elaborate and mature as any recorded in history. He belongs to a social order, which dates far back into the depths of time, with innumerable well-defined grades and classes; with titles which were borne by his forefathers, when the ancestors of English dukes still paddled about in wicker canoes, when wild in woods the noble marquis ran. He professes a religion compared with which all other creeds are mere parvenus; which looks down on the venerable faith of Buddhism as a modern heresy, and watches the varying fortunes of Mahommedanism with the same contemptuous curiosity as that with which the Church of England regards the progress of the Revival movement. He still may recognise at every turn the traces of a system of government, justice, and finance, as comprehensive and minute, though not so philosophical, as that which we have founded in its place. His countrymen were bankers, and merchants, and shopkeepers, long before the renaissance era of European commerce; ere Venice had yet supplanted Amphitrite in the affections of Neptune; ere Britannia was aware of the charter which had been drawn up for her benefit on the occasion of her rising from the azure main amidst a flattering but somewhat monotonous chorus of guardian angels. Broking, and discounting, and forestalling, and retailing were going on briskly along either bank of the Ganges while Gurney and Overend were squabbling over the skin of a badger which they had trapped on the ground where the Exchange now stands; while Fortnum and Mason were driving a bouncing trade in acorns, and Swan and Edgar were doing a good thing in woad; while Rothschild was compounding for his last grinder with some fierce chieftain in Franconia. Who can wonder that the member of such a society should differ radically from a Frenchman or a German;—not as a savage differs from a civilized man, but as one man differs from another who has been brought up amidst an entirely dissimilar set of ideas, scenes, associations, and influences? The day has long passed when the Bengalee could be disposed of by being termed a "mild Hindoo," and I trust that it will not be long before he will cease to be disposed of by being called a " damned nigger."

In the constitution of the native mind, the fundamental characteristic is want of stamina, and this defect is the favourite text of the abuse levelled against the Hindoo by his enemies. The secret of our rapid conquest and secure tenure of the country is the absence of energy among the inhabitants. In every action of his life, the Bengalee makes it manifest that he is entirely without the earnestness of purpose which a Briton carries into his business, his pleasures, even his vices. Your native is perfectly contented to glisten and bask in the sun for days and weeks together, dozing, waking to scratch his arms and turn over, and dozing again. Conceive a Scotchman, not under the influence of whisky and unprovided with tobacco, lying on his back for two hours of daylight! He would never be able to recover his lost ground and catch up his brother Scotchman in the race of life. John Stuart Mill has shown that the " standard of comfort indispensable in the people of the " labouring classes" is the ruling principle of social progress. Now, in India, that standard is lamentably low. A penny or twopence a day will provide a man with rice enough to produce a pleasing sense of plethora. A single coarse cotton garment, a mat, and a brass lotah require no large outlay. He digs a great hole in the

LOW STANDARD OF COMFORT. 219

ground, and makes a dirt pie, which he calls a house. He grinds his curry on a stone prigged from an English graveyard, cooks his rice in an extempore oven on a fire of dried cow-dung, and eats till he "swells visibly " before your very eyes." One good fit of dyspepsia, tempered by a pipe and a siesta, suffices for his sustenance. The great mass of the population will do just as much work as will earn them their simple but flatulent dinner, and not a stroke more. The distinctive traits of the Oriental and the Frank are strongly marked in their respective methods of limiting their exertions to their wants. An English navvy will work like a horse for four days out of the seven, and spend the other three in an Elysium of beer, bird's-eye, pugilism, and bull-terriers. A ryot lounges and snoozes over his business every day and all day long, except on some high festival, when he splotches his turban with pink paint, and sets off to drink the water of the holy river in an exalted state of piety and bang, in the company of twenty or thirty of his neighbours, a tomtom, and two females of bad reputation.

The ordinary Hindoo has no feeling about the sacredness of toil. Honest, faithful performance you will expect from him in vain. A drunken debauched mechanic in our own country will turn out what work he does, in first-rate style. A knavish, dissipated groom will bring your horse to the door in perfect condition, with not a hair out of place, as fresh as he himself was the evening before. A native, on the contrary, must be watched from morning till night. He has no sense of shame in the matter of laziness, and considers himself horribly ill used if he is kept to his duty. I learnt this fact during my first night on these shores. After half an hour's sleep, I began to dream that I was Dante, and that I was paying a visit to the Infernal realms under the guidance of Martin Tupper. Protected by his divine presence, I traversed the regions of torment, escaping with difficulty from the clutches of minor demons, who bore a strong resemblance to the Lascars in the service of the P. and O., until we arrived at the sanctum of the Father of Lies, who received us very cordially. The atmosphere was hot, very hot; so hot that I had begun to think of negotiating a retreat, when an imp came up to his majesty, touched his horns respectfully, and said, " More coals, please sir, for General Butler." At this moment I awoke in a fearful state of perspiration, to see the punkah hanging motionless overhead. I sallied forth, and there was the bearer rolled up in his blanket, fast asleep; and this fellow had absolutely nothing else to do besides pulling a string for three hours and a half every night. The rest of the twenty-four he had at his own disposal. If you go to sleep on a journey, nothing is more usual than to find your palanquin on the ground at the side of the road, while half the men are gone to a village a mile off for a drink of water, and the other half are smoking in a circle and listening to a disquisition of the torch-carrier, who has just pronounced to the satisfaction of his audience that you are of a lower caste than the Sahib at the last dawk bungalow, because he wore a collar and waistcoat, while you travel without those badges of rank. It is difficult to imagine how any business was done before we came into the country —how any one ever made a road, or a boat, or a journey. The other day I was on a visit to the house of a Maharajah. We were to set off at three in the morning, in palanquins, to catch a train at a distant station. Most minute arrangements had been made over night. Our servants were to start on an elephant at one A.M.; our baggage on the heads of coolies an hour after that; while we were to find breakfast ready at a quarter before three. At five minutes before three I awoke by chance, and, out of a household of a hundred and more, not a soul was stirring. They had all gone to bed, not with a determination to oversleep themselves, but absolutely indifferent whether they overslept themselves or not. This utter want of conscience in everything that concerns industry is very trying to men who employ natives in large numbers; and a natural indignation is too apt to render such men oblivious of the fact that the most idle, worthless, servile, timid ryot is the equal of the Viceroy himself in his rights of man and citizen.

Unfortunately, this want of truthfulness leavens the whole being of the Bengalee. And here, though I use the language of the most cruel foes of the native, I entreat you to believe that the same language may be employed with very different ends. Facts are facts. The deduction to be drawn from them is the vital point. Is a firm friend of the Hindoo, a devout believer in the destinies of the race, to blink his eyes to grand faults of the Hindoo character, because those faults form a pretext for those who desire to lower the peasant-proprietor to the condition of a serf? Let us boldly take the native as he is, compare him with what he was, and we shall find no reason for despair as to what he will be. It is not too much to assert that the mass of Bengalees have no notion of truth and falsehood. During the earliest weeks of Indian life one is amused or irritated, as the case may be, by the transparency or ingenuity of the lies which meet one at every turn. The first Mofussil town at which I spent any time was Patna. When my servant heard that we were going thither, he appeared to be in high glee, and said that he had a papa and mamma at Patna. Pleased at his filial piety, I gave him some hours' leave in the course of every day, little dreaming that his parents were represented by a hideous venal sweetheart of eight-and-thirty. At Mofussilpore his papa and mamma were succeeded by his brother and sister, at Chupra by his uncle and aunt. As we went from station to station he had reason to regret that he had been so extravagant with his relations at first setting out. By the time we came to Gya he had exhausted the whole connexion, and was reduced to the clumsy expedient of transporting the author and authoress of his being from Patna in search of employment. You are obliged to engage a servant with your eyes shut. It is a hundred to one that the testimonials which he brings for your inspection refer to some other man. A lady told me that three ayahs applied to her consecutively, one dirtier than another, with precisely the same set of testimonials. But, however deeply engrained in the Hindoo nature are habits of mendacity, there is good ground for believing that those habits may be corrected or modified in time. Under favourable circustances a native can refrain from saying the thing that is not. Powerful Rajahs and high-born Zemindars are too proud and independent to lie and cozen. There are abundance of signs which must convince those who do not in their heart of hearts wish their dark brethren to continue " always liars, evil beasts, " slow bellies," that the Hindoo is capable of speaking the truth, just as he is capable of reading Gibbon, wearing peg-top trousers, and drinking bottled ale. Bengalees who have received an English education, and who mix much with Englishmen, have learnt to appreciate the English feeling about veracity. The Jemmadar, or headman of a factory, who is high in the confidence and much in the company of his master, is often every whit as trustworthy as a Norfolk or Yorkshire bailiff. Who can doubt, then, that among the many blessings which England will have conferred upon India, Truth will not be wanting? At present she is certainly lying with Hope at the bottom of the tank in Short's bazaar.

The love of gain is strong in the Hindoo, but not so strong as to counteract his aversion for what an Englishman would call work. His covetousness displays itself in a penchant for saving money that almost amounts to a mania, and in the popularity of all occupations which afford an opportunity for turning two-thirds of an anna without any great exertion of mind or body. Your Bengalee dearly loves a contract. He is the ideal contractor, as far as his own interests are concerned. He will spare no trouble or time to buy the article at an absurdly low price, and of the worst quality that can by any possibility pass muster. If there is any quiet little knavery practicable, he marks it with the glance of a vulture. The universal " dustoorie " is a singular monument of the petty peculation which has been going on throughout Bengal for thousands of years. Every agent employed to make a purchase, great or small, pockets a commission unknown to his principal. This commission is called "dustoorie," or "the customary "sum;" the amount being regulated by the impudence of the buyer, and the anxiety of the seller to dispose of his goods. A native prince, who agreed to take the house and furniture of a gentleman about to leave the country, claimed to make a deduction from the price, on the ground that he was his own agent. The rascality and acuteness of the servants in European families are something stupendous. A bad servant cheats you right and left. A good servant takes less and less every year that he lives with you, but he will always take something. He could not reconcile it with his conscience to impugn the institution of the dustoorie. If you give your man a rupee to pay a cab, he puts the coin in his pouch, and arranges the matter when your back is turned. If you bid him throw a few pice into a beggar's lap, he takes his percentage after a bargain made at great length and with much heat. But it never occurs to the cabman or the beggar to dispute his right to a commission. The other day, a treasury messenger was sent to buy some stamps. Not being aware that this commodity is supplied by the Government, which is more apt to take dustoories than to give them, he demanded his discount, which was summarily disallowed by the clerk. Shocked and scandalised by a refusal, which appeared to him monstrous and unreasonable, he jumped over the counter, knocked the functionary on the head with his own official ruler, and carried off the ledger in triumph as a hostage back to the treasury. A lady, who lately set up house here, paid the wages of twelve bearers into the hands of the Sirdar or headman during the first month. At the end of that time, she himself, "We employ perjury, it is true, but the other "side employ both perjury and forgery. We bring "forward fifteen witnesses, who would not speak truth "if they could, but the other side brings forward as "many who could not speak truth if they would." Last month, at Mofussilpore, I witnessed a case which came before Benson, and which he referred to Tom. A shopkeeper complained that, as he was walking across the street, one of his neighbours fell on him, knocked him down with a cudgel, and, as he lay insensible on the ground, robbed him of thirteen rupees. He produced seven witnesses, who confirmed circumstantially his whole statement. It eventually turned out that the prisoner struck the prosecutor on the back with a slight switch, and that the rupees and the insensibility were an episode which had no foundation in fact. The proceedings in a case where natives are concerned always remind me of the scene at a public school, when a disputed point occurs during an interesting match. Last winter, I witnessed a game of football at Harrow between two boarding-houses, in which twelve boys of known probity (that is to say, the eleven players and their umpire) swore that the ball had flown midway through the base; while twelve other boys, of equally known probity, swore that it had touched one of the poles. What would Paley say to this? Which of these two pre-judications would he find himself unable to resist?

Mildred, my Mofussil friend, who has lived for twenty years in constant communication with the people of the country, at times seeing none but black faces for six months on end, has a very low opinion of native evidence. He is a credible authority on this point, inasmuch as he is a real friend of the Hindoo, and is adored by the population of the neighbourhood. Ryots who have a suit in court are very importunate to have him called as a witness in their favour. A man lately entreated the magistrate to summon my friend to testify to his character. On being asked whether he had ground for believing that Mildred knew anything about him, he replied that the Sahib had once fined him ten rupees for cattle stealing! When Mildred was a very young man, he bought a village from a zemindar, who sold it cheap because the inhabitants had for some years past refused to pay a pice of rent. As the new proprietor was well aware that his tenants enjoyed a very evil reputation for theft, dacoity, and manslaughter, he called his friends and neighbours together, and rode over with some force to collect the arrears. It happened that cholera was rife in the village; so the party encamped for the night on a spot about a mile distant. Late in the evening, the head man, accompanied by six or seven others, came to Mildred, and told him that, unless he cleared off in the course of the morrow, they would bring the corpse of a ryot who had died of the epidemic, cut the throat, throw it into the camp, and go in a body to the magistrate, to accuse the Sahibs of a murder!

On another occasion, Mildred, in company with two planters of his acquaintance, drove over to visit a friend, who lived at a considerable distance from the station. They had given him no previous intimation to expect them, but people in India can be hospitable on very short notice, and he soon set before them curry, and fowls, and beer, and cheroots. As they were chatting over their tobacco, after a jolly tiffin, they heard the howl of a jackal in the vicinity of the bungalow, and it was proposed to sally forth and have a shot at him. The firearms in a planter's house are always in a condition for immediate use; so the host loaded a rifle, and went out with one of his guests, while Mildred and the other remained among the soda-water bottles. After some time a shot was heard, and soon after the pair returned, pale and agitated. The master of the house said, " Mildred, I believe I have shot a man, but " we did not dare to go and look." It appears they could not find the jackal : so, in the wantonness of men who were full of meat, and drink, and smoke, they took a shot at a sheep which was feeding about a furlong off. As the gun was fired, a man sprang up out of the grass behind the animal, and dropped again before he was well on his feet. Mildred went to the spot, and found a peasant stone dead, with a ball through the heart. Now for the sequel. The relations of the poor fellow prosecuted the planter for murder, and swore that he had tied the deceased to a tree, beaten him cruelly, outraged him in the most foul manner, and finally put him out of his misery by deliberately firing at him from the distance of a few yards. This vindictive wicked lie was supported in every particular by a number of the villagers. The presence of his three countrymen, —a happy chance, and nothing more,—alone saved the. prisoner from condemnation. " From that day forward " (such was the conclusion which Mildred drew from the circumstance) " I resolved, if ever I was on a jury, " never to convict a European of a capital crime on "native testimony." I endeavoured to show him that his resolution was illogical, and that the consequences of it would be most disastrous; that, if we rejected the evidence of Hindoos when the life of an Englishman was in question, we must refuse to admit it on any other occasion whatsoever; the result of which would be that, instead of providing the people of India with justice of superior quality to that dealt out by their own countrymen, we should banish law and order from the land, until an insulted Providence sent us about our business. He was not convinced.

By the most scrupulous care our officers cannot prevent their names being used for purposes of the grossest corruption. For instance, a native gentleman calls on the magistrate, and then goes straight to the house of some one who has a suit pending, and says: "I sit "down in the presence of the Sahib. He has a greater "respect for me than for the sub-inspector of police, and "loves me better than he loves a lieutenant and two "ensigns in the cantonments, and he will soon love me "better than one of the captains. Give me five hundred "rupees." And, though the poor fool must know that if he gave away his whole fortune in presents he would not alter a tittle of the magistrate's verdict, he pays the money under a hazy conviction that some benefit will ensue. Rich baboos will vie with each other for the post of deputy-treasurer, which is worth fifty or sixty rupees per mensem, and will gladly deposit eighty or a hundred thousand rupees as security for the faithful discharge of the functions. They are attracted, not so much by the honour of being in the service of Government, as by the knowledge that an official position will enable them to drive harder bargains, to obtain higher interest, to oppress their poorer neighbours, and intimidate their equals. And yet every dealer in the town knows that if he was to come to the English authorities, and say: "Baboo Chunder Boss, the deputy-treasurer, "told me yesterday that if I refused to let him have my "saltpetre at his own price I should repent it," Baboo Chunder Boss would not be deputy-treasurer another twenty-four hours. They know this, but they cannot act upon it. Habit is too strong for reason. Besides, your native positively likes to fee Jacks-in-office. During the progress of a Governor through his province, all the rajahs and zemindars who come to pay their respects to the great man are never content unless they pay their rupees to his servants. They would not enjoy their interview thoroughly if they got it gratis. The sirdar-bearer or the head messenger of a member of council makes a wonderfully good thing of his place. Out of his pay of a pound a month he manages to dress well, feed of the best, and maintain a sufficiency of wives and parasites. If he hears of a good investment on a small scale, he can generally come down with a fat bag of rupees. Surely the fellow's clients and patrons can hardly imagine that he has the ear of his master. Their munificence is dictated by "dustoor," or custom, the most powerful of all the motives which actuate the conduct of a native.

Dustoor is the breath of a Hindoo's nostrils, the mainspring of his actions, the staple of his conversation. A ryot is never so happy as when he is squatted amidst a circle of neighbours, smoking a mixture in which powdered dung is the most fragrant ingredient, and talking about dustoor. The spirit of conservatism, powerful everywhere except among the conservative leaders in the English House of Commons, is rabid in the East. In European countries men keep up old practices and habits which reason cannot approve because familiarity has rendered them attractive. In India men do things which they know to be absurd, and which they excessively dislike, because custom so enjoins. An English family, an hour after their usual bedtime, perform an elaborate toilette, and start off to dance and flirt themselves into a state of unnatural wakefulness. The son is routed out from a quiet corner, where he has been employed over a surreptitious cigar, and hounded up to his dressing-room with threats and execrations. A daughter, who is on ordinary occasions a model of piety, rudely tears the kerchief from the face of her sleeping father, and rouses him from sweet visions of middling fair Pernambuco and ditto transfer stock, to the fearful reality of a four hours' lounge in a back drawing-room, sweetened by fine supper-sherry at twenty-eight and six. And yet they go forth to the sacrifice a troop of willing victims, proud of the fillet, and in fond expectation that they will enjoy the rite. A shopkeeper or clerk, when club-night comes round, duly pays half-crowns which he can ill afford, and swallows four times as much liquor as he can well digest. But, while he is seated at midnight in the midst of a noisy, boozy company, with an incipient headache and the prospect of a crapulous colic, smoking his fourteenth pipe and sipping his ninth—no, tenth—no, eleventh—brar-r-ry war-r-rer, he is all the time under the impression that he is doing something uncommonly jolly and Bacchanalian. Now this is not the case with the Hindoo. Groaning and repenting, he follows whithersoever dustoor may lead him. This thrifty, temperate race, who deny themselves every pleasure and comfort without a sigh, at the command of fashion fling away sums which would keep them and theirs in luxury for a lifetime. To procure these sums they are forced to have recourse to money-lenders, who are the bugbears of Indian social life. A sepoy, whose pay is seven rupees a month, has often been known to sell himself, body, soul, and pension, to a baboo, in order to spend three hundred rupees on a marriage feast. The other day, an ayah, whose wages are those of a London servant-of-all-work, invited a European lady's-maid to a dinner, where covers were laid for thirty guests, with champagne, and beer *à discrétion*. Mildred told me that native gentlemen frequently came to him to borrow some thousands of pounds on the security of a great slice of their estate. He would say: " My good fellow, I am well aware what you want this " loan for; and you are well aware that you will never " be able to pay it, and that you will have ruined your- " self and your descendants in order, once in a way, to " cut a figure in the district. You will gain much more " respect by being known to be able to spend all your " rents." The zemindar would own the truth of everything my friend stated, shrug his shoulders, and go off muttering something about " dustoor." A few days after, the land would be in the clutches of some harpy from Patna.

A curious instance of the pernicious effects of " dus-" toor" is afforded by the fortunes of the family of my friend the Maharaja. His ancestors were enormously wealthy, and were, besides, the purest of pure Brahmans, and at the head of the religious community for a hundred miles round. If Lord Fitzwilliam were likewise Archbishop of York, his position in the country would be much that of the old Maharajas of Kishenagur, in the tract which lies along the left bank of the Hooghly. The grandfather of the present man brought himself to the brink of ruin by the most reckless and aimless extravagance. On one occasion he sold the battle-ground of Plassey for two lacs (20,000*l*.), and expended the proceeds on gold and silver cups, which he scattered broadcast among the mob from the summit of his sacred car during the procession on a solemn feast-day. The father received the estate much involved and reduced to very small dimensions. Nevertheless he spent thirty thousand rupees on the marriage of his son. Happily that son had received an English education, and had acquired a taste for English habits and society. He lives freely, keeps open house from year's end to year's end, and is very popular with the residents at the station; and meanwhile he has paid off debts to the tune of seventeen thousand pounds, has cleared the property, and intends to indulge himself in a visit to England next March, as a reward for his sense and forethought. He has much more fun for his money than ever his grandfather had, and yet he manages to eat his chupatty, and have it too. When he had once emancipated himself from the toils of "dustoor," prosperity followed as a natural consequence. Being so very exalted a Brahmin, he may eat and drink in the company of Europeans without blame or stain. Nay, hundreds and hundreds of natives come to him in the course of the year, to have their caste restored for a price. It is the old story. I fancy Tetzel got his indulgences uncommon cheap. There are some who say that, if we left India to-morrow, the only traces of our occupation would be the empty beer-bottles; just as there are some who say that it is all over with the army since the amalgamation, and who make other affirmations of about equal value with the statement that Balbus is building a wall. Let no one assert that we have ruled, and fought, and panted, and perspired, and permanently settled in vain, as long as we have taught one Maharaja the absurdity of "dustoor."

Yours ever,

H. BROUGHTON.

LETTER IX.

BRITISH TEMPER TOWARDS INDIA, BEFORE, DURING, AND SINCE THE MUTINY.

CALCUTTA, *May* 11, 1863.

DEAR SIMKINS,—I lately read through a file of the *Friend of India,* for 1836, with great pleasure, not unmingled with regret. The value of such a paper in these days would be incalculable. The tone of the articles indicated the existence in Anglo-Indian society of a spirit which has passed away and left but faint traces. In those times the well-being of the Hindoo was the first and dearest care of our leading civilians. Their successors honestly do their duty by the native population; but that duty is no longer a labour of love. Thirty years ago the education of the people of the country was the favourite subject of conversation in the best circles, and occupied the spare time of men who had little enough of that commodity. Hindoo history, Hindoo literature, Hindoo social life, were discussed with inexhaustible ardour; and the hopes entertained concerning the future of the race were proportionate to the interest which it excited. Of course this feeling, like all that is noble and unselfish in the mind of man, partook of a strong dash of illusion. But the same may be said of every successive stage in the progress of knowledge and civilization. Philanthropists are a sanguine class; and it is well for them that they are so. The generation which was determined to show that Englishmen came to India with other ends than that of making money, and swaggering about the great "Anglo-"Saxon race," might well be forgiven for over-rating the merits of Sanskrit poetry or the attainments of a Bengalee Bachelor of Arts. Once every week, Marshman, the editor of the *Friend of India,* would come down from Serampore for a conversation with the Secretary to Bengal; and the salutary fruits of this close understanding between the executive power and the press were evident, both in the acts of the Government and the articles in the *Friend.* Public measures were dictated by a spirit of enlightened philosophy, and the suggestions and disquisitions in the journal were practical and temperate, and acquired additional value from the fact that they were understood to represent the views of men in power. A noisy and enthusiastic breakfast-party frequently met to discuss the subject which was next their hearts. Of these men some are still doing good work well, while others have passed away, leaving their mark more or less deeply impressed on their generation. There was Sir Edward Ryan, then Chief Justice of Bengal, now President of the Civil Service Commission, whose hearty address and kindly advice are among the most agreeable associations which a young civilian carries from the shores of England. I remember well, that, on emerging from his pleasant presence, I remarked in the hall a bust of Dwarkanath Thakur, a Hindoo gentleman for whom Sir Edward entertained a strong regard; for our officers were then not ashamed to call a native by the name of "friend," and would have been very much ashamed to talk of him by the appellation of "nigger," even without the customary prefix. Then there was young Trevelyan; and young Colvin, whose destiny was to die sick and weary in the darkest hour of the great mutiny, at a time when his authority as Governor of the North-West Provinces was confined to the space commanded by the guns of the fort of Agra: Sir Benjamin Malkin, an able judge and a ripe scholar, a man eminently distinguished by "public "spirit, ardent and disinterested, yet always under the "guidance of discretion:" and Ross Mangles, who, when chairman of the Court of Directors during that eventful year 1857, could never be convinced that the mass of the population of India had been suddenly transformed into felons and rebels, preordained by Providence to afford food for powder and the gallows. And there too was Macaulay, in high delight at finding himself in a country where so much was to be learned; keeping the company far on towards noon over the cold curries and empty tea-cups, until the consciousness of accumulating boxes drove them one by one to their respective offices. Now-a-days such a reunion would be reviled in the local papers as a parcel of conspirators assembled to hatch dark plots against the English Name, the Planting Interest, and the Development of the Resources of India. Under the auspices of Lord Dalhousie, the harvest which had been sown by these men and those who thought with them, was reaped in a series of wise and beneficent reforms. But during the reign of the next viceroy things took a fatal turn.

At the commencement of 1857, humanity and philanthropy were the order of the day. We had just brought to an end the Russian war, which had been fought throughout in a spirit of generous chivalry, in spite of the efforts of those who endeavoured to turn a contest waged to preserve the balance of power into a murderous struggle of embittered nations. It was not many years since we had put down, in a cheery off-hand style, an Irish rebellion, which would have furnished our forefathers with a welcome excuse for barbarous severity and prolonged and increased oppression. In 1798, the victorious Orangemen could not be induced to spare the lives of a parcel of clever schoolboys, who talked a little too much about Brian Boru, and Harmodios and Aristogiton. In 1848 we transported the leader of the revolt for a few years, rather because we did not know what else to do with him, than from any desire to make him suffer for his presumption. When Smith O'Brien was sentenced to be hanged, drawn, and quartered, any one who knew the temper of the nation was perfectly aware that the value of the life of the condemned rebel, in an annuity office, was as good as that of any other man of his age in the three kingdoms.

Then came the tidings of the outbreak at Meerut, of the massacre of Delhi. The first impression produced by the intelligence was curiosity mingled with pity, and surprise that any interesting thing could come out of India. But as every mail brought a fresh story of horror and disaster, a significant change came over the face of society. If the sympathy and indignation inspired by an outrage is intense in proportion to the faculty of suffering in the victim, here was a case in which indignation and sympathy could know no bounds; for the victims belonged to the most refined and enlightened class of the first nation in the world. Ladies, bred and nurtured amidst all that wealth and affection could afford, were dragged along, under a June sun, in the ranks of the mutineers, in hourly expectation, and soon in hourly hope, of death. Officers, who had been trained to the duties of government by the best education which the mother-country could supply; judges, magistrates, men of science, men of letters, were pelted to death with brickbats, or hung, amidst shouts of laughter, after a mock trial. Then from the lowest depths of our nature emerged those sombre, ill-omened instincts, of whose very existence we had ceased to be aware. Intense compassion, intense wrath, the injured pride of a great nation—those combative propensities against which Mr. Bright has so often testified in vain—surged in upon the agitated community. It was tacitly acknowledged that mercy, charity, the dignity and sacredness of human life—those great principles which, at ordinary times, are recognised as eternally true—must be put aside till our sway was restored and our name avenged. It is well that nations, as men, should pray to be delivered from temptation. Two months of Nana Sahib brought about an effect on the English character at the recollection of which Englishmen at home have already learned to blush, but the lamentable consequences of which will be felt in India for generations yet unborn or unthought of.

Who does not remember those days, when a favourite amusement on a wet afternoon, for a party in a country house, was to sit on and about the billiard-table devising tortures for the Nana; when the palm was given to that ingenious gentleman who proposed that he should be forced, first, to swallow a tumbler of water in which all the blue papers in a seidlitz-powder box had been emptied, and then a tumbler with the contents of all the white papers in a state of solution? when every one chuckled to hear how General Neill had forced high Brahmans to sweep up the blood of the Europeans murdered at Cawnpore, and then strung them in a row, without giving them the time requisite for the rites of purification? It is singular that he imitated in every particular the conduct of Telemachus towards the maidservants who had lent too kind an ear to those suitors who were content to fly at low game, with a view, I presume, to keep their hands in during the intervals of their more ambitious courtship. Every one chuckled, with the exception of a certain evangelical paper, which remonstrated with the General for depriving these poor men of their chances of salvation! "Have you heard the news?" said a celebrated author to an acquaintance, as they stood together under the porch of the Athenæum. "The Sepoys have taken to inflicting the most exquisite "cruelties upon the Sikhs, and the Sikhs in return "swear that they will stamp the Company's arms in "red-hot pice over the body of every Sepoy who comes "in their way. These are the sort of tidings that now- "a-days fill every heart in England with exultation and "thankfulness." During the first debate at the Union Society, in my first term, an orator wound up with these words: "When the rebellion has been crushed out from "the Himalayas to Comorin; when every gibbet is red "with blood; when every bayonet creaks beneath its "ghastly burden; when the ground in front of every "cannon is strewn with rags, and flesh, and shattered "bone;—then talk of mercy. Then you may find some "to listen. This is not the time." This peroration was received with a tumult of applause by an assembly whose temper is generally characterized by mild humanity, modified by an idolatrous attachment to the memory of Archbishop Laud. If you turn over the volume of *Punch* for the latter half of 1857, you will probably open on a picture representing a big female, with a helmet and a long sword, knocking about a black man, in appearance something between a gorilla and a soldier in one of our West Indian regiments, who is standing over a dead woman and child. Two palm-trees in the back-ground mark the locality, and the whole production is labelled "Justice," or "Nemesis," or "O God of Battles, steel my soldiers' hearts!" What must have been the fury of the outburst which could transport to such lengths that good-natured and sensible periodical, which so admirably reflects the opinions of a good-natured and sensible nation!

Such was the feeling in England; and, being such, it was only the faint shadow of the state of things in India. For out here men were influenced, not only by pity and wrath, intensified by the immediate presence of the objects of those passions, but by shame, by the bitterness of bereavement and ruin, by an ever-present fear, by the consciousness of an awful risk which they had barely escaped, and of innumerable perils still to come. History shudders at the recollection of the terrible "Spanish fury" which desolated Antwerp in the days of William the Silent; but the "English fury" was

more terrible still. With the grim determination and
the dogged pertinacity of their race, men went forth
over the face of the land to shoot, and sabre, and hang,
and blow from guns till the work should be accomplished. It was generally understood that no one would
be called in question for having erred on the side of
severity. Many a one of those good-humoured agreeable
civilians with whom you canter along the course, or
play billiards at the club; who are so forgiving when
you revoke palpably and inexcusably, and so ready with
their letters of introduction and offers of hospitality—
many a one of them has witnessed strange scenes, and
could tell strange tales. He could tell how he has
ridden into some village in Shahabad or the Dooab,
with a dozen troopers at his heels; how he has called
for a drink of milk, and taken his seat under a tree,
pistol in hand, while his men ferreted out the fugitive
mutineers who had found their way home to seek concealment and sustenance among their relations and
neighbours; how very short a trial sufficed to convict
those who were accused of housing and abetting the
rebels; and how, as he left for the next camping-ground,
he pretended not to observe his followers stealing back
to recover their picket-ropes.

There is a degree of mutual terror which almost necessitates mutual extermination. At a time when the
safety of India depended on the Punjab, and the safety
of the Punjab hung on a single hair (and, thank God,
that single hair was a strong one, for it was Sir John
Lawrence), a native regiment quartered in that province,
unable to resist the epidemic of sedition, mutinied and
left the cantonments. An energetic civil officer started

off in pursuit with the slender force of sixty-six policemen, brought the mutineers to bay, and, by a rare display of audacity and craft, captured them to a man. It is more easy to blame what followed than to say how he should have acted under the circumstances. It would have been madness to send off a compact and numerous force with tickets of leave to recruit the rebel garrison of Delhi. At the same time, Sir Joshua Jebb himself would have hesitated before he undertook to guard a battalion of regular troops with a handful of native policemen, who were themselves at that moment on the eve of an outbreak. One course remained. There is a closer prison than a Government jail: a surer sentry than a Punjabee chokedar.

When first I came out there were two gentlemen here who were considered the most welcome addition to Calcutta society. One was a jolly comical-looking chap, an excellent officer, and a capital man for a small dinner-party. The other was most refined and intelligent, with a remarkably courteous and winning address. It was said that these two had hung more people than any other men in India. Mr. Hume, of Etawah, who was blamed by many for excess of leniency, but who so bore himself that no one could blame him for want of courage, distinguished himself by keeping down the number of executions in his district to seven, and by granting the culprits a fair trial. These he treated with fatherly tenderness, for he invented a patent drop for their benefit; so that men prayed—first, that they might be tried by Mr. Hume, and next, that, if found guilty, they might be hanged by him.

One morning I was lounging in the room of a very

good friend of mine, one of the youngest captains in the army, who went through as much rough-and-tumble fighting as could be squeezed into twelve months, and who came out of the business with the reputation of being a first-rate cavalry officer. We were overhauling his collection of guns, trying the locks, and criticizing the grooving, as men do on such occasions, when I remarked, suspended in the place of honour, an archaic rickety revolver, and an old cut-and-thrust sword, with a bright notched blade, and a well-worn leathern handle. Those were not holiday weapons. Once, when charging a couple of hundred of the famous Dinapore mutineers, he left that sword in the head of a sepoy. While dismounting to recover it he was separated from his squadron, and surrounded by a party of desperate Pandies, who, being perfectly aware that their last hour was come, were desirous of opening to themselves the gates of the celestial Zenana by the sacrifice of so redoubted a Sahib. My friend sheltered himself as best he could behind his horse's neck, and kept the assailants off with his revolver, till two faithful Punjabees galloped back to his assistance. Meanwhile, he had shot three men dead on the spot, each with a bullet through the brain. He took part in the pursuit of Coer Sing from Lucknow to the Ganges. On the night before that old warrior succeeded in passing the river, a picket was posted to keep watch upon the rebels, who were quartered in and near a populous village. From time to time the country-people came in with the intelligence that the enemy were still there, until their importunate desire to give information roused a suspicion that all was not right. We advanced cautiously, and found that

Coer Sing had stolen away, and was already well on his road towards the ferry. After the affair had terminated in the escape of the mutineers, our commanding officer sent back his cavalry, with orders to take signal vengeance on the peasants whose treachery had foiled his carefully-concerted plan. The regiment surrounded the village, set the roofs on fire, looted the dwellings of what cloth and grain they contained, stripped the women of their bangles and anklets, and put all the males to the edge of the sword. This was only one among many like deeds, deeds of which every one approves at the time, but which afterwards no one cares to justify or to discuss. We little dream what a dire and grim significance is attached by many a widow and orphan in Oude or Bahar to the names of some who appear to us the mildest and most loveable of human beings. In the eyes of only too many Roman matrons Cæsar was the most attractive and insinuating among the young swells of his day; whether amiability and tenderness formed the leading features of his character, as conceived by a Helvetian or a Nervian, may reasonably be doubted.

Things had now come to a terrible pass. During the first weeks of the mutiny the murders were perpetrated by the "budzarts," or black sheep, of the regiment, with a view to implicate their comrades beyond the hope of pardon; to place between themselves and their former condition of life a gulf filled with English blood. Their scheme met with entire success. The minds of our countrymen were so agitated and distorted by anger and uneasiness, that even those battalions which remained true to their salt began to be apprehensive for their safety whenever they found themselves in the same cantonment with European troops. In a station where this state of things existed, suspicion and dislike reigned supreme. The officers of the native corps slept in the European lines with loaded revolvers under their pillows; the guns, unlimbered and charged to the muzzle with grape, faced the quarters of the sepoys; a strong force was at all times under arms, and the very air seemed heavy with an impending storm. Under such circumstances, an outbreak would have been regarded rather as a relief than as a misfortune. But if our people were anxious, the supposed mutineers had far more reason to be nervous. On occasions of this description, there is nothing which men so constantly underrate as the terror which they themselves inspire in the breasts of others. During a town and gown row, I always used to think that the hostile column looked most formidable and impressive, while I was only too conscious that the fighting power of our own array was lamentably defective. Who could depend on Screwington, who had descended by hebdomadal steps from the second to the sixth boat, until he finally retired into the illimitable? on Dufferly, who cried three weeks before he left school, when the fags mutinied and pelted him with pennyrolls? on Timkins, who had never taken a walk a mile long since he spent the day at Shelford to escape being condoled with after missing his scholarship? And yet the effect produced on the imagination of the town by our onward charge was, doubtless, very demoralizing. A cloud of tall forms, in square caps and flowing gowns, bearing down through the fog, must test the courage of the hardiest Barnwell cooley, or the most vindictive college kitmutgar, burning to take out his unpaid wages in undergraduate gore. Once, or more than once, it befell that, when the suspected troops were ordered out to be disarmed or discharged, the loaded cannon, the lighted matches, the line of frowning white faces, proved too much for their nerves. Convinced that they had been assembled to be butchered, the poor devils broke and took to their heels, under a crashing fire of shrapnel and canister. By the time it came to this, the only chance of existence for the one party lay in the utter destruction of the other. Quarter was not given, and, indeed, hardly could be said to be worth the asking. An Englishman knew well that, though one set of Pandies were to spare his life, the next lot who came across him would cut his throat; and a sepoy knew well that, if his captors took the trouble to drag him about in their train for a few days, the magistrate at the first station on the road would infallibly hang him before the officer in command of the party had finished his dinner.

The presence of a military officer, however, seldom afforded much comfort to a prisoner. None of their persecutors were so dreaded by the natives as the royal troops lately arrived from England. No civilian armed with the thunderbolts of the law, able to ascertain at a glance whether the culprit was a pensioned sepoy, a Mahommedan fanatic, or a peaceable cultivator, was half so terrible a judge as a beardless subaltern, fresh from the depôt at Chatham, whose experience of the population was summed up in the statements that "nig-" gers were all blasted liars," and that, "when a feller " said he was a ryot, he was sure to be the greatest " scoundrel unhung:" a distinction which he was not likely long to retain. The knowledge of the servants of the Company was far less formidable than the ignorance of the servants of the Crown. No Sikh burning to avenge Aliwal and Sobraon on the revolted mercenaries who had been used by the Feringhees as tools to accomplish the humiliation of his race, inspired such horror in the souls of the village people, as the British private, who saw a probable murderer, and an undoubted subject for " loot," in every " Moor" who came in his way—for in those days the rank and file of our army always spoke of the inhabitants of India by the appellation of " Moors." As the men landed at Bombay, they expressed vexation and disappointment at not being allowed to go in at the Moors who were taking their *siesta* upon the beach. They had been brought all the way from England to kill Moors, and why should they not begin at once? One Moor in the hand was worth two in the bush, or rather the jungle. At one time it became necessary to double the guards at Fort William, in order to prevent the soldiers from sallying forth at night to avenge the atrocities committed in Oude and Rohilcund upon the syces of Chowringhee, and the palkee-bearers of the China-bazaar. A corporal, who had travelled up with a party from Bombay to join his regiment in the field, on his arrival at head-quarters reported that in the course of the journey a mutiny had taken place among the bullock-drivers. On inquiry, it appeared that the hero of the affair was an honest fellow, who had disembarked with his head full of the Nana and the fatal well. His story was simple:—" I seed two Moors talk-" ing in a cart. Presently I heard one of 'em say " ' Cawnpore.' I knowed what that meant; so I fetched

"Tom Walker, and he heard 'em say 'Cawnpore,' and
"he knowed what that meant. So we polished 'em
"both off."

It is observable that civilians, as a rule, described the operation of killing as "accounting for," or "disposing "of:" as if to express the perfunctory and exact performance of official work. Military men preferred the term "polishing off" as a more jovial and rollicking synonym for the extermination of their fellow-creatures. Men spoke of executions and massacre in the tone which a certain class of medical students are supposed to adopt with reference to surgical operations. It must have been a curious state of things in which English Christians could talk to other English Christians of "fine bags," not of hares and pheasants, but of human beings.

At Buxar, which, you may remember, is on the Ganges, a little above Arrah, there lived a native, well known to all the residents by the name of "Coony "Baboo," who was employed by the Government in a subordinate capacity. He was a Bengalee, and as such had just as much reason to be alarmed for his safety as any Englishman at the station. One day he was pursuing his avocation at a wharf on the river, armed with a pistol, which he kept to protect his life and property against the stray mutineers, and other vagrants, who swarmed in those troubled regions, when a steam-flat came up the stream carrying a detachment of English troops. The commanding officer sent a boat to communicate with the authorities on shore. The crew, seeing a man who, to their eyes, presented a suspicious appearance, hanging about the jetty, took it into their heads that he might just as well hang on board their steamer, and accordingly seized him and searched his person. When the pistol came to light, they made no doubt but that he was a mutineer who had in some unaccountable manner been delivered into their hands. They forthwith took him on board, where, after a short but satisfactory investigation, the poor Baboo was ordered for immediate execution. Happily, in the nick of time, a civil officer appeared on the scene, who, when he saw the prisoner, exclaimed, " Why, it is Coony Baboo ! " What are they doing to you, Coony ? " It was with great difficulty that the captors could be induced to believe the assurances of the civilian, whom they evidently regarded as an emissary of Lord Canning, and a representative of that clemency policy which was the bugbear of the day.

At a place hundreds of miles distant from the seat of war, some brinjarries, or corn-dealers, came into the camp of a regiment which had been a very short while in the country. The men on guard observed that the heads of the strangers were shaved, and knew by instinct that they must be sepoys. A hastily-constituted tribunal took cognizance of the matter, and called in a sergeant who had the reputation of a profound knowledge of India. Pleased at being consulted, he cocked his eye, and, after due inspection, pronounced that the prisoners were undoubtedly sepoys. A civilian, who was present, remonstrated most vehemently, but was answered with the *primâ facie* argument, " You see their heads are " shaved ! They must be sepoys." At length his importunity prevailed, and the colonel ordered the soldiers to take the brinjarries to the outskirts of the camp and let them go. These orders were obeyed to the letter. The men were led beyond the tents, set free, and shot down as they ran away.

A story was current at the time, which, if not true, had at any rate so much the air of truth, that people did not take the trouble to refuse it credence. Some troops, fresh from England, were marching up country under the orders of an old brigadier. One morning, just before the tents were struck, a couple of dirty miserable beings were detected lurking outside the line of sentries. They were seized, and brought before the commanding officer, who questioned them closely. Whether from the consciousness of guilt, or an inability to understand Aldershott Hindoostanee, the poor wretches answered only by uncouth gestures and disjointed exclamations. The verdict was: " Spies, spies ! " Hang 'em up ! " and the word was given to march. At the next halting-place the colonel's bed was missing. The old fellow stormed, and fretted, and cursed his servants freely, but with no result. At length his sirdar-bearer came forward trembling, and putting his hands together in an attitude of supplication, as their wont is when addressing a superior, said in a tone of deprecatory explanation: " Master done give order hang up " bed-coolies."

The events of those times have left their trace in our military vocabulary. During the year and a half which followed the outbreak at Meerut, to "loot" and to " polish off " became household verbs in the British army. It was only the other day that I was present while a party of military men were discussing the beauties and antiquities of Benares. " Gad," exclaimed

one of them, "what a town it would be to loot. They
" say that nobody knows when it was looted last.
" There must be at least ten crore of jewels and coin
" somewhere about the place." The notion seemed
wonderfully palatable to the company, and afforded
a pregnant subject of conversation. Meanwhile, I sat
with my mouth wide open, marvelling how on earth
English officers could entertain the idea of plundering
a city which was exactly as much an English city as
York or Exeter. Talk of this description is childish
enough, but, when indulged in frequently, it becomes
significant. The sterling qualities of our army alone
rescued it from utter demoralization. No other soldiers
in the world could have preserved their self-respect
amidst so fearful an ordeal. Eighteen months in such
a school would have turned the French line-regiments
into Zouaves, the Zouaves into Turcos, and the Turcos
into cannibals.

After all, however, the best hope of the miserable
natives lay in the justice and moderation of official
men. The stern and cold animosity of the civilians,
the reckless and unscrupulous retribution dealt out by
the military, were as nothing to the rabid ferocity of the
non-official community. These men had come to the
shores of India for the sole purpose of making money.
They were under no professional obligation of providing
for the prosperity and happiness of the population, and
indeed were too apt to regard their dark fellow-subjects
simply as tools for promoting their own ends. Now that
their lives and fortunes were brought to the extreme of
jeopardy, in consequence of a wide-spread and most
formidable revolt of the despised race, their fury and

hatred knew no measure. In one or two instances the Government was constrained by the pressure of circumstances to place power in the hands of men of this class. In one great city some low Europeans were vested with full magisterial authority. The unhappy place was delivered over to a Reign of Terror. Whatever misery could be inflicted by cupidity, private malice, and vulgar barbarity, was endured to the full by the wretched natives at the hands of this triumvirate of snobs.

The tone of the press was horrible. Never did the cry for blood swell so loud as among these Christians and Englishmen in the middle of the nineteenth century. The pages of those brutal and grotesque journals published by Hébert and Marat during the agony of the French Revolution, contained nothing that was not matched and surpassed in the files of some Calcutta papers. Because the pampered Bengal sepoys had behaved like double-dyed rascals, therefore every Hindoo and Mussulman was a rebel, a traitor, a murderer; therefore, we were to pray that all the population of India might have one neck, and that all the hemp in India might be twisted into one rope. It would be wearisome to quote specimens of the style of that day. Every column teemed with invectives which at the time seemed coarse and tedious, but which we must now pronounce to be wicked and blasphemous. For what could be more audacious than to assert that Providence had granted us a right to destroy a nation in our wrath?— to slay, and burn, and plunder, not in the cause of order and civilization, but in the name of our insatiable vengeance, and our imperial displeasure? The wise ruler, whose comprehensive and impartial judgment preserved him from the contagion of that fatal frenzy, was assailed with a storm of obloquy for which we should in vain seek a precedent in history. To read the newspapers of that day, you would believe that Lord Canning was at the bottom of the whole mutiny; that upon his head was the guilt of the horrors of Cawnpore and Allahabad; that it was he who had passed round the chupatties and the lotahs, and spread the report that the Russ was marching down from the north to drive the English into the sea. After all, the crime charged against him was, not that he had hindered the butchery, but that his heart was not in the work. No one had the face to say, or, at any rate, no one had the weakness to believe, that Lord Canning had pardoned any considerable number of condemned rebels. His crying sin was this, that he took little or no pleasure in the extermination of the people whom he had been commissioned by his Sovereign to govern and protect.

After Lord Canning, Sir John Peter Grant had the gratification of being the personage most profusely and fiercely maligned by the enemies of the native: which honourable position he long retained, until of late Sir Charles Wood put in his claim,—a claim which has been instantly and fully recognised. A certain journal made the brilliant suggestion that Sir John Peter, had he dared, would very likely have released the sepoys whom General Neill had ordered for execution, and then proceeded to abuse him as if he had actually so done. This hypothetical case soon grew into a fact. It was stated positively in all quarters, that Sir John Peter Grant had set free the murderers of Cawnpore, with a bombastic proclamation, containing the words "in virtue of my high authority," an expression which at once discredited the story in the estimation of all who knew the man. Sir John and his high authority were reviled and ridiculed in the daily and weekly papers of England and India, in conversation, on the stage, and on the hustings. Meanwhile, with native laziness and good-humour, he said nothing, and allowed the tempest to whistle about his ears without moving a muscle. At length the Home Government wrote out to the Governor-General, directing him to take cognisance of the affair; and he accordingly requested the accused party to explain how the matter stood. Then Sir John spoke out, and affirmed that the report was a pure fabrication; that he never enlarged a single sepoy; and that, had he desired to thwart General Neill, such interference would have been entirely out of his power. Hereupon, the press in general proceeded to make amends in a full and satisfactory manner. One newspaper, however, had no intention of letting him off so easily, and put forward an apology which was exquisitely characteristic, and which probably diverted the object quite as much as it was designed to vex him. The gist of it was, that Sir John had undoubtedly been falsely charged in this particular instance, but that he was such a confirmed and abandoned friend of the native as quite to deserve everything he had got; and that no contumely, whether rightly or wrongly bestowed on him, could by any possibility come amiss.

And now who can wonder that among a generation which has gone through such a crisis philanthropy is somewhat at a discount? It is unjust to blame men who have lost their fortunes and friends and health in the desperate struggle, because the moment the victory is decided, they cannot set to work heart and soul at concocting and promoting plans for the benefit of their conquered foe! That struggle irresistibly reminded us that we were an imperial race, holding our own on a conquered soil by dint of valour and foresight. Cantonments and arsenals, field batteries, and breaching batteries, seemed more essential to the government of the country than courts of law, normal schools, and agricultural exhibitions. The questions of the day were, not whether Sanskrit should be taught at the Presidency College, or to what extent the pure mathematics of Hindoo men of science were borrowed from European sources; but whether artillery might safely be posted at a station where no English cavalry were quartered; whether the advantages of massing troops at central points compensated for the sanitary dangers of that measure. As long as human nature remains what it is, men who have just made a great and successful effort will ask themselves whether they and theirs are not to profit by their exertions. Had we poured forth our blood like water in order that the children of sepoys might receive a better education than they would have obtained in the event of their fathers having overturned the British supremacy? In order that the disaffected Rajpoots of Shahabad might reap the advantages of a more speedy and equitable administration of justice than they would have enjoyed under the rule of Coer Sing? What was England to gain in return for her millions of money and thousands of lives? Did she not merit some more substantial recompense for having recovered India, than the privilege of governing the Indians in a spirit of wisdom and unselfishness? Echo and the planters answered "yes!" though equity and humanity steadily continued to assert that the events of 1857 and 1858 had not altered a whit our position in India—that our re-conquest could be justified in the sight of God and Europe only by the same conditions as had justified our original conquest. We must still govern the land in the interest of the inhabitants. We must still provide them with everything that is essential to their well-being and happiness. We must still pay rent and taxes, keep the roof tight and the drains open, or out we must turn as unprofitable and dishonest tenants.

It is greatly to the credit of the civilians that they hearkened to the voice of equity and humanity. The natives cannot accuse their governors of neglect or injustice. They have no reason to regret having exchanged Munro and Elphinstone for Grant and Beadon. Most of our officers would do all and suffer all rather than betray their trust. Some have already done much, and suffered not a little. But the new order of things is not as the old. The children of the soil are no longer regarded with the lively interest, the credulous partiality of yore. Those are plants which do not flourish amid the rank weeds and rushes, the sand and rubble that overspread the land which was lately submerged by the deluge of civil strife. Men cannot at will cast aside the recollection of those times when all was doubt and confusion and dismay; when a great fear was their companion, day and night; when the mother and children were in sanctuary at the headquarters of the Division; when the husband worked with a loaded revolver among his papers, a horse standing saddled in the stable, his feet resting upon a pair of saddle-bags crammed with his most valuable property. The distrust and dislike engendered by such an experience are too deeply rooted to be plucked up by an act of volition.

Though the civilians do not allow the impressions left by the events of the mutiny to influence their opinions and their conduct, the case is far other with the non-official society. And here I may remark that there is some difficulty in finding an appellation for the members of that society. They themselves insist upon it that the civilians have given them the name of " inter- " lopers," and grow extremely wroth over this imaginary grievance. I solemnly declare that I never heard the word used in conversation by a civilian, and never saw it in print, except when it occurs in the effusions of the " interloping" party. On occasions, when they are very angry indeed, they will have it that they are called " adventurers." Perhaps "settlers" is the least objectionable and most comprehensive title.

The European settlers in India speedily acquired that contempt for the Bengalees which it is a law of nature that the members of a conquering race should entertain for the subject population among whom they live. As the Norman baron regarded the Saxon churl, as the Dutch boer regarded the Hottentot, so it was inevitable that the English planter should regard the ryot and the cooly. No one can estimate very highly the moral and intellectual qualities of people among whom he resides for the single purpose of turning them to pecuniary account. But in the course of time a new element was added to the feelings which the settler displayed towards the Hindoo. Dislike appeared by the side of disdain. The Dutchman might treat the Hottentot as he pleased, without the interposition of Government, as represented by a numerous and able body of public servants paid to protect and cherish the ancient population of the country. Front-de-Bœuf and Brian Bois de Guilbert did what was right in their own eyes, without fear of being charged with dacoity and abduction under the revised penal code before the civil and sessions judge of the district. But the English settler became aware that he must behave towards the Bengalee as towards a fellow-citizen and fellow-subject, or the local magistrate and the Supreme Court would know the reason why. This discovery did not raise his opinion of the natives, but caused him to look on them in the light of enemies, possessed of rights and privileges whereto they had no just claim, and which, as time went on, they might be tempted to employ against him as weapons of annoyance. His state was much that of a boy at school who is prevented by an wholesome dread of the monitors from fagging a stupid, cowardly fellow in the same bedroom with himself to the extent which the eternal fitness of things appears to him to demand—a position which is not calculated to foster the most kindly sentiments of our nature.

At the period of the mutiny the feeling of aversion was intensified into deadly hatred. For a season this hatred was shared by the entire mass of our countrymen. Invectives against the treacherous, blood-thirsty Mussulman, ironical sneers about the " mild Hindoo," were nuts alike to the civilian and the planter. The latter rejoiced to hear the world acknowledge that his estimate of the native had been correct throughout. But this glimpse of happiness was too bright to last. This sweet vision of a Utopia of rampant Anglo-Saxons and "damned niggers" melted away as swiftly as it had arisen, and disclosed the stern reality in all its horrid nakedness : a land flowing indeed with ghee and indigo, but peopled by a race of free peasants, possessed of an ancient interest in the soil, and by an oppressed and disheartened community of Englishmen, whose unnatural mother-country refused to recognise any distinction in civic rights between a nigger doomed to everlasting torment and a white man in a state of salvation. At home the reaction against a severe and retributive policy set in with irresistible strength. People fell to repenting their recent excesses, in sackcloth and ashes ; or, to speak more accurately, in pamphlets and May meetings. The official society out here soon followed suit, and the unfortunate settler found himself in the plight of a colonial Abdiel, "faithful only he" to the great principles of the debasement of the native, the domination of the Anglo-Saxon, and the "development of the resources " of India" into English pockets. Always sore upon the question of the social and political condition of the native, he now became positively raw and festering. The events of the last few years have certainly not been of a nature to soothe his injured soul. His morbid detestation of the Bengalees, as displayed in the pages of the local journals, would be ludicrous, if there could be a ludicrous side to a phenomenon so painful and ill-omened. One unfortunate correspondent, who happened to make use of the expression, " our native brethren," was lately treated to a column of indignant remonstrance and ill-tempered satire. A certain official, in answer to an affectionate address presented to him by a large number of wealthy and influential Hindoos, spoke of " the two great races" who occupy India. Next morning he was taken to task firmly but respectfully for having been weak enough to call the natives a " great " race," and place them by implication, on an equality with Englishmen. As if this gentleman, in order to gratify the vanity and spite of any class in existence, would have chosen to insult a body of worthy men who had assembled to give him a mark of respect and devotion, by reminding them that they belonged to an inferior and subject people !

It is only natural that the protectors of the native should come in for a share of odium. Though the great majority of planters live on the most cordial terms with the officials in their neighbourhood, it cannot be denied that the *meneurs* of the party have worked themselves up into a state of violent excitement against the very name of civilian. I said above that the events of the last few years have not been of a nature to calm the agitation of the public mind. In fact, from the day that law and order were restored throughout the land, one vexed question has followed another in swift and baneful succession.

First came the great indigo row. Now, if you cannot touch pitch without being defiled, you certainly cannot touch indigo without being made to look uncommonly blue. Besides, I am not one of those who enjoy walking " through fires placed under the crafty cinder ; " so I will confine myself to stating boldly that over vast tracts of Bengal the ryots cultivated indigo under a system which, in the hands of shrewd and energetic European planters, had become an instrument of intolerable oppression. Many of these poor fellows (excited, as some think, by the general up-turning of society occasioned by the rebellion) objected to grow indigo, on the ground that other crops paid them better. Upon this their employers, in many cases, sowed the lands by the hands of their myrmidons, who meanwhile kept the unfortunate proprietors at a distance by terror of sword and cudgel. This went on until a young magistrate, the Honourable Ashley Eden, of all the friends of the native the most consistent and audacious, (no unimportant quality in a state of society where philanthropy is useless unless backed up by audacity), like the worthy son of an English Bishop, stepped in with the following order:—

" Since the ryots can sow on their lands whatever
" crop they like, no one can without their consent and
" by violence sow any other crop; ordered, therefore,
" that the original petition be sent to the Deputy-
" Magistrate of Mitterhaut, in order that he may send
" policemen to the ryots' land to prevent any disturb-
" ances that are likely to ensue from any compulsory
" cultivation of their lands, and instruct them—if the
" land is really that of the ryots—not to allow any one
" to interfere with it. *If the ryots wish to sow indigo*
" *or anything else, the policemen will see that there is no*
" *disturbance.*"

This occasioned the appointment of the Indigo Commission; which, after a searching and patient investigation, brought to light a vast number of facts which proved the horrible tendency of the existing system. There can be no object in boring or shocking you, as the case may be, with a long array of grievances and abuses. Suffice it to say that the Commission reported that "the planters, *as a body*, are not acquitted of the "practice of kidnapping and illegally confining indi-"viduals;" and that (while thirty thousand cultivators of the poppy, within the limits of a single agency, had in the course of a few years thrown up their opium contracts, and resumed them only on obtaining a considerable advance in price from the Government) out of the hundreds of thousands of ryots who grow indigo *not one could be produced who had cleared his accounts with his employer, and been permitted to break off his connexion with the factory.* It was likewise ascertained, though not inserted in the Report, that certain of the planters were in the habit of carrying about a "Sham Chand," or leathern instrument of flagellation, with which to flog the free peasant proprietors with whom they had dealings. And these are the sons of the men who thought the abolition of negro slavery cheap at twenty millions sterling!

In the heat of the mêlée the Rev. Mr. Long published a translation of a vernacular drama, entitled, "Nil Durpan," or, "The Mirror of Indigo," giving the aspect of the question as seen from a native point of view. In so doing he acted in accordance with the spirit of the Missionaries, "whose conduct," says the Report, "during the late controversy and crisis, is not "blameworthy, and that of many has been straight-"forward, manly, and considerate." In the preface Mr. Long reflected in severe but just terms upon the line taken by the two leading Anglo-Saxon journals. By the exertions of the "Planters' Association" he was brought to trial, and indicted on two counts: first, for having libelled the *Englishman* and the *Bengal Hurkaru* in the preface; and, secondly, for having libelled "*the* "*general body of planters*," in the play itself. The passages which excited the most animadversion were the following. The first occurs in a conversation between two native women.

"*Reboti*. Moreover, the wife of the indigo-planter, " in order to make her husband's case strong, has sent " a letter to the magistrate, since it is said that the " magistrate hears her words most attentively."

"*Aduri*. I saw the lady. She has no shame at all. " When the magistrate of the Zillah (whose name " occasions great terror) goes riding about through the " village, the lady also rides on horseback with him. " Riding about on a horse! Because the aunt of Kezi " once laughed before the elder brother of her husband " all people ridiculed her: while this was the magistrate " of the Zillah."

The second runs as follows. The Daroga, or police-sergeant, says to the jemmadar of the jail:—

"Did not the magistrate say he will come here this " day?"

"*Jemmadar*. No, sir. He has four days more to " come. On Saturday they have a champagne-party " and ladies' dance. Mrs. Wood can never dance with " any one but our Sahib. I saw that when I was a " bearer. Mrs. Wood is very kind. Through the in- " fluence of one letter she got me the jemmadary of the " jail."

With reference to these passages the judge on the bench spoke to the following effect, as reported in the contemporary papers:—

"His Lordship approached the subject with sorrow "and disgust, as any man must. Reading these pas- "sages, it was impossible to speak of them otherwise "than as a foul and filthy slander against a society of "helpless women, who, under the mask of a general "type, were cruelly stabbed in the dark. If it meant "anything, it was not merely a slander against the "wives of planters, *but it was for the jury to consider* "*whether it was not intended as a reproach on the whole* "*middle class of the women of England*, whence they "came. *The jury*, the civilians, the soldiers, the "merchants in this country, alike had their origin from "that middle class whose daughters were here so "shamefully maligned. Those women came to this "country to share a life of toil and hardship with their "husbands, far from the friendships and protection of "their native land."

By the way, talking of the protection of their native land, was Mr. Thackeray indicted for calumniating under the mask of the general type of Becky Sharp, the whole middle class of the women of England, whence she came?

The Judge proceeds, or rather is said by the papers to have proceeded, thus:—

"Would they believe that those women were in the "habit of prostituting themselves in order to gain the "decision of magistrates who were bound by oath to "administer the law with strict impartiality? Would "they believe that those magistrates were in the habit

" of violating the solemn obligations of their duty and
" conscience to gratify licentious desire?

" Would the reverend gentleman point out how far
" he thought this *filthy* statement was calculated to
" bring about improvements in social morals. When
" he read those *filthy* passages he blushed to think that
" a clergyman of the established Church of England
" could have lent himself to the propagation of so
" malicious and unfounded a slander. That state-
" ment would go forth to the mothers and daughters
" of the middle class in England to make them think
" that is the fate of their daughters here. Not a
" gentleman in any station but would tear the *filthy*
" production; but, above all, every civilian, soldier,
" and merchant, and he hoped every clergyman, would
" agree that it should never reach the firesides of
" England."

The best comment on these last words is afforded by a lady famous for her virtues and charities, who, writing to a friend in India, declared herself unable to form a judgment on the impropriety of the objectionable passages, as her husband had received an expurgated copy. It is needless to say that the filthy production had reached her fireside in all its revolting integrity.

The jury did not require to be stimulated from the bench. Mr. Long was thrown into jail and heavily fined; though I have reason to believe that certain good friends did not allow the expense to fall upon his slender wages as a missionary. One juryman was said to have held out against the verdict for a short space. This same man, *this very year*, though a scholar and a gentleman of high official rank and blameless character, was blackballed at the Bengal Club, whither men connected with indigo do most resort.

Close upon the heels of the indigo row came the rent dispute. Some planters, who at the same time were landholders, raised the rents of their tenantry, on the principle of doing what they liked with their own; while the civilians, as a class, maintained that the ryots had an undefined but undoubted right in the land, which had been confirmed by Act Ten of '59. This complication was not calculated to throw oil on the troubled pools. When the matter was laid before the Lord Chief Justice of Bengal, he decided broadly and roundly against the ryot; a decision which, if carried into effect, would reduce millions upon millions of peasant proprietors to the condition of Irish cottier tenants, ground to the earth by a rack-rent, and a sense of humiliating dependence without aim or hope. The civilian magistrates and judges, however, so arrange matters that the planters have got very scant satisfaction from this decision of the Chief Justice.

Then came the renewed demand for a criminal contract law, a subject with regard to which a planter is as touchy as a Buckinghamshire farmer in the matter of Free Trade and Protection. The modification of the resolutions concerning the sale of waste lands did not tend to heal the breach; and the ringleaders of the European settlers, now regard the civilians as their sworn foes, and have firmly persuaded themselves that, in their public acts, our officers are influenced by an inveterate hatred of all English capitalists and Zemindars. Read the following extracts from the writings of

one of the shining lights of what he himself calls the
" interloping " party :—

"I feel compelled to protest against the supineness on
"the part of interlopers, which has been permitting the
"Government, now, as formerly, under the rule of the
"Traditional Policy Party, to undo all that has been
"done, and to return by degrees to the state of things
"which prevailed before the mutinies. Not two years
"ago, interlopers had conquered and dismissed a lieu-
"tenant-governor, had overcome the prejudices which
"the governor-general had been imbibing for five years
"from his civilian advisers, and had seen their old
"enemy, Mr. Cecil Beadon, introducing that horror of
"civilians, a Contract Act, into the Legislative Council.
"I shall not call to your recollection at present the
"minor circumstances of their triumph, such as the
"discomfiture of Mr. Seton-Karr and others. Not two
"years ago interlopers were in the zenith of their power;
"but, having arrived to that proud eminence, they seem
"to have lain down and slept there, till their old
"enemies, recovering, ventured to give them a shove,
"and sent them down the hill much faster than they
"climbed it."

Then follows a jeremiad on the falling-off of Mr.
Beadon, who appears to have "relapsed into the pure
"civilian which he had always been, guided by the prin-
"ciples and maxims of civilianism, which had become
"his second nature." Happily, whatever may be the
second nature of that worthy successor of Sir John Peter
Grant, his first nature is as noble and genial as any being
on earth is blessed with. After this comes a description
of "the civilian policy, which never dies, but is handed

"down from one generation to another, more than a
"match for the tactics of a society whose members are
"ever changing, and whose leaders are even now scat-
"tered, though but such a short time has elapsed since
"the date of their greatest victories; and I am sorry to
"say that we have but little chance of seeing them re-
"united, or of seeing another band of men fighting like
"them, until civilian misrule again destroys a great
"industry, or inflicts some unbearable oppression upon
"a race which is but too long-suffering." And so on,
and so on, *usque ad nauseam*. There is plenty more of
this to be had at the same shop. It is wearisome work,
morning after morning wading through huge masses
of balderdash, in which her Majesty's servants are
held up to execration because they prevent one class
of her subjects from oppressing and enslaving another
class.

The theory that the native is his equal in the eyes
of the law is of itself sufficiently aggravating to the
European settler; but, when the occasion comes for that
theory to be put in practice, when justice demands that
one of our countrymen should be brought to account for
outrage or oppression, then class hatred breaks forth into
a paroxysm of illogical fury; then is the great Anglo-
Saxon spirit neither to hold nor to bind; then are the
"English name," and the "development of the resources
"of India," unlimbered, and trundled out to overawe the
civilian magistrates and the judges of the High Court.
It was bad enough not to be permitted to hang
natives at discretion, but what if it came to hanging
a member of the imperial race? Last year, one Rudd,
who was in the service of a Mr. Jellicoe, was desired by

his master to procure a sheep for the use of the household. He accordingly selected one from the flock of a shepherd of the name of Fazil, who objected to his choice, saying, " Sir, do not take the sheep; she is with " young, and I will give you another." To this piece of Indian perversity Rudd replied by carrying off the animal *vi et armis*. The owner followed him to the bungalow, and appealed to Mr. Jellicoe, who, after hearing of the story, gave back the sheep, and reproved his servant for his want of consideration. The weak and un-English behaviour of his master gave great offence to Rudd, whose righteous and Anglo-Saxon soul was vexed to such a point that he could vent his indignation by no milder measure than that of pelting Fazil with stones, and kicking him in the loins—a proceeding which excited sympathy rather than surprise among the bystanders, who were probably accustomed to Rudd's method of conducting a purely commercial transaction. Apparently imagining that enough had not been done to avenge the English name upon this insolent nigger, our countryman soon afterwards took a gun from the house and fired in the air, over Fazil's head; and then, having brought out another gun, shot the poor fellow through the back as he ran away. The murderer returned to the bungalow " very pale:" a pallor which was much insisted on by his admirers as a proof of the kindliness of his disposition. His victim died soon after, and Rudd was put upon his trial, and overwhelmed by a mass of evidence, native and English, which could leave no doubt of his guilt on the minds of the most indulgent jury. Sir Charles Jackson (who, by the way, has never been forgiven for the part which he played on this occasion), in spite of his evident compassion for the prisoner, summed up like a true English judge who does not fear what man or the Calcutta press can do unto him. Rudd was convicted of wilful murder—murder all the more horrible from the wanton brutality which considered no punishment too severe for a native who dared to have a voice in the disposal of his own property.

Then the *Bengal Hurkaru*[1] spoke out: "We discern "signs that Calcutta will be stirred to its utmost depths "in a day or two, all classes and conditions of men "banding together for a common object, to achieve the "gain of a human life, an existence which is forfeit to "the public strangler. Marvellous, indeed, is the power "of the instinct of mercy. Mightier and holier the wish "to save than the yearning to destroy." And this was the very journal which but three short years before cried the loudest and longest for blood, and yet more blood! which howled at Lord Canning as a traitor because he displayed no marked satisfaction at the consciousness that more natives had been hung during his reign than under all the former Viceroys together! which called down fire from heaven upon every civilian who refused to degrade himself from a judge into a "public strangler!" Marvellous, indeed, was the power of "the instinct of

[1] Wherever throughout these pages reflections occur on the *Bengal Hurkaru*, no allusion is intended to anything that has appeared since the paper came into the hands of Mr. James Hutton, who has edited it with considerable ability, and in a spirit of true philanthropy, from the date of March 1st, 1863. An exception has been made in the case of the English Correspondence, written, as generally supposed, by a former editor now resident at home. This Mr. Hutton, according to the custom of the Indian press, has been bound to publish, without alteration or omission.

"mercy" in the months that followed the mutiny. That quality, as far as the Sepoys were concerned, was certainly strained uncommonly fine. The relation between the might and holiness of the wish to save and the yearning to destroy, in the year 1862, was exactly what it had been in the year 1857. This talk about "human life," and "marvellous instincts," and "holy "wishes," ill became those who had so lately been the foremost to hound on the slayer. It would have been more honest to have refrained from these generalisations, and boldly to have declared that the sentence of the law must not be carried out because, villain as he might be, Rudd belonged to the Anglo-Saxon race—because the murdered man was no better than a damned nigger.

When such was the state of feeling in the European community there was no difficulty in obtaining a vast number of signatures to a petition urging the Governor-General to commute the sentence. Naturally enough the educated Hindoos, who had but just now been accustomed to see multitudes of innocent natives hung simply because they were natives, were scandalised at the notion that a guilty Englishman must be spared, simply because he was an Englishman. One of these men expressed the sentiments of his class in a temperate and well written article, containing the following passage:—" If the offender has deserved the extreme " penalty of the law, in the name of justice and humanity " let the forfeit be extorted. Let blood be shed for blood. " To attempt in such a case to mitigate the punishment " is to attempt to pervert justice, to shake the staple " foundations upon which society rests." These expressions, in the eyes of the *Hurkaru,* savoured of blasphemy and ferocity, and called forth an invective, of which the following lines are a specimen :—" The editor " is a sable Christian—one who has grafted upon the " traditional mildness of the Hindoo character the " charitable tendencies of the Gospel. Christian Cali " desires blood, and denounces the immorality which " would afford a criminal the chance of sobbing out his " life in ignominy and pain."

What would this humane gentleman have said if Sir John Peter Grant, in virtue of his high authority, had packed off General Neill's prisoners to " sob out their " lives in ignominy and pain" on the shores of the Andamans? To my mind the writer had better have thought twice before he had accused his neighbours of impiety. Another statement in the same columns is only saved from being revolting by its extreme absurdity :—" The Mosaic dispensation is dispensed with by " the Christian era. A mightier than Moses is Prince of " Justice." Does this mean that it was under the Law that we hung ryots in 1857, and that in obedience to the Gospel we are to spare murderers in 1862 ? Was the Mosaic dispensation in force during the mutiny, and was the Christian era coincident with the pacification of India ? After puzzling over the matter for some time, I at length came to the conclusion that the writer was of opinion that the Mosaic dispensation went out with the old Company, and that the Indian Council and the Evangelists came in together.

The Governor-General, to his infinite credit, refused to use his prerogative of pardon, and, as a natural consequence, the people who had reviled Lord Canning for saving from the gallows one out of a thousand con-

COURAGE OF LORD ELGIN.

demned natives, now reviled Lord Elgin for sending to the gallows a single Englishman. The Viceroy, however, was proof against that outcry, to which even the stern spirit of his predecessor at length yielded—a concession that produced such lamentable results during the last months of his otherwise spotless administration. So, finding that he was not likely to be frightened into compliance or repentance by any amount of bluster—conscious, too, that it was impossible to deprive Sir Charles Wood of the honour of being the enemy *par excellence* of the English name, and invest Lord Elgin with that title on so short a notice—the votaries of Rudd changed their tack, and fell foul of the native community for having instituted the martyrdom of their saint.

" Give him " (the native) " an English life. His fore-
" fathers offered up human sacrifices to ensure good
" harvests, and their descendants ask that the gallows
" and the cord may aid in the same good work of pro-
" moting Bengalee happiness."

" The convict Rudd is to be hanged in spite of the
" earnest prayers of more than 3,000 people. Well,
" when the gods are to be propitiated, it is well to have
" a victim at hand, and the offering will be all the more
" acceptable if they are not angry at the moment of
" sacrifice. Rudd will die because he is an English-
" man."

" We hesitate not to say that nine-tenths of those
" who vote for the public strangling of the unhappy
" wretch have done so because if Rudd is not hanged
" the native population will be dissatisfied. They will
" do injustice if the heavens threaten to fall."

And here occurs an interesting speculation. Why is a native always "polished off," and an Englishman " publicly strangled ?" The operation is the same in both cases.

Unfortunately, within the last few months, circumstances have taken place, which have called forth those bad passions that have slept since the execution of Rudd. An English family, who possess a large and thriving estate in the Delta of the Ganges, had long been desirous of purchasing a village which would have rounded off their property. The inhabitants, however, stoutly refused to sell. The servants of the disappointed landholders did their best to annoy and terrify these poor people into acquiescence. On one occasion they made an attack on the village, and got a sound thrashing for their pains. They were now irritated to such a degree, that they resolved to take a signal revenge on these obstinate peasants, and especially on the head man of the place, a Bengalee Naboth, called, as far as I can remember, Raneemoollee. Be it observed that the employers of this pack of rascals had no cognizance whatever of these iniquitous proceedings. They are universally acknowledged to be kind-hearted loyal English gentlemen. One night a strong force assailed the village, brutally ill-used the ryots, murdered Raneemoollee, and carried off two women of his family. It was strongly suspected that a young Irishman of the name of Dennis Hely had been the ringleader. He disappeared immediately after the affair, and the police long searched for him in vain.

Now here was an occurrence which, one would think, should have stirred the compassion and indignation of every honest man in Bengal and Behar. Oppression, violence, abduction, murder, brutal satellites, innocent peasants slaughtered for refusing to sell the homesteads of their fathers—no element of horror and villany was wanting. On what conditions do we hold India? What is the strongest plea by which we may justify our occupation of the country in the eyes of rival nations and impartial posterity? Surely, that we have enthroned order and the law, where rapine and the sword once reigned supreme; that we have banished from the land, to the best of our power, the curse of brigandage and dacoity. But what gang of dacoits ever committed a more flagrant outrage than this atrocity, which had been perpetrated under the supposed instigation of one of our countrymen? The sin of Ahab and Jezebel was a trifle to it, for they, at any rate, preserved the forms of justice, and forbore to take the law into their own hands. Would not the first sentiment of every true Englishman be profound pity, and an earnest desire that Hely might be brought to account, in order that if guilty he might expiate his crime, and if guiltless might establish his innocence, and wipe off a foul suspicion from the English name?

What, then, was the view of the subject taken by the anti-native portion of the Calcutta press? What was the theme upon which they especially delighted to dwell? Pity for the sufferers? No, indeed. Solicitude for the honour of our rule and nation? Far from it. The fear lest Hely should be condemned by the machinations of the friends of the Hindoo, and the deduction that the Bengalees were damneder niggers than ever, occupied their thoughts so entirely, that no room was left for more noble or humane sentiments. Hely was at last secured, and put to trial on a charge such that no jury in the world would have convicted him. Instead of indicting him as having been present at and engaged in a murderous riot, the prosecutor undertook to prove that the fatal shot had been fired by the prisoner's own hand. The hopeless confusion of a night attack, and the confusion, far more hopeless, of native evidence, would have prevented such a charge from being substantiated had the accused been ten times guilty. The jury declined to hear the defence, and at once returned a verdict in his favour. Then appeared a series of leading articles from which we have selected the following extract :—

"The Conciliation Policy, Lord Canning's great "stumbling-block and infatuation, pensively declined "to cut the cords which bound the victim to the altar, "lest the native population should be baulked of the "wished-for immolation. Their instinctive antipathy "to the Feringhee might, it is presumed, be danger- "ously excited without that sacrifice. An annual "tragedy, with a European to do the death-scene, is "a capital contrivance for obviating rebellion. The "tranquillizing entertainment can hardly now be dis- "continued. Cerberus must have his sop, or the in- "fernal regions will become intolerable from his hungry "howlings."

Now I do not hesitate to brand the expression, "an "annual tragedy," as a foul mis-statement. From the columns of this very journal I learn that the last Englishman who suffered the extreme penalty of the law in Calcutta, was a soldier, who was executed as far back as 1858 for the murder of a comrade and a countryman. Since Rudd, no European has died on the gallows.[1]

Yours ever,
H. BROUGHTON.

[1] It is satisfactory to observe that the leading Calcutta journals, which had hitherto spoken of the "Competition Wallah" in terms of extravagant and unmerited eulogy, immediately on the publication of this letter, discovered that he was an ignorant, conceited coxcomb, "fresh from college," whose effusions could only be received with silent contempt, expressed in leading-articles an ell long. It is not easy to see what freshness from college has to do with the matter. The passages quoted in the above letter would be equally objectionable if the extracts had been made by a literary veteran as old as Methuselah.

LETTER X.

CHRISTIANITY IN INDIA.

DEAR SIMKINS,—On my return from a visit to Chandernagore, I found two letters full of your reflections on the questions of the advisability of our keeping India. One had come through Bombay, and the other by Point de Galle, and I am anxiously expecting another round the Cape. The problems which you select for discussion are certainly rather antiquated. Some three months ago you gave me your opinion about the annexation of Oude, in a treatise that displayed profound political wisdom, which more than compensated for a slight want of familiarity with the details of your subject. At first I was surprised and gratified to find that you had turned your attention to an event so recent; but it gradually began to dawn upon me that the annexation of Oude, which you had undertaken to justify in the sight of God and man, was not that accomplished by Lord Dalhousie, in 1856, but the arrangement which was effected by Lord Wellesley, as far back as 1801. While reading your letters I seem to resemble the traveller, who, during a tour in Southern Russia, in the year 1819, came to a Cossack village, somewhere between the Don and the Volga. He found the population in a state of wild excitement and exhilaration. Bonfires were blazing, and oxen roasting whole. The

A LITTLE BEHINDHAND. 283

gutters ran with raki and train-oil. Peasants who had never tasted anything daintier than a rushlight now had their fill of long sixes. It was evidently some great occasion. Perhaps the birthday of an archduke. Perhaps a victory over the Circassian. Possibly the return of an influential member of the tribe from a temporary sojourn in Siberia. The tourist inquired what had given rise to these demonstrations. " Haven't " you heard ? " was the answer. " Napoleon has abdi- " cated ! The allies have entered Paris ! Our brethren " are living at free-quarters in a land flowing with lard " and tallow. Hourah ! Alexander for ever ! "

Now, you are at least as much behind the world as these honest Cossacks. Some four or five years ago, when the financial state of our Eastern Empire seemed desperate to the most sanguine of political economists, there was some little talk about the inconvenience and danger of retaining our hold upon India. Men might reasonably question the advantage of a possession which cost more than it brought in. No one will thank you for leaving him an estate encumbered with mortgages, and entailing on him a yearly lawsuit; and the condition of such an estate was much that of our dominions in Asia, loaded with a debt of a hundred millions, surrounded by such litigious neighbours as Burmese and Afghans, thronged with tenants as turbulent and impracticable as Sikhs and Santhals. India might be the brightest jewel of the English crown, but she certainly was one of which the cutting and setting came uncommonly expensive. There was very little encouragement and satisfaction in the prospect of a budget which showed a pretty steady annual deficit of five millions; or, worse than that, in the prospect of an annual deficit of five millions without any budget at all. Until the appointment of poor Mr. Wilson, the public resources of India were administered on the most happy-go-lucky system that perhaps ever existed in any civilized country. That grand old Company displayed very little mercantile accuracy in the management of the finances. It would almost seem as if the Anglo-Indian government was ashamed of its commercial origin, and sought to rival the majestic profusion of ancient and time-honoured dynasties. Then, the work of conquest and annexation went on so briskly, there were so many independent princes to be turned into allies, and so many allies to be degraded into subjects, that our rulers had neither time nor inclination for the manufacture of financial statements. They found it easier to pay their contractors and their mercenaries with the first money that came to hand, and borrow whenever the treasury was not in cash—a contingency of by no means rare occurrence. Even if the powers that then were had been overtaken by a fit of economy, even if they had felt the paramount necessity of effecting a comprehensive and minute survey of the resources and expenses of the State, it is doubtful whether they would have found in the ranks of the Civil Service men endowed with the experience and knowledge which such a task would demand. As long as there were vast conquests to be organized and governed, mighty potentates to be cajoled into friendship or bullied into vassalage, justice to be administered, codes to be digested, no one cared to descend from the *rôle* of a governor, an envoy, a judge, a lawgiver, and assume the less splendid, but certainly not less useful, character of an accountant or an auditor. Who would condescend to the office of quæstor, when he might be a prætor or a pro-consul? Napoleon the Great acted on a very different principle. He knew well that a power which owes its origin to a period of general confusion, and its grandeur to successful and successive wars, can least of all afford to neglect the finances. Nothing short of the most rigorous economy, the most anxious and constant scrutiny into details, could have kept afloat through so many eventful years a Government at once revolutionary and aggressive, whose chief was hated by all the monarchs of Europe as a usurper and a *parvenu*, and by all the nations of Europe as a grasping and unscrupulous Jupiter Scapin. While with his terrible right hand he was dealing home-thrusts at the heart of Austria and Brandenburg, his left hand was for ever in his breeches-pocket jingling the francs and centimes. Unfortunately there was no Buonaparte in India. Things went as providence chose to order them—providence, that is to say, represented by Armenian stockjobbers and Hindoo contractors. The budget made itself as best it could. Acting Governors-general wrote home by one mail in a flurry to announce a deficit of forty lacs of rupees, and by the next mail informed the honourable Court that a slight error had been detected in the accounts, and that instead of a deficit there turned out to be a surplus. Unfortunately in far the greater number of instances the case was reversed, and instead of a surplus there resulted a very tangible and palpable deficit. By the year 1859, the prospects of India were so hopeless, as far as the financial eye could reach, that even those who could view our occupation of this country from other points than that of pounds, shillings, and pence. began seriously to doubt whether we were not paying too dearly for the privilege of governing and civilizing the East.

Now everything is changed. Mr. Wilson brought in the first Indian budget; and, before two years were out, the astonished world beheld the last Indian deficit. Three years ago a Governor of Madras prophesied that the vast resources of the country, fostered by judicious economy and administered by trained financiers, regulated and adjusted by means of an exact and sweeping annual estimate, would more than suffice to meet all demands. And yet we may well believe that even he would have been astounded could he have foreseen the state of things which it has fallen to his lot to announce. In 1859–60 the Revenue was £39,705,822, and the Expenditure £50,475,683. In 1862-63 the Revenue was £45,105,700, and the Expenditure £43,825,104. The questions which occupy our Eastern Chancellor of the Exchequer are no longer how this deficit is to be met, how that loan is to be negotiated; but whether an increased grant may be allotted to education, whether an oppressive monopoly may be abolished with advantage, whether the surplus should be absorbed in repealing taxation, paying off debt, or advancing reproductive public works.

It appears, then, that we can afford to hold India: but how do we establish our right of tenure? There is no need to justify our occupation in the eyes of the world in general. The commercial interests of all

DO WE DO OUR DUTY BY INDIA?

nations imperatively demand that the government of Hindostan should be in the hands of a great and enlightened power. As long as Bombay and Calcutta are free ports; as long as the navigation of the Ganges and the Indus is as safe as the navigation of the Elbe and the Rhone; as long as the tea-plantations in Assam are as secure as the sugar-plantations in Jamaica, and the cotton-fields of Central India a great deal more secure than the cotton-fields of South Carolina; so long the merchants of Marseilles, of Hamburg, of Baltimore, of Manilla will thank us for taking upon ourselves the trouble of keeping the Ghorkas out of Bahar, and the Burmese out of Silhet. Monsieur Thiers may grumble, and Monsieur Lesseps may rant, but almost every Frenchman of sense would be very sorry to see our commissioners and collectors succeeded by prefects and receivers-general. During the crisis of the mutiny we enjoyed the hearty sympathy of the civilized world; and we may say with pride, and without ingratitude, that that sympathy was not entirely disinterested. The Americans of the North, who see a parallel between their present position and that of England in 1857, bitterly complain that we have requited their good-will with our cold neglect. As far as India is concerned, we do our duty by the commonwealth of nations. It remains to inquire whether we do our duty by the inhabitants of India.

We are, as a nation, agreed that the greatest benefit we can confer upon our subjects is Christianity. Our heart's desire and prayer for India is, that she may be saved. Is that desire soon to be accomplished? Is that prayer in the course of fulfilment? Let us ask our missionaries who, with true Protestant honour and fidelity, publish to the light the results of their labours, be they great, or be they insignificant. The Report of the Church Missionary Society for 1862-63 contains the following summary :—

"Taking the statistics of the three presidencies of
" India, we find that, besides hundreds of thousands of
" listeners to the Gospel message, there were ten years
" ago 94,145 registered Christians, and that there are
" now 138,543."

That is to say, there is something less than one Christian to every thousand heathen, and this after European missionaries have been sixty years in the country.

As I know, by personal observation, nothing at all of the presidency of Bombay, and little of Madras, I will confine my remarks on the progress of Christianity to the North of India. The Report of the Church Missionary Society places the number of native Christians in the North India Mission at 8,523 ; that is to say, at barely one Christian to every ten thousand heathen.

Like brave and worthy Englishmen, the labourers in this ungrateful vineyard are not afraid of acknowledging their failure. Let us take the three Mofussil missions of Bengal. The Rev. S. Hasell, of Burdwan, owns in his report that, " but very few converts have been bap-
" tized from the Zillah itself."

The Rev. R. P. Greaves, in his annual review of the mission at Kishnagur, writes :—

" One of the most unsatisfactory characteristics of
" the congregations in this district at present is their
" non-expansion. They are showing but little light, and

" producing but little good around. For a series of
" years they have been stationary, not to say stagnant."

The Rev. E. L. Puxley, of the Bhaugulpore and Santhal mission, furnishes a statement containing the following passage:—

"As to future prospects, humanly speaking, I feel
" much less hope now for the rapid conversion of the
" Santhals than I did at the beginning of last year. I
" was then new to the work, and judged more by reason
" than experience. The religion of the Santhals is a
" religion which they cherish as derived from their
" fathers, and to which they cling with far greater
" tenacity than I had expected. I cannot help ex-
" pressing my hope that I am totally in the wrong con-
" cerning our future prospects, and that events may
" prove that my original opinion was the most exact.
" We derive courage from the thought of the unseen
" things—God's power, and the promises which are
" behind."

Gallant words these, and good words: but what a hopeless state of things do they imply! The cause of Faith must, indeed, be in a bad way when such men despair. To fight an uphill fight; to finish his course without joy; to sow where he cannot reap; to strew where he may not gather; to work honestly and stoutly to the end, and to work in vain; such is the fate of the English missionary in the Northern Provinces of India. It is idle to close our eyes against the fact, that with all the advantages of civilization and domination, we have hitherto succeeded in converting to our own creed only one in ten thousand of the subject-people. Why is the most pure and consistent of religions powerless against the most foul and fanciful of superstitions? Why is Truth worsted in the battle, though science and authority, the power of the intellect, and the power of the sceptre, are ranged at her side in close alliance? Why, under the very shadow of the Christian churches and colleges, do men cry aloud to Seeva, and cut themselves after their manner with knives and lancets, till the blood gushes out upon them? Why does Christ count His followers by units, while Vishnu numbers his worshippers by myriads? The failure is due partly to defects inherent in our system of evangelization; partly to overwhelming obstacles without, against which the most perfect organization would unsuccessfully contend.

The very excellence and perfection of our religion constitutes our first and most serious difficulty. The creed which our missionaries preach would be far more readily adopted if it were not so much too good for the men to whom they preach it. The days of wholesale conversion are long gone by. It is natural to regret the golden age when tribes of Huns and Vandals embraced, with easy unanimity, the faith of the empire which they had invaded—when strings of captive Danes were led from the field of battle to the nearest stream before the blood had dried upon the weapons of the victors. But we must not forget that our Christianity differs from the Christianity of the dark ages at least as much as the belief of Socrates differed from the belief of Homer. Ours is an elevated and philosophic religion, adapted to the wants of an enlightened and progressive society: and a philosophic religion cannot be a proselytizing religion. The Church in old time offered very different attractions to converts of rank and power, and demanded from them a far easier test than do the Protestant missionary societies of our own day. The bounty was so high, and the discipline in her ranks so lax, that she found no difficulty in procuring recruits. St. Cuthbert's bishop knew well what he was about when he undertook to enlist the old northern rover.

> "Broad lands he gave to him on Tyne and Wear,
> To be held of the Church by bridle and spear:
> Part of Monkwearmouth, of Tyndale part,
> To better his will, and soften his heart.
> Count Witikind was a joyful man,
> Less for his faith than the lands which he wan.
> The High Church of Durham is dressed for the day,
> And the clergy are ranked in their solemn array.
> There came the Count in a bearskin warm,
> Leaning on Hilda his concubine's arm.
> He kneeled before St. Cuthbert's shrine
> With patience unwonted at rites divine;
> But such was the grisly old proselyte's look,
> That the priest who baptized him grew pale and shook."

Nor did the churchman demand any very marked outward manifestation of the good work that was going on within the breast of his convert. Sir Walter tells us how—

> "—— E'en the good bishop was forced to endure
> The scandal which time and instruction might cure.
> It were dangerous, he deemed, at the first to restrain
> From his wine and his wassail a half-christened Dane.
> The mead flowed around, and the ale was drained dry,
> Wild was the laughter, the song, and the cry;
> With Kyrie Eleison came clamorously in
> The war-song of Danesman, Norweyan, and Fin."

He must have been a very thick-headed old Viking who could not appreciate the advantages of a conversion in which the only drawback consisted in a short rite followed by a long drinking-bout, and the practical result was a fat fief in Durham or Northumberland. If he had been required to give up habits of brutality and self-indulgence; to stint himself in mead and ale, and make Hilda an honest woman; to become charitable, devout, and unselfish; to have a decided opinion on the doctrine of the Real Presence, and an undecided opinion on the question of Eternal Punishment; to profess, and at the same time to profess with reservation, his belief that, if his ancient brethren in arms held that the Holy Ghost was not proceeding, but either made, created, or begotten, without doubt they would perish everlastingly —if such were the conditions exacted of him by his new teachers, he would probably be not quite so ready to renounce the pleasing prospect of tippling through all eternity in the congenial society of Odin.

As a general rule, the religion of a people is ceremonial in inverse proportion to their advance in knowledge and civilization. Among rude and degraded nations the outward and visible sign is regarded far more than the inward and spiritual grace. The preponderance of the spiritual element in the national religion of Scotland is, in no small measure, due to the canniness of her inhabitants. Weak human nature craves for a rite, until by thought and effort it has attained to the power of seeing God through, and not in, His creatures. Our Lord was not unmindful of this craving when He bade His disciples, in remembrance of Him, do as He had done on the last sad night in that large upper room within the city. The very simplicity which, to the educated mind, constitutes the chief grace and virtue of Protestantism, renders it distasteful to the Oriental. How can we expect that men glutted with the coarse and grotesque pomp of the Brahminical worship can be attracted by the unadorned ritual of our Church? How can we expect that men who have been encouraged by their priests to run riot in debauchery and crime can submit to bring their bodies into subjection, and their minds into true devotion? What is there in common between the faith of Heber and Swartz and a creed which enjoins suicide and self-mutilation, prostitution and murder; whose monks are fakeers; whose knights-errant are Thugs; and whose temples are little better than consecrated brothels?

There can be little doubt that, if we would consent to return to the system of the Church in past ages, we might Christianize the Hindoos as fast as our clergymen could get through the Ministration of Baptism to such as are of riper years. If we were to entice the great chiefs by liberal grants of waste lands, and intimidate them with threats of fine and confiscation; if we were to attach no conditions to admission into the fold save the mere naked rite of baptism; if we were to permit the neophytes to indulge to their hearts' content in lust, and perjury, and bang, and litigation; if we were to wink at their marrying a plurality of wives during life, and burning their favourites after death,—I do not hesitate to assert that we might convert Maharajas by the dozen, and Zemindars by the hundred: and the populace would soon follow the example of their natural leaders. But, thank God, we have not so learned Christ. We do not profess to do evil that good may come; least of all, so certain an evil for a good so illusory. Better one true convert to ten thousand heathen, than a whole continent of mongrels, Brahmins in heart and in deed, and Christians only in name.

Our missionaries would succeed better if they were in certain respects inferior men. According to one theory very generally received, the nature of the land in India does not repay deep-soil ploughing; and the character of the people seems to resemble that of the soil which they till. In the moral world, as well as the agricultural, work may be done too scientifically. It is to be feared that we are using tools of too fine an edge. The men to impress and influence Oriental populations are not scholars and gentlemen, but devotees. The mass of the people of Hindostan are of much the same grade intellectually and morally as the mass of the Western populations in the darkest centuries of the Christian era —those centuries have produced such an abundant crop of saints and martyrs. The peasant of Bengal could appreciate the self-humiliation of St. Paul of Thebes, the self-torment of St. Simeon of the Pillar; but logic and learning, argument and illustration, are yet, and will long be, to him but the dead letter. If an English clergyman chose to stand for twenty years at a stretch on the top of the Ochterlony monument, or take up his abode under a cocoa-nut tree in the Sunderbunds, he would have thousands of worshippers and millions of admirers; but the Bishop of Oxford or Dr. Guthrie might preach through all the cities in the north of India without making two dozen proselytes. In what terms can you appeal to the conscience or the good sense of men who canonize a bloated sensual scoundrel for no other reason than because he has never been known to wash himself or to wear a rag of clothing? What can you do with people who see virtue and merit in the performances of a fakeer? The highest phase of earthly existence, according to the Menu books, is the contemplation for seven years of the divine essence as represented by the tip of your own nose. If our priests would conduct the service with their right foot held over their left shoulder, if our bishops would make their visitations by rolling along the Grand Trunk Road from one station to another, we should soon have converts enough and to spare; the high festivals of our religion would be among the most popular Poojahs of the year; our churches would reek with frankincense, and glitter with the offerings of wealthy baboos; and the doors would be too small to admit the same painted, drunken, perspiring, yelling mob which crowds the temples of Juggernauth and Tripety.

However, it is possible for those who recognise this defect in the native character to make a worthy use of their knowledge. From time to time there have been men who have not hesitated to sacrifice comfort, society, so-called respectability, to the chance of doing some great thing for the cause of Christ. Sleeping in native huts, living on native food, going afoot from village to village through the sun of June and the exhalations of September, talking of Jesus to the ryots in the field, to the women at the well, under the gipsy tent in the lonely jungle, beneath the eaves of the coffee-shop, in the crowded bazaar, they have shown to the heathen, and shown not in vain, that a Christian apostle may equal a Hindoo eremite in endurance and devotion. Such a man need not fear the rival influence of the most punctilious Brahmin or the most disgusting fakeer. When once the people of the country have learnt to revere him as one who courts privation and suffering, his humility and disinterested zeal give him an unspeakable advantage over the ostentatious, self-seeking professors of the baser religion.

I speak not my own opinion, but that of men who have gained by long experience the most intimate acquaintance with the native population, when I say that our missionaries will never obtain a thorough hold on the Hindoo mind until they renounce that way of life which is considered essential to the health of the European in this climate. The barbarous people around us refuse to submit their belief to instructors who live in spacious houses hung with punkahs to cool the air, and muslin netting to keep off the mosquitoes; who eat fish, and flesh, and fowl, and drink beer and wine; who bathe and change their linen twice in every twenty-four hours. *We* are well aware of the devotion of these our countrymen. *We* know that their poor little luxuries only render this country something less miserable and unwholesome to men brought up in the Sixth Form Rooms of Rugby and Marlborough, and the quadrangles of Merton and Baliol. But the people for whose sake they have come into willing exile understand none of these things. The man they go out to the wilderness to see must not be clothed in soft raiment. He must carry no silver in his purse, nor bread, nor change of coat; but into whatsoever village he enters, he should abide in the house of the most worthy, eating and drinking such things as are set before him—boiled rice, and peas, and coarse river fish, and water from the tank; and then he need not fear lest he should find occasion to shake the dust off his feet for testimony against that village. Our Saviour did not preach abstinence and self-mortification. He placed no merit in fasting or penance. But He knew that, when simple souls are to be won, it does not do to count the cost too closely. It was but seldom in those three years that the Son of Man had where to lay His head.

Certain societies of German Lutherans have obtained a remarkable influence over the people of the country. These men bear up the battle under the pressure of the most abject poverty, and a very good fight they make of it. At Chupra, the children of these good folk live on rice and curried lentils like the young Hindoos among whom they are brought up. The parents are most thankful if the collector sends them a parcel of half-worn white trousers, or if the judge's wife looks up some frocks belonging to her little girl who sailed for England at the end of the last cold weather. Very touching are the stories which peep through the records of these small communities—how brother Friedrich was carried off by the epidemic of March; and brother Bernard, whom we had hoped to be able to afford to send to the hills during the rains, sank under a third attack of dysentery in the last week of August. But the lives of these men, and their deaths, are not without their due effect. Talking the vernacular languages with admirable fluency and precision; sympathising with the sorrows and joys of the children of the soil; fearing nothing; doubting nothing; they go everywhere, and are everywhere welcome. A friend of mine was present at the baptism of a Brahmin of high rank, who had been convinced by the exertions and example of the German missionaries. The proselyte publicly renounced his religion in the presence of a large assembly of his friends and retainers amidst general and profound emotion. When, at a certain stage in the ceremony, he snapped with his own hands the Brahminical cord which hung about his neck, the sacred badge of his faith and grade, a long and deep moan of horror and wrath ran through the multitude. That very night the convert's house was burnt to the ground.

The searching and incessant oppression to which a native Christian is subjected by his countrymen at present forms an insurmountable impediment to the efforts of our missionaries. Among the hardy nations of the North of Europe, persecution which stops short of extermination would seem to be the most favourable condition under which a young religion can develop itself. But the mild and flexible nature of the Hindoo shrinks from an ordeal which would only add zest to the religious emotions of a Scotchman. The Free Church nowhere counts among its votaries so large a proportion of the population, as in the districts where, at the period of the secession, the secular authority was in the hands of violent opponents of the movement. In a village, where the attendance at the worship of the Establishment is exceptionally thin, the chances are that you will be told, on inquiry, that the father of the present laird, honest man, had always steadily refused to grant a site for a Free Kirk. But it may be questioned whether even an ardent Free Kirker would not think the most unpremeditated discourse, from the mouth of a preacher of his own choosing, dearly purchased at the cost of the suffering undergone by a converted Hindoo. The poor fellow is exposed to a subtle and constant social tyranny, which might well break a heart of sterner stuff than his. The words, "loss of caste," convey to an English gentleman's mind no more terrible idea than that of marrying his laundress; while to an English lady they imply the consequences attached to an elopement with her music-master. But they have a far more ominous sound in the ears of a Hindoo Christian. In the dark hour of obloquy and outrage he does not possess the sweetest and most effective of consolations,—the sympathy of those who are the nearest to him, and who should be the dearest. The Covenanter who gave testimony to the death before his own hearthstone looked boldly down the barrels of the Southron carbines, because he was secure of the respect, the love, the compassion of his neighbours; because his widow would cherish the memory of her goodman with proud sorrow; because his children would never tire of telling how their sire played the man in the time of the great troubles. But the Hindoo martyr has no more bitter foes than they of his own household. His parents disown him. His wife is taught to loathe him. His very children rise up and call him cursed. It would be vain for him to ask his new masters to suffer him to go and bury his father, for the unconscious form of the sire would almost shrink on the funeral pile from the defiling touch of the outcast son. He has not with whom to eat or drink; with whom to sit down or stand up; with whom to go on a journey or rest at an inn. If he offers to smoke or chat with the loungers in the bazaar, the meanest coolies would refuse to squat in the same circle as the Christian. It is hard to be unable to appear in public without being hailed as an eater of pig, and a wearer of hats, by men with whom he lived, but a month ago, in intimate converse. It is hard to be pelted through the street of the village in which he was born and nurtured with showers of dried mud and broken pottery, and unsavoury and most ungrounded assertions concerning his female connexions of many generations back. Such a trial would be severe enough for the most strong-willed Teuton; but to the native, whose childish mind, singularly tenacious of associations, dotes upon "dustoor" or custom, this sudden breach of all the ties of family and social life is especially painful.

A native convert of rank and wealth may perhaps have no cause to dread personal violence, but his position is none the less most trying and melancholy. It is not too much to say, that the condition of an English barrister or clergyman who had turned Brahmin would be enviable compared with that of a Brahmin who had turned Christian. If it was to be announced in all the daily papers that a Peer of the Realm or a Bishop of the Church intended to submit on a certain day to the rite of circumcision, and publicly to testify his adherence to the Mahommedan faith, we should only have a faint idea of the horror, the scandal, the indignation occasioned by the baptism of a rich and high-born Hindoo. In fact, it may be questioned whether a swell who had adopted the Brahminical creed would not find his position in society improved by his conversion; whether his betel-box and turban would not be considered essential ingredients in every evening party of note; whether the beauties of the season would not treat him to the nautch of his adopted country as he puffed his bubbling hookah among the cushions of many a back drawing-room in May-fair. The native society of India, however, has not yet arrived at such a pitch of civilization as to consider singularity synonymous with fashion, and the proselyte must be prepared to surrender everything which he once held dear—the company of his equals, the respect of his inferiors, social distinction, home affection. Unless he is ready to own whosoever shall do the will of his Father which is in Heaven as brother, and sister, and mother, he must go through the dreary remainder of life uncheered by friendship and unsoothed by love.

The penalty attached to conversion is so awful, the loss of status and reputation so certain, that the majority of converts belong to that class which has little or no reputation or status to lose. The missionaries acknowledge with grief the inferior character of many among their congregations. Small as the flock is, they scorn to reckon the black sheep among the valuable stock. Mr. Greaves, of Kishnagur, says : " By with-" drawing unwise and indiscriminate temporal aids from " our Christians, we shall be able much better to discern " the wheat from the chaff. Among our people there " are not a few on whom it is worse than useless to " spend our time, labour, and money. They never have " been Christians, but in name. The pity is that they " ever received the name." Hence arises the unfortunate prejudice against native Christians, so general in Anglo-Indian society. It is a positive disadvantage to a servant who is looking for an engagement to give himself out as a Christian. I well remember hearing some members of the Civil Service discussing the identity of a Hindoo. One of the number, a most religious and estimable man, made use of the following expression: "The fellow I mean was an awful blackguard. He turned Christian;" and the sentiment appeared so perfectly natural that it passed without comment either from the speaker or his audience.

There remains one stumbling-block in the path of those who would bear to the Hindoo the good tidings of great joy—a stumbling-block which we have placed there with our own hands, and which we do not seem in a hurry to remove. How can the heathen appreciate the blessings of English Christianity while the practice of English Christians is what it is? Here is a peasant who, under a Hindoo landlord, has lived on the produce of a plot of ground which has been in his family for generations; who has paid a moderate rent, fixed by custom more revered than any law, and has learnt under the mild and equitable rule of his countrymen to respect himself as an independent yeoman. The estate is purchased by an Englishman, who, bragging all the while of Anglo-Saxon energy and public spirit, twists to the ruin of his tenant some one clause in a law which was compiled for his protection; and before twelve months have passed the poor fellow is a homeless pauper. With what face can an Anglo-Saxon missionary preach to that man in the name of the Teacher who warned His followers to lay not up for themselves treasures upon earth? Here is a village, whose inhabitants, time out of mind, have grown indigo for a Hindoo capitalist with profit to themselves and satisfaction to their employer. An Englishman buys the factory—an Englishman, strong in the consciousness of the great principle of the Development of the Resources of India—and within a few short years the thriving little community finds itself changed into a society of poverty-stricken hopeless serfs, bound to their new masters by indissoluble bonds, forged by unscrupulous shrewdness and selfish foresight. Let an Anglo-Saxon evangelist go down to that village, and stand under the ancient peepul-tree at the hour of the evening meal, and proclaim that our God is love, and that our most cherished virtue is that charity which doth not behave itself unseemly, and seeketh not her own ! Here is the widow of a poor shepherd who has been butchered by the wanton violence of a European loafer, and whose cries for vengeance are answered by the statement that the murderer was as respectable, as humane, as singularly amiable, as the murderers of natives always are in the eyes of some of our countrymen, and by the complaint that those brutes of niggers have such delicate spleens. Go to her and tell that our religion is too pure to take count of murder, because we hold that whosoever is angry with his brother without a cause is in danger of his immortal soul !

In vain do the missionaries preach the gospel of love, and humility, and self-sacrifice, as long as the *Bengal Hurkaru* preaches the gospel of national hatred, national insolence, and national cupidity. In vain do one class of our countrymen call the converts "Christian " brethren," as long as another class persist in dubbing them " damned niggers." To undertake the great charge of governing an alien population, and to fulfil that charge by abusing our subjects as if they were our most bitter foes; to coin their sweat into rupees, and speak of them all the while in private and public as a pack of treacherous, worthless scamps; to revile those who protect them; to hunt down and fling into jail any poor missionary who may strive to interest the people of the mother country in their behalf:—a worthy comment this upon the words of Him who bade us love our enemies, bless them that curse us, and do good to them who requite that good with hate!

Even in those cases in which the errors of Hinduism have been extirpated by a liberal education there seems to be little or no disposition to admit the truths of Christianity in their place. The most ignorant and debased ryot is a more hopeful subject for the missionary than a young Brahmin loaded with prizes won at a Christian college, who talks like Samuel Johnson, and writes like Addison, and will descant by the hour upon the distinction between Original Grace and Prevenient Grace. For the Hindoo mind is singularly acute and subtle, and dearly loves to disport itself in the intricate mazes of Western controversy. The cultivated native is irresistibly attracted by the curious and complicated theological problems which at present occupy so much of the attention of all our most earnest men. He regards the doctrines of Eternal Punishment and verbal inspiration much as the Christian schoolmen regarded Plato's doctrine of ideas; that is to say, as a training-ground for the intellect, as an excellent field for mental gymnastics. While the mass of the people, like the Jews of old, desire a sign, the upper classes seek after wisdom as eagerly and insatiably as the Greeks of

Athens and Alexandria. The missionaries have not failed to observe this trait. The Rev. James Vaughan, of Calcutta, writes:—" Perhaps the saddest feature of "all which strikes us in dealing with the educated "classes is the extent to which European infidelity "influences them. Newman and Parker have long been "household words with them. German and English "rationalism also wonderfully strengthen their position "of unbelief; and now they triumphantly point to a "mitred head, and cry, 'Behold a bishop of your own "Church cannot believe the Bible as inspired!'"

The nature of the process by which the weeds of Brahminism are rooted out and cleared away does not prepare the ground favourably for the reception of the seed of Christianity. The most effective spell with which to exorcise the demons of the Hindoo mythology is physical science. A native who has taken the degree of Doctor of Medicine, or who has learnt at the Presidency College all that can be taught him by a crack Cambridge Wrangler, must regard the astronomy and geography of his old religion with a contempt which will very soon include that religion itself. But, when he has surrendered his ancient creed because the priests of that creed are at strife with the European astronomers, is he likely to accept a new creed whose priests are at strife with the European geologists? Until our clergymen make their peace with Huxley they must not expect to meet with any success among the educated Hindoos. To aggravate the evil, the leading Anglo-Saxon journals are furious partisans of orthodox geology. The *Bengal Hurkaru* seems unable to make up its mind which is the most heinous crime—to express sympathy with an evicted Bengalee peasant, or doubts on the extent of the Noachian Deluge. The doctrines of Sir Charles Lyell are but one degree less damnable than the doctrines of Sir Charles Wood, and the name of Professor Owen is only less execrable than the memory of Lord Canning. So that there occurs the extraordinary phenomenon of a Hindoo journalist praising the leading geologists of the day as men of profound learning and acute insight, and an English journalist sneering at them as shallow, conceited, impious blockheads.

It is most unfortunate that the present Governor of Madras should have so warmly and openly espoused the cause of the clergy against the geologists. When a man who, from his position and ability, holds so great a place in the eyes of India, goes out of his way to proclaim that the dearest interests of the Church are incompatible with the newest theories of Science, his subjects naturally enough trust him to the extent of believing that it is impossible for them to serve two masters between whom such an antipathy exists, and hasten to make their choice between Science and the Church. And how can men who have but just cast off one faith, because the tenets of that faith are inconsistent with Physical Truth, accept another faith whose tenets are declared, by the Englishman who but lately held the highest rank in our Eastern dominions, to be inconsistent with what is held to be Physical Truth by the most eminent savans of the day? What is now passing among the upper classes in India is an admirable illustration of that glorious simile by which a great and good man rebukes those who stake the truth of religion on the event of a controversy regarding facts in the physical world. "Like the Israelites in their "battle with the Philistines, they have presumptuously, "and without warrant, brought down the ark of God "into the camp as a means of ensuring victory;—and "the consequence is, that, when the battle is lost, the "ark is taken."

The struggle which must be gone through before a man can expel a crowd of false, but cherished, opinions, and abandon a host of idle, but familiar ceremonies, is so intense and painful, as to leave the mind languidly incredulous, and, for a time at least, incapable of new and prolonged exertion; and the exertion of ascertaining, sifting, and accepting the varied and involved doctrines of English Protestantism, is no slight one. For Protestantism insists that her doctrines shall be judged separately on their own merits, and finally swallowed in the lump—a process which requires a peculiar conformation of intellect, which, unfortunately, is rare indeed. If we put the Bible into the hands of a man who was brought up a Brahmin, and now has no faith at all, can we, humanly speaking, be confident that such a man will evolve from the pages of the Sacred Book exactly the creed which we profess? Will he, after an unprejudiced study of the Word of God, be absolutely certain to light upon all the doctrines held by the Church of England, and miss all the doctrines which she eschews? Will he, without fail, hit off exactly that theory of the Eternity of Punishment which will put him out of danger of the Council—exactly that distinction between the conversion of the Godhead into flesh and the taking of the Manhood into God which will put him out of danger of hell-fire? Rome has this immeasurable advantage, that she can say to the weary wounded soul: "I am the true and ancient Church, "whose authority has descended in unbroken stream "from the rock on which Christ himself built. Do not "trouble yourself to weigh and investigate this rite "and that tenet. Perform faithfully whatever I bid; "believe humbly whatever I enjoin; and it cannot but "be well with you. Come unto me, all ye that labour "and are heavy laden, and I will give you rest." Beautifully, indeed, has this idea been expressed by one in whose conversion she may well take pride:—

> "What weight of ancient witness can prevail
> If private reason holds the public scale?
> But, gracious God, how well dost Thou provide
> For erring judgments an unerring guide!
> Thy throne is darkness in the abyss of light,
> A blaze of glory, that forbids the sight.
> Oh, teach me to believe Thee thus concealed,
> And seek no farther than Thyself revealed;
> But her alone for my director take
> Whom Thou hast promised never to forsake!
> My thoughtless youth was winged with vain desires;
> My manhood, long misled by wandering fires,
> Followed false lights; and, when their glimpse was gone,
> My pride struck out new sparkles of her own.
> Such was I, such by nature still I am;
> Be Thine the glory, and be mine the shame!"

With such an element of discord as the proud and bigoted Mahommedan population scattered throughout the country, it is greatly to the credit of our Government that religious disturbances are of such rare occurrence. If you can conceive the Catholics and Orangemen of Ireland, each multiplied by twenty, and planted under a zone where the passions are at blood-heat, you will have an idea what the state of things out here would be if it were not for the heavy hand of English authority. In all sectarian squabbles our magistrates behave with the same cold justice and magnificent indifference that was displayed by the provincial officers of old Rome in the days of Paul and Barnabas, and I have no doubt but what they get the same hard measure from the enthusiasts whom they prevent from tearing each other in pieces. In all probability, the records and traditions of the respective creeds preserve the name of more than one judge or collector, who was rewarded for having saved the life of some bold preacher, by being handed down to posterity as the personification of "carelessness." There are few personages in history who have been so unjustly used as these Roman deputies and chief captains. They seem to have borne themselves with rare courage and judgment, to have stood on every occasion between the persecutors and their prey, and to have given way only when nothing short of concession could avert a general uprising of a fierce and determined nation of fanatics. The conduct of Lysias and Festus seems to have been eminently just and prudent; and, after all, poor Gallio's fault simply consisted in this, that when he found no mention in the revised code, of the crime charged against Paul, he bundled both parties out of his cutchery.

During the most awful and melancholy scene that the world has ever witnessed—when the earth trembled with horror, and the kindly sun veiled his face before the cruelty of man—after the Divine victim, and those women whose perfect love cast out their fear, the character who most deserves our pity is the timid, feminine, compassionate ruler, who pleaded hard for that sacred life against the murderous and turbulent mob of Jerusalem; who yielded at last in an agony of remorse and shame; and who restored to His disciples the body of their Master in the teeth of those implacable bigots, who desired to pursue their revenge beyond the limits of the grave. His cowardice seems far more venial than the dastardly desertion of those men who, after living in daily intercourse with our Saviour for the space of three years, hanging on His words, eating with Him at the same table, sleeping at His side, sharing His every toil and privation (made light indeed by so blessed a presence, and so deep an affection), at the first sight of sword or staff, "forsook Him and fled." The conduct of Judas, of Caiaphas, of Herod, of Pilate, may be explained by (alas!) ordinary human motives. But who can account for the conduct of Peter and James, Andrew and Philip? In the most stormy tumult, with outrage and massacre staring them in the face, a faithful band of followers and admirers always stuck by Paul to the last. On the day when "the best of men who "knew not God" was mobbed by deadly enemies before a prejudiced tribunal, Plato and Crito, Apollodorus and Critobolus stood around their companion and teacher, pressed him with loving importunity to accept their money and their services; and, at the risk of their lives, schemed his escape from prison, loth to acquiesce in his fixed determination to submit to the laws of his country, however unjustly they might have been wrested by his adversaries to ensure his destruction. And yet Paul and Socrates, great and noble as they were, were nothing more than men. How then could those who had been permitted to call themselves the friends of a Divine and perfect being stoop to a baseness from which ordinary men of the world would be preserved by sentiments of honour and self-respect? It indeed required a life as long as that of John, and a fate as painful as the fate of James and Peter, to wipe out such a stain from their own conscience and from the memory of mankind.

The immediate prospects of missionary enterprise in India are, indeed, discouraging; but it does not follow that there is no hope for the future. However little we may have succeeded in doing towards introducing Christianity, we have done a great deal towards driving out Brahminism. The fresh air of European civilization circulates freely through every pore of this vast community. That gross and grotesque system of religion which has prevailed through so many ages of semi-barbarism, cannot hold its ground in the face of our art and science, our energy and good sense, our liberal views and purer morality. The gigantic edifice of class exclusiveness is shaken to the very foundation. The Government School had already done much, and the railroads seem likely to complete the work. A Brahmin who travels from Burdwan to Calcutta cheek by jowl with a butcher, in order to see his son go up to receive a prize at the Presidency College in company with the offspring of a sweeper, is likely to go home with some new ideas on the question of caste. Striking symptoms of the great change which is working itself out in the minds of men meet us at every turn. The ladies of one of the most ancient and respected Hindoo houses

in Calcutta lately exchanged visits with the families of
the leading English public servants; and at the Agricultural Exhibition of Alipore a day, or rather a night,
will be set apart for the native women who can prevail
on their lords to trust them away from the Zenana
amongst Christian prize-cattle and steam-ploughs. A
school has been set up for female children, to which
Brahmins, of high consideration among their fellows,
have promised to send their daughters; and the more
enlightened natives are agitating for the abolition of
the time-honoured custom which condemns the Hindoo
widow to life-long solitude and retirement, than which
the genial and exciting martyrdom of the Suttee would
be hardly more terrible.

The missionaries have noticed this state of things,
particularly in the more immediate neighbourhood of
European influences. Mr. Vaughan says: " I have at
" different times preached east, west, north, and south
" of Calcutta, and the same grand features strike one
" everywhere. Hinduism is dying; yea, is *well-nigh*
" *dead,* as respects the hold which it has upon the
" minds of the people. It is no longer the battle-
" ground. During the whole tour, I have hardly met
" with a man who stood forth as its champion!"

It is not too much to say that an educated Hindoo
almost inevitably becomes a Deist. Even the great
sect of Dissenters, who began by professing to extract
a rational religion from the sacred books of the Veda,
soon gave over playing Niebuhr, and confined their
belief to the pure and eternal God. The introduction
of western learning has produced upon the Hindoo
religion the same effect that was produced upon the

ancient classical creeds by the progress of civilization. The leading men of old Rome preserved as much of the outward forms of Paganism as their social standing and comfort might demand. They canvassed vigorously for the offices of Pontiff and Flamen. In their parliamentary harangues they used the Immortal Gods copiously enough for purposes of allusion and appeal. They never hesitated to accept a legacy on account of the sacrifices and ceremonies with which it might be saddled. They drove triumphal cars along the Via Sacra, and annual nails into the wall of the temple of Jupiter Optimus Maximus. But, in secret, their allegiance was given to the Academy, the Porch, the Garden, or the Tub.

There are 'some who admire the great men of Greece and Rome, because they united philosophy to the conduct of public affairs. How beautiful to behold Pericles learning from Anaxagoras that the universe in general, and Aspasia in particular, was composed of homogeneous atoms! Cato, on the eve of death, assuring Plato that he reasoned well! Cicero, in the interests of self-glorification, writing academic treatises, and receiving consolatory letters from people who had sailed from Ægina to Megara! There would be just as much sense in praising Bright for being a Protestant as well as a demagogue, or Pelissier for being a Roman Catholic as well as a marshal. A man must nave a belief, or disbelief, of some sort or kind; and when, as in the case of Jupiter and Vishnu, the national religion is too absurd for an enlightened man to swallow, he must profess himself something, were it only an atheist.

When Lentulus and Atticus entertained their colleagues of the Sacred College of Augurs, it may be doubted whether the conversation ever turned on the mysteries of their art. It would be much if the master of the feast muttered the name of some favoured deity as a preliminary to the first toast, as he dashed on the tesselated pavement a few drops of wine drawn from a cask which remembered the Marsian War: if indeed any good liquor had escaped the notice of Spartacus the Contraband. The talk ran fast and free concerning the nature of Pain and Pleasure, the Acatalepsy of Arcesilaus, and the Cataleptic Phantasm of Zeno. The Wheel of Ixion, or the Elysian Fields, were matters which concerned such men as little as the Jewish Sabbath or the prophecies of Isis. In the same manner, a Brahmin is unwilling to surrender the estimation which he holds in the eyes of his countrymen in virtue of his religious rank and dignity. That he may not shock his weaker brethren, he continues to perform the family rites, to wear the prescribed dress, and abstain from the forbidden meats. At the great festivals he keeps open house, and fills his corridors with garlands and torches, and hires the crack dancer from Rajpootana for five hundred rupees and a pair of Cashmere shawls. But at heart he cares for none of these things. His creed is drawn, not from the rolls of the Veda, but from the pages of Locke, and Adam Smith, and Buckle. As Cicero said of the augurs of his day, it is hard to conceive how one Calcutta Brahmin can look another in the face without a smile.

And herein lies the best hope for those whose desire is set upon Christianizing India. Not in our lifetime, nor mayhap in the lifetime of our sons, will the good work come to its accomplishment. It will require many a decade to batter down the stronghold of tradition, and cut away the barriers of caste. When that end is attained ; when a new generation has arisen that knows not Vishnu; when men who have emancipated themselves from the trammels of Brahminism rear up sons who know of those trammels only by hearsay ; then, if that crisis finds us still in possession of the reins of government, we may trust that the majority of cultivated Hindoos will not be averse to accept the creed of their rulers.

To educate, to enlighten, to strike off the fetters of custom and superstition, this is the grand duty the fulfilment of which we must further by all honest means. Colleges and railroads, libraries and newspapers, national justice and moderation, national charity and conscientiousness—such are the forces with which the battle of Truth is at present to be fought. The time will surely come when we may bring up our reserves with happy effect ; but that time is not now, and to anticipate the favourable moment would be to secure us nothing save disappointment, chagrin, and despondency. Let us not despair because India is not yet ripe ; because, being men, we must stoop to human means ; because the wind bloweth where it listeth, and not where we list. The world is so ordered that we cannot Christianize the heathen of Bengal as the Apostles Christianized the heathen of Greece and Asia Minor. To none of us is given the working of miracles, nor prophecy, nor discerning of spirits, nor divers kinds of tongues. We must labour in the way in which it is given us to labour, or not at all. And at those times when our soul grows faint within us, when the toil seems excessive, and the end remote and doubtful, we may comfort ourselves with the thought that, though there be differences of administrations, there is the same Lord, and, though there be diversity of operations, it is the same God that worketh all in all.

Yours ever,
H. BROUGHTON.

LETTER XI. AND LAST.

EDUCATION IN INDIA SINCE 1835; WITH A MINUTE OF LORD MACAULAY.

MOFUSSILPORE, *July* 20, 1863.

DEAR SIMKINS,—You will be glad to hear that I passed my second examination some three weeks ago, and have since been settled here as an assistant to Tom Goddard. He set me to work at first upon the Government School, which was not in a satisfactory state; and I have gained some valuable experience about the operation of our system of public instruction. The natives of India do not seem willing to adopt Christianity as a compensation for the loss of national independence; but there can be no question whether or not they appreciate the blessings of a sound European education. That we have been enabled to offer to our subjects in the East a boon so acceptable, is due mainly to the exertions of a great man, who, for the space of more than three years, laboured to direct the whole course of instruction into the channels which it at present occupies. To describe with my feeble pen the nature of the change which he introduced would be vain and presumptuous indeed, when he has left a monument of that change in his own immortal words. Strange it is, while rummaging among the dusty records of the Public Offices at Calcutta, to light upon a yellow bundle of foolscap, tied up with frayed and faded tape, and honeycombed by the ravages of generations of white ants. To judge from the appearance, it might well be an ancient minute upon the question of Half Batta, or the spread of 'Russian influence in Affghanistan, indited by some bygone councillor who now lies under the grass of a churchyard at Cheltenham, or dozes over " Allen's Indian Mail " in the subscription reading-room at Torquay. Unfold the packet, and every page teems with the vivid thought, the glowing fancy, the grand yet simple diction which has already become classic wherever the English tongue is spoken or the English literature studied; which ages hence will be familiar, whether to the New Zealander, who from that broken arch of London Bridge contemplates the ruins of St. Paul's, or (as is far more probable) to the student in some Anglo-Saxon college founded on the site of a stockade of the Maori race, already long extinguished by the combined influence of fire-water and progressive civilization.

At the commencement of the year 1835, the operations of the Committee of Public Instruction, of which Macaulay was President, were brought to a stand by a decided difference of opinion. Half of the members were in favour of Arabic, Persian, and Sanscrit learning; the other half in favour of English and the vernacular. The battle was fought over a sum of ten thousand pounds, set apart by Parliament for the promotion of literature and science. When the matter came before the Council, Macaulay drew up the following minute, which is endorsed thus :—

A MINUTE.

" I give my entire concurrence to the sentiments
" expressed in this minute.

"W. BENTINCK."

"*2d February,* 1835.

"As it seems to be the opinion of some of the gentlemen who compose the Committee of Public Instruction, that the course which they have hitherto pursued was strictly prescribed by the British Parliament in 1813, and as, if that opinion be correct, a legislative Act will be necessary to warrant a change, I have thought it right to refrain from taking any part in the preparation of the adverse statements which are now before us, and to reserve what I had to say on the subject till it should come before me as a member of the Council of India.

"It does not appear to me that the Act of Parliament can, by any art of construction, be made to bear the meaning which has been assigned to it. It contains nothing about the particular languages or sciences which are to be studied. A sum is set apart 'for the revival and promotion of literature and the encouragement of the learned natives of India, and for the introduction and promotion of a knowledge of the sciences among the inhabitants of the British territories.' It is argued, or rather taken for granted, that by literature the Parliament can have only meant Arabic and Sanscrit literature, that they never would have given the honourable appellation of a 'learned native' to a native who was familiar with the poetry of Milton, the metaphysics of Locke, and the physics of Newton; but that they meant to designate by that name only such persons as might have studied in the sacred books of the Hindoos all the usages of cusa-grass, and all the mysteries of absorption into the Deity. This does not appear to be a very satisfactory interpretation. To take a parallel case; suppose that the Pacha of Egypt, a country once superior in knowledge to the nations of Europe, but now sunk far below them, were to appropriate a sum for the purpose of 'reviving and promoting literature, and encouraging learned natives of Egypt,' would anybody infer that he meant the youth of his pachalic to give years to the study of hieroglyphics, to search into all the doctrines disguised under the fable of Osiris, and to ascertain with all possible accuracy the ritual with which cats and onions were anciently adored? Would he be justly charged with inconsistency, if, instead of employing his young subjects in deciphering obelisks, he were to order them to be instructed in the English and French languages, and in all the sciences to which those languages are the chief keys?

"The words on which the supporters of the old system rely do not bear them out, and other words follow which seem to be quite decisive on the other side. This lac of rupees is set apart, not only for 'reviving literature in India,' the phrase on which their whole interpretation is founded, but also for 'the introduction and promotion of a knowledge of the sciences among the inhabitants of the British territories,'—words which are alone sufficient to authorize all the changes for which I contend.

"If the Council agree in my construction, no legislative Act will be necessary. If they differ from me, I will prepare a short Act rescinding that clause of the Charter of 1813, from which the difficulty arises.

"The argument which I have been considering affects only the form of proceeding. But the admirers of the Oriental system of education have used another argument, which, if we admit it to be valid, is decisive against all change. They conceive that the public faith is pledged to the present system, and that to alter the appropriation of any of the funds which have hitherto been spent in encouraging the study of Arabic and Sanscrit would be downright spoliation. It is not easy to understand by what process of reasoning they can have arrived at this conclusion. The grants which are made from the public purse for the encouragement of literature differed in no respect from the grants which are made from the same purse for other objects of real or supposed utility. We found a sanatarium on a spot which we suppose to be healthy. Do we thereby pledge ourselves to keep a sanatarium there, if the result should not answer our expectation? We commence the erection of a pier. Is it a violation of the public faith to stop the works, if we afterwards see reason to believe that the building will be useless? The rights of property are undoubtedly sacred. But nothing endangers those rights so much as the practice, now unhappily too common, of attributing them to things to which they do not belong. Those who would impart to abuses the sanctity of property are in truth imparting to the institution of property the unpopularity and fragility of abuses. If the Government has given to any person a formal assurance; nay, if the Government has excited in any person's mind a reasonable expectation that he shall receive a certain income as a teacher or a learner of Sanscrit or Arabic, I would respect that person's pecuniary interests—I would rather err on the side of liberality to individuals than suffer the public faith to be called in question. But to talk of a Government pledging itself to teach certain languages and certain sciences, though those languages may become useless, though those sciences may be exploded, seems to me quite unmeaning. There is not a single word in any public intructions from which it can be inferred that the Indian Government ever intended to give any pledge on this subject, or ever considered the destination of these funds as unalterably fixed. But, had it been otherwise, I should have denied the competence of our predecessors to bind us by any pledge on such a subject. Suppose that a Government had in the last century enacted in the most solemn manner that all its subjects should, to the end of time, be inoculated for the small-pox : would that Government be bound to persist in the practice after Jenner's discovery ? These promises, of which nobody claims the performance, and from which nobody can grant a release ; these vested rights, which vest in nobody ; this property without proprietors ; this robbery, which makes nobody poorer, may be comprehended by persons of higher faculties than mine—I consider this plea merely as a set form of words, regularly used both in England and India, in defence of every abuse for which no other plea can be set up.

"I hold this lac of rupees to be quite at the disposal of the Governor-General in Council, for the purpose of promoting learning in India, in any way which may be thought most advisable. I hold his Lordship to be quite as free to direct that it shall no longer be employed in encouraging Arabic and Sanscrit, as he is to direct that the reward for killing tigers in Mysore shall be diminished, or that no more public money shall be expended on the chanting at the cathedral.

"We now come to the gist of the matter. We have a fund to be employed as Government shall direct for the intellectual improvement of the people of this country. The simple question is, what is the most useful way of employing it ?

"All parties seem to be agreed on one point, that the dialects commonly spoken among the natives of this part of India contain neither Literary or scientific information, and are, moreover so poor and rude that, until they are enriched from some other quarter, it will not be easy to translate any valuable work into them. It seems to be admitted on all sides that the intellectual improvement of those classes of the people who have the means of pursuing higher studies can at present be effected only by means of some language not vernacular amongst them.

"What, then, shall that language be ? One half of the Committee maintain that it should be the English. The other half strongly recommend the Arabic and Sanscrit. The whole question seems to me to be, which language is the best worth knowing ?

"I have no knowledge of either Sanscrit or Arabic.—But I have done what I could to form a correct estimate of their value. I have read translations of the most celebrated Arabic and Sanscrit works. I have conversed both here and at home with men distinguished by their proficiency in the Eastern tongues. I am quite ready to take the Oriental learning at the valuation of the Orientalists themselves. I have never found one among them who could deny that a single shelf of a good European library was worth the whole native literature of India and Arabia. The intrinsic superiority of the Western literature is, indeed, fully admitted by those members of the Committee who support the Oriental plan of education.

"It will hardly be disputed, I suppose, that the department of literature in which the Eastern writers stand highest is poetry. And I certainly never met with any Orientalist who ventured to maintain that the Arabic and Sanscrit poetry could be compared to that of the great European nations. But, when we pass from works of imagination to works in which facts are recorded and general principles investigated, the superiority of the Europeans becomes absolutely immeasurable. It is, I believe, no exaggeration to say, that all the historical information which has been collected from all the books written in the Sanscrit language is less valuable than what may be found in the most paltry abridgments used at preparatory schools in England. In every branch of physical or moral philosophy the relative position of the two nations is nearly the same.

"How, then, stands the case? We have to educate a people who cannot at present be educated by means of their mother-tongue. We must teach them some foreign language. The claims of our own language it is hardly nceessary to recapitulate. It stands pre-eminent even among the languages of the West. It abounds with works of imagination not inferior to the noblest which Greece has bequeathed to us; with models of every species of eloquence; with historical compositions, which, considered merely as narratives, have seldom been surpassed, and which, considered as vehicles of ethical and political instruction, have never been equalled; with just and lively representations of human life and human nature; with the most profound speculations on metaphysics, morals, government, jurisprudence, and trade; with full and correct information respecting every experimental science which tends to preserve the health, to increase the comfort, or to expand the intellect of man. Whoever knows that language, has ready access to all the vast intellectual wealth, which all the wisest nations of the earth have created and hoarded in the course of ninety generations. It may safely be said that the literature now extant in that language is of far greater value than all the literature which three hundred years ago was extant in all the languages of the world together. Nor is this all. In India, English is the language spoken by the ruling class. It is spoken by the higher class of natives at the seats of Government. It is likely to become the language of commerce throughout the seas of the East. It is the language of two great European communities which are rising, the one in the south of Africa, the other in Australasia; communities which are every year becoming more important, and more closely connected with our Indian empire. Whether we look at the intrinsic value of our literature, or at the particular situation of this country, we shall see the strongest reason to think that, of all foreign tongues, the English tongue is that which would be the most useful to our native subjects.

"The question now before us is simply whether, when it is in our power to teach this language, we shall teach languages in which, by universal confession, there are no books on any subject which deserve to be compared to our own; whether, when we can teach European science, we shall teach systems which, by universal confession, whenever they differ from those of Europe, differ for the worse; and whether, when we can patronise sound Philosophy and true History, we shall countenance, at the public expense, medical doctrines which would disgrace an English Farrier—Astronomy, which would move laughter in girls at an English boarding school—History, abounding with kings thirty feet high, and reigns thirty thousand years long—and Geography, made up of seas of treacle and seas of butter.

"We are not without experience to guide us. History furnishes several analogous cases, and they all teach the same lesson. There are in modern times, to go no further, two memorable instances of a great impulse given to the mind of a whole society—of prejudices overthrown—of knowledge diffused—of taste purified—of arts and sciences planted in countries which had recently been ignorant and barbarous.

"The first instance to which I refer is the great revival of letters among the Western nations at the close of the fifteenth and the beginning of the sixteenth century. At that time almost everything that was worth reading was contained in the writings of the ancient Greeks and Romans. Had our ancestors acted as the Committee of Public Instruction has hitherto acted; had they neglected the language of Cicero and Tacitus; had they confined their attention to the old dialects of our own island; had they printed nothing and taught nothing at the universities but Chronicles in Anglo-Saxon and Romances in Norman-French, would England have been what she now is? What the Greek and Latin were to the contemporaries of More and Ascham, our tongue is to the people of India. The literature of England is now more valuable than that of classical antiquity. I doubt whether the Sanscrit literature be as valuable as that of our Saxon and Norman progenitors. In some departments — in History, for example — I am certain that it is much less so.

"Another instance may be said to be still before our eyes. Within the last hundred and twenty years, a nation which had previously been in a state as barbarous as that in which our ancestors were before the Crusades, has gradually emerged from the ignorance in which it was sunk, and has taken its place among civilised communities—I speak of Russia. There is now in that country a large educated class, abounding with persons fit to serve the state in the highest functions, and in nowise inferior to the most accomplished men who adorn the best circles of Paris and London. There is reason to hope that this vast empire, which in the time of our grandfathers was probably behind the Punjab, may, in the time of our grandchildren, be pressing close on France and Britain in the career of improvement. And how was this change effected? Not by flattering national prejudices; not by feeding the mind of the young Muscovite with the old woman's stories which his rude fathers had believed: not by filling his head with lying legends about St. Nicholas: not by encouraging him to study the great question, whether the world was or was not created on the 13th of September: not by calling him 'a learned native,' when he has mastered all these points of knowledge: but by teaching him those foreign languages in which the greatest mass of information had been laid up, and thus putting all that information within his reach. The languages of Western Europe civilized Russia. I cannot doubt that they will do for the Hindoo what they have done for the Tartar.

"And what are the arguments against that course which seems to be alike recommended by theory and by experience? It is said that we ought to secure the co-operation of the native public, and that we can do this only by teaching Sanscrit and Arabic.

"I can by no means admit that, when a nation of high intellectual attainments undertakes to superintend the education of a nation comparatively ignorant, the learners are absolutely to prescribe the course which is to be taken by the teachers. It is not necessary, however, to say anything on this subject. For it is proved by unanswerable evidence that we are not at present securing the co-operation of the natives. It would be bad enough to consult their intellectual taste at the expense of their intellectual health. But we are consulting neither —we are withholding from them the learning for which they are craving; we are forcing on them the mock-learning which they nauseate.

"This is proved by the fact that we are forced to pay our Arabic and Sanscrit students, while those who learn English are willing to pay us. All the declamations in the world about the love and reverence of the natives for their sacred dialects will never, in the mind of any impartial person, outweigh the undisputed fact, that we cannot find, in all our vast empire, a single student who will let us teach him those dialects unless we will pay him.

"I have now before me the accounts of the Madrassa for one month —the month of December, 1833. The Arabic students appear to have been seventy-seven in number. All receive stipends from the public. The whole amount paid to them is above 500 rupees a month. On the other side of the account stands the following item : Deduct amount realized from the out-students of English for the months of May, June, and July last, 103 rupees.

"I have been told that it is merely from want of local experience that I am surprised at these phenomena, and that it is not the fashion for students in India to study at their own charges. This only confirms me in my opinion. Nothing is more certain than that it never can in any part of the world be necessary to pay men for doing what they think pleasant and profitable. India is no exception to this rule. The people of India do not require to be paid for eating rice when they are hungry, or for wearing woollen cloth in the cold season. To come nearer to the case before us, the children who learn their letters and a little elementary Arithmetic from the village schoolmaster are not paid by him. He is paid for teaching them. Why, then, is it necessary to pay people to learn Sanscrit and Arabic ? Evidently because it is universally felt that the Sanscrit and Arabic are languages the knowledge of which does not compensate for the trouble of acquiring them. On all such subjects the state of the market is the decisive test.

"Other evidence is not wanting, if other evidence were required. A petition was presented last year to the Committee by several ex-students of the Sanscrit College. The petitioners stated they had studied in the college ten or twelve years ; that they had made themselves acquainted with Hindoo literature and science ; that they had received certificates of proficiency : and what is the fruit of all this ? 'Notwithstanding such testimonials,' they say, 'we have but little prospect of bettering our condition without the kind assistance of your Honourable Committee, the indifference with which we are generally looked upon by our countrymen leaving no hope of encouragement and assistance from them.' They therefore beg that they may be recommended to the Governor-General for places under the Government, not places of high dignity or emolument, but such as may just enable them to exist. 'We want means,' they say, 'for a decent living, and for our progressive improvement, which, however, we cannot obtain without the assistance of Government, by whom we have been educated and maintained from childhood.' They conclude by representing, very pathetically, that they are sure that it was never the intention of Government, after behaving so liberally to them during their education, to abandon them to destitution and neglect.

"I have been used to see petitions to Government for compensation. All these petitions, even the most unreasonable of them, proceeded on the supposition that some loss had been sustained—that some wrong had been inflicted. These are surely the first petitioners who ever demanded compensation for having been educated gratis—for having been supported by the public during twelve years, and then sent forth into the world well-furnished with literature and science. They represent their education as an injury which gives them a claim on the Government for redress, as an injury for which the stipends paid to them during the infliction were a very inadequate compensation. And I doubt not that they are in the right. They have wasted the best years of life in learning what procures for them neither bread nor respect. Surely we might, with advantage, have saved the cost of making these persons useless and miserable; surely, men may be brought up to be burdens to the public and objects of contempt to their neighbours at a somewhat smaller charge to the state. But such is our policy. We do not even stand neuter in the contest between truth and falsehood. We are not content to leave the natives to the influence of their own hereditary prejudices. To the natural difficulties which obstruct the progress of sound science in the East we add fresh difficulties of our own making. Bounties and premiums, such as ought not to be given even for the propagation of truth, we lavish on false taste and false philosophy.

"By acting thus we create the very evil which we fear. We are making that opposition which we do not find. What we spend on the Arabic and Sanscrit colleges is not merely a dead loss to the cause of truth: it is the bounty-money paid to raise up champions of error. It goes to form a nest, not merely of helpless place-hunters, but of bigots prompted alike by passion and by interest to raise a cry against every useful scheme of education. If there should be any opposition among the natives to the change which I recommend, that opposition will be the effect of our own system. It will be headed by persons supported by our stipends and trained in our colleges. The longer we persevere in our present course, the more formidable will that opposition be. It will be every year re-inforced by recruits whom we are paying. From the native society left to itself we have no difficulties to apprehend; all the murmuring will come from that oriental interest which we have, by artificial means, called into being and nursed into strength.

"There is yet another fact, which is alone sufficient to prove that the feeling of the native public, when left to itself, is not such as the supporters of the old system represent it to be. The Committee have thought fit to lay out above a lac of rupees in printing Arabic and Sanscrit books. Those books find no purchasers. It is very rarely that a single copy is disposed of. Twenty-three thousand volumes, most of them folios and quartos, fill the libraries, or rather the lumber-rooms, of this body. The Committee contrive to get rid of some portion of their vast stock of Oriental literature by giving books away. But they cannot give so fast as they print. About twenty thousand rupees a year are spent in adding fresh masses of waste paper to a hoard which, I should think, is already sufficiently ample. During the last three years, about sixty thousand rupees have been expended in this manner. The sale of Arabic and Sanscrit books, during those three years, has not yielded quite one thousand rupees. In the mean time the School-book Society is selling seven or eight thousand English volumes every year, and not only pays the expenses of printing, but realizes a profit of 20 per cent. on its outlay.

"The fact that the Hindoo law is to be learned chiefly from Sanscrit books, and the Mahomedan law from Arabic books, has been much insisted on, but seems not to bear at all on the question. We are commanded by Parliament to ascertain and digest the laws of India. The assistance of a law commission has been given to us for that purpose. As soon as the code is promulgated, the Shasters and the Hedeya will be useless to a Moonsiff or Sudder Ameen. I hope and trust that, before the boys who are now entering at the Madrassa and the Sanscrit college have completed their studies, this great work will be finished. It would be manifestly absurd to educate the rising generation with a view to a state of things which we mean to alter before they reach manhood.

"But there is yet another argument which seems even more untenable. It is said that the Sanscrit and Arabic are the languages in which the sacred books of a hundred millions of people are written, and that they are, on that account, entitled to peculiar encouragement. Assuredly it is the duty of the British Government in India to be not only tolerant, but neutral on all religious questions. But to encourage the study of a literature admitted to be of small intrinsic value only because that literature inculcates the most serious errors on the most important subjects, is a course hardly reconcilable with reason, with morality, or even with that very neutrality which ought, as we all agree, to be sacredly preserved. It is confessed that a language is barren of useful knowledge. We are told to teach it because it is fruitful of monstrous superstitions. We are to teach false history, false astronomy, false medicine, because we find them in company with a false religion. We abstain, and I trust shall always abstain, from giving any public encouragement to those who are engaged in the work of converting natives to Christianity. And, while we act thus, can we reasonably and decently bribe men out of the revenues of the state to waste their youth in learning how they are to purify themselves after touching an ass, or what text of the Vedas they are to repeat to expiate the crime of killing a goat?

"It is taken for granted by the advocates of Oriental learning that no native of this country can possibly attain more than a mere smattering of English. They do not attempt to prove this ; but they perpetually insinuate it. They designate the education which their opponents recommend as a mere spelling-book education. They assume it as undeniable, that the question is between a profound knowledge of Hindoo and Arabian literature and science on the one side, and a superficial knowledge of the rudiments of English on the other. This is not merely an assumption, but an assumption contrary to all reason and experience. We know that foreigners of all nations do learn our language sufficiently to have access to all the most abstruse knowledge which it contains, sufficiently to relish even the more delicate graces of our most idiomatic writers. There are in this very town natives who are quite competent to discuss political or scientific questions with fluency and precision in the English language. I have heard the very question on which I am now writing discussed by native gentlemen with a liberality and an intelligence which would do credit to any member of the Committee of Public Instruction. Indeed, it is unusual to find, even in the literary circles of the continent, any foreigner who can express himself in English with so much facility and correctness as we find in many Hindoos. Nobody, I suppose, will contend that English is so difficult to a Hindoo as Greek to an Englishman. Yet an intelligent English youth, in a much smaller number of years than our unfortunate pupils pass at the Sanscrit college, becomes able to read, to enjoy, and even to imitate, not unhappily, the composition of the best Greek authors. Less than half the time which enables an English youth to read Herodotus and Sophocles ought to enable a Hindoo to read Hume and Milton.

"To sum up what I have said : I think it clear that we are not fettered by the Act of Parliament of 1813 ; that we are not fettered by any pledge expressed or implied ; that we are free to employ our funds as we choose ; that we ought to employ them in teaching what is best worth knowing; that English is better worth knowing than Sanscrit or Arabic; that the natives are desirous to be taught English, and are not desirous to be taught Sanscrit or Arabic; that neither as the languages of law, nor as the languages of religion, have the Sanscrit and Arabic any peculiar claim to our encouragement; that it is possible to make natives of this country thoroughly good English scholars, and that to this end our efforts ought to be directed.

"In one point I fully agree with the gentlemen to whose general views I am opposed. I feel, with them, that it is impossible for us, with our limited means, to attempt to educate the body of the people. We must at present do our best to form a class who may be interpreters between us and the millions whom we govern; a class of persons, Indian in blood and colour, but English in taste, in opinions, in morals, and in intellect. To that class we may leave it to refine the vernacular dialects of the country, to enrich those dialects with terms of science borrowed from the Western nomenclature, and to render them by degrees fit vehicles for conveying knowledge to the great mass of the population.

"I would strictly respect all existing interests. I would deal even generously with all individuals who have had fair reason to expect a pecuniary provision. But I would strike at the root of the bad system which has hitherto been fostered by us. I would at once stop the printing of Arabic and Sanscrit books; I would abolish the Madrassa and the Sanscrit college at Calcutta. Benares is the great seat of Brahmanical learning; Delhi, of Arabic learning. If we retain the Sanscrit college at Benares and the Mahomedan college at Delhi, we do enough, and much more than enough in my opinion, for the Eastern languages. If the Benares and Delhi colleges should be retained, I would at least recommend that no stipend shall be given to any students who may hereafter repair thither, but that the people shall be left to make their own choice between the rival systems of education without being bribed by us to learn what they have no desire to know. The funds which would thus be placed at our disposal would enable us to give larger encouragement to the Hindoo college at Calcutta, and to establish in the principal cities throughout the Presidencies of Fort William and Agra schools in which the English language might be well and thoroughly taught.

"If the decision of his Lordship in Council should be such as I anticipate, I shall enter on the performance of my duties with the greatest zeal and alacrity. If, on the other hand, it be the opinion of the Government that the present system ought to remain unchanged, I beg that I may be permitted to retire from the chair of the Committee. I feel that I could not be of the smallest use there—I feel, also, that I should be lending my countenance to what I firmly believe to be a mere delusion. I believe that the present system tends, not to accelerate the progress of truth, but to delay the natural death of expiring errors. I conceive that we have at present no right to the respectable name of a Board of Public Instruction. We are a Board for wasting public money, for printing books which are of less value than the paper on which they are printed was while it was blank; for giving artificial encouragement to absurd history, absurd metaphysics, absurd physics, absurd theology; for raising up a breed of scholars who find their scholarship an encumbrance and a blemish, who live on the public while they are receiving their education, and whose education is so utterly useless to them that, when they have received it, they must either starve or live on the public all the rest of their lives. Entertaining these opinions, I am naturally desirous to decline all share in the responsibility of a body which, unless it alters its whole mode of proceeding, I must consider not merely as useless, but as positively noxious."

The event has more than justified the opinions expressed in this minute. The natives of India have, with marvellous eagerness and unanimity, abandoned the dead or effete learning of the East for the living and vigorous literature of England. Whoever can spare the time and money greedily avails himself of the instruction which we offer. "To such an extent, " indeed, is this the case" (I quote the Report on Public Instruction for Bengal Proper), "that many of " our best native scholars can write English and even " speak it with greater facility than their mother- " tongue." Interest and ambition, the instinct of imitation and the thirst for knowledge, urge on the students; and, by the aid of a delicate taste, and a strong power of assimilation, their progress is surprising to one accustomed to the very slender proficiency in the classical tongues obtained by the youth of England after a boyhood devoted almost exclusively to Xenophon and Cicero. Of two hundred scholars who leave Eton in the course of a year, it is much if some three or four can construe a chorus of Euripides without the aid of a translation, or polish up with infinite pains a piece of Latin prose which a Roman might possibly have mistaken for a parody of the "De Officiis," composed by a Visigoth in the time of Diocletian. A young Hindoo who has made the most of his time at college will write by the hour a somewhat florid and stilted English with perfect ease and accuracy; and will read, enjoy, and criticize any of our authors, from Chaucer down to Robert Browning and Carlyle. The works of our greatest historians and philosophers have penetrated to every corner of our dominions, and, wherever they pass, shed somewhat of the wisdom, the good sense, and the pure morality which stamp a peculiar character upon our noble literature. The Mahommedan gentlemen, whose pride does not allow them to study the language of their conquerors, have begun to be painfully aware that they are fast losing their moral and intellectual superiority over the Hindoos, who do not profess any such scruples.

The aptitude of educated Bengalees for philosophic and literary pursuits is indeed remarkable. Their liberal and elevated opinions, their love of truth and contempt for bigotry, would go far to satisfy the most ardent lover of the human race, were he only certain that these splendid qualities are more than skin-deep. That instinct for imitation, which I mentioned above, is so dominant in the native, his desire to please so constant, that you never know whether his sentiments are real or artificial. In fact, it may be doubted whether he knows himself. When he speaks, you cannot be sure whether you are listening to the real man, or to the man whom he thinks you would like him to be. The feebleness and the servility which render Hindoo testimony so singularly untrustworthy forbid us to put too much confidence in Hindoo civilization. The Bengalee witness, who has no motive to lie, will distort the facts if he imagines that he can by so doing give one tittle of pleasure to the barrister who is examining him, or the judge who is taking notes of his evidence. The Bengalee journalist, with equal facility, will adopt the tone which he has reason to believe may suit the greatest number of Sahibs. All the great discoveries in Political and Social Science which have been wrought out by successive generations of European thinkers he picks up and appropriates with almost pathetic simplicity and conceit. He never writes an article on Trade or Taxation which, as far as the opinions are concerned, might not have been the work of John Stuart Mill. He never writes an article on Creeds or Subscription which might not have been the work of Goldwin Smith or Maurice. He has his choice of all the theories which have ever been current, and he finds it just as cheap to take the most advanced and the most recent as to borrow one which already has been a little blown upon. In the hardy rugged minds of northern men, liberality is a plant which springs from seed sown amidst doubt and fond regret; which strikes root downward, and bears fruit upward. Here, it lies on the surface, and sprouts to right and left with easy profusion; but its produce is mighty tasteless and surfeiting. In the days of the Reform Bill, when the great soul of England was in woful anxiety and misgiving as to the course which it behoved her to pursue, every little Hindoo Bachelor of Arts was most glib and positive about the absurdity of Gatton and old Sarum returning Members, while vast marts of industry, gigantic emporia of commerce, cities teeming with a countless population, remained still unrepresented.

It is hopeless to attempt to give a true idea of what these people think, and wish, and love, and hate. It was but yesterday that I called upon a native, with the view of obtaining some information concerning the reign of terror which succeeded the capture of Delhi. To my certain knowledge, this man, who had been worth more than 30,000*l*. the day before the assault, had been plundered by our soldiery of everything he possessed, though he had distinguished himself by marked proofs of his attachment to our rule. I asked him whether some severities had not been committed which our cooler judgment might regret.

"Oh, no, Sahib! The rebels were punished, and "the good people rejoiced."

"But did not the whole population desert the city "through fear of being hung?"

"Yes, Sahib; but they had sinned so grievously in "that they had allowed the sepoys to enter Delhi at "the first. The people repented very much that they "had done so. The sepoys were budmashes, Sahib. "They used to take goods worth six annas, and only "give four annas in payment."

Upon this I asked him how much our soldiers used to give in payment when they had taken goods worth six annas from the shopkeepers of Delhi: but the question distressed him so cruelly that it would have been unkind to persist.

On another occasion I was anxious to learn from a native gentleman what effect the great heat produced upon the comfort and health of the people of the country. No persuasion, however, would induce him to describe his own sensations. He persisted in speaking of the climate from what he imagined to be my point of view. I kept asking him whether he suffered from cold in December; whether he became languid and weak in the hot weather: while he continued to inform me that the temperature was unbearable during nine months in the year, but that in the cold season life was tolerable provided you stayed in-doors from eight in the morning till five in the afternoon. This was at least as absurd as if an Englishman, in talking of the climate of our own island, were to say that it was possible to bear the out-door cold for two or three hours in the middle of the day during the months of July and August.

We certainly have not yet got to the bottom of the native character. Facts crop up daily which prove incontestably to all, save those who reduce everything to some Procrustean theory of civilization, that the depths of that character cannot be fathomed by our ordinary plummet, or marked with certainty on the chart by which we navigate in European waters. Take for instance those extraordinary symptoms which preceded the great mutiny; the marvellous organization of that vast plot; the mysterious but intimate connexion between the mutineers and the independent native powers; the dim prophecies and ghastly rumours which foreshadowed the outbreak; the secresy; the unanimity; the tokens passed from hand to hand throughout a million villages. Within the last few years, on one and the same day along the whole course of the Ganges the women flung their spindles into the river, and to this hour no European has the most remote conception of their motive in so doing. Some imagine that the sacrifice was made with the idea of expiating a national shortcoming; others suppose that it was intended to avert a drought; others, again, of a more practical turn of mind, believe it to have been a superstition invented by the manufacturers of spindles. There is something very striking in these rumours. No one knows where they originate, or what their purport may be; but they are passed on, from house to house and city to city, spreading throughout the length and breadth of the land agitation and anxiety, a wild terror and a wilder hope. Shortly after the pacification of the country, it was said everywhere in the Lower Provinces, that within three months there would be no "white thing" throughout Bengal. Nobody had the slightest clue as to what this "white thing" might be. Some held it to be the poppy, and supposed the prophecy to refer to the extremely improbable contingency of the abolition of the opium traffic. Some took a more gloomy view, and would have it that it pointed to the approaching extermination of our race. It was useless to question the natives, for they knew no more than we. The rumour had been set a-going, and it became, therefore, a sacred duty to do their best to spread it. At this moment there is a universal belief all over the Punjaub that our rule is to come to an end before this very year is out.

Some of these are uudoubtedly idle reports, set on

foot in mere wantonness, or, perhaps, springing up almost spontaneously from the talk of men, and indicating at most an unhealthy, excited condition of the popular mind. But, beyond all question, some secret influence was at work, to advertise, as it were, the coming horrors of 1857. The ringleaders of that gigantic conspiracy deliberately undertook to impress upon the world in general the idea that something was coming the like of which had not been known before : just as, when we see in Piccadilly a file of men with blank boards on their shoulders, we become aware that a sensation drama has been put in hand at one of the leading theatres. It has been ascertained that the Mahommedans throughout the whole of the north of India received instructions, from an unknown hand, to sing at all their social meetings a ballad which described in touching strains the humiliation of their race, and the degradation of their ancient faith, once triumphant from the Sutlej to the Burrampootra, but now in subjection and bondage to the Christian and the stranger. Each village in turn received a handful of chupatties or bannocks, by the hands of the post-runners, with orders to bake others, and pass them on to the next village ; and in the month of January, 1857, a saying was universally current :—" Sub lal hogea hai "—" Everything " is to become red." On the first of February a satirical poem appeared in a Calcutta journal, intending to ridicule the fears of those who paid attention to this prophecy. The concluding passage, which no doubt was thought droll enough at the time both by the writer and his readers, when studied by the light of subsequent events has the air of a ghastly prediction :—

> "Beneath my feet I saw 'twas nought but blood,
> And shrieking wretches borne upon the stream
> Struggled and splashed amidst a sea of gore.
> I heard a giant voice again proclaim,
> 'Mid shouts of murder, mutiny, and blood,
> 'SUB LAL HOGEA HAI,' and I awoke."

In the meantime people ate, and drank, and married, and gave in marriage, and danced, and flirted, and speared hogs, and acted "Cocknies in California," at the amateur theatre in Fort William, and wrote letters to the newspapers complaining that the military men in civil employ gave themselves airs, and abusing the Municipal Board for not seeing that the course at Calcutta was properly watered, and condoling with a popular physician of Cawnpore who was forced to go to England for the benefit of his health. There is an irony in history surpassing in depth the irony of Sophocles.

During the April of 1857, the English Society at Delhi was convulsed by the conduct of a peppery colonel, who, at the station-ball for some fancied insult from a civilian, turned his band out of the room and stopped the dancing, but expressed himself willing to relent if the official of highest rank present would apologize to the bandsmen. On the 17th of the same month comes a complaint that :—

" The bigwigs get the strawberries from the station-
" garden, while a new subscriber cannot get a sniff at
" the flowers."

Likewise—

" A wedding talked of as likely to take place soon,
" but the names of the aspirants to hymeneal bliss I
" will refrain from mentioning just yet, lest anything

"should occur to lesson their affection for each other "before the knot is tied."

On the fifth day of May, a correspondent writes from that doomed place:—

"As usual no news to give you. All quiet and dull. "Certainly we are enjoying weather which at this "season is wonderful. The morning and evening are "deliciously cool. In fact, punkahs are hardly come "into use."

On the eleventh day of May the English quarter was given over to murder, and rapine, and outrage. The Commissioner lay hewn in pieces inside the palace. Metcalfe, the collector, was flying for his life through the streets of the city where his family had ruled for more than half a century. The mangled bodies of the officers of the 54th Native Infantry were heaped in a bullock-cart outside the walls. The fanatic troopers from Meerut, with all the scum of the bazaar at their heels, were hunting down and butchering the members of the quiet Christian community. The teachers had been slain in the lecture-room ; the chaplain in his study ; the telegraph-clerk with his hand still on the signalling apparatus. The Editor of the *Gazette*, with his mother, wife, and children, died in the office of the journal. At the Delhi Bank fell Mr. Beresford, the manager, with all his family, after a gallant and desperate resistance. Of those ladies, who a few days before were grumbling at the bearishness of the old colonel, some were dragging themselves towards Meerut or Kurnaul, under the fierce noon-day sun, bare-headed and with bleeding feet ; while others were lying unconscious in death, and therefore less to be pitied, on the platform in front of the police-office in the principal boulevard.

Early in the year 1857, a new church was consecrated at Sealkote, which is described in a letter to the *Englishman* from that place as "the most chaste and "beautiful structure of Modern Gothic in India." No high praise, by the way. It was only the other day that we Calcutta people were gratified by the information that Mr. Fergusson, in his work on Modern Architecture, had given drawings of our Cathedral, both inside and out; but our delight was qualified by the subsequent discovery that he had inserted those drawings as specimens of what he pronounced to be the most debased style extant. The writer from Sealkote takes occasion to say that:—

"The future historian, when he traces the career of "our rise, and perchance our fall, in this wondrous land, "will love to dwell upon a picture like the present— "a few score strangers dedicating their churches to be "set apart from all profane uses for ever with such "fixity of purpose, and with minds so assured as never "for one moment to doubt the fulness of their faith in "the future; and this in the midst of millions distinct "from them in race, religion, and feeling. The strength "of the many made subservient to the will of the few, "not by crushing armies from foreign lands, but by "sowing the seeds of peace and order around—a land "a few years ago bristling with bayonets, an enemy's "country, now cheerfully acknowledging our rule, and "avowing it to be a blessing—is a truth that has been "sealed by the ceremony just concluded."

Then comes a remarkable postscript:—

" The other day a telegraphic message was received, "noted 'Urgent.' The news ran like wildfire round the "station, that the troops here were to march at once "for Herat.[1] But, alas! it was—can it be guessed? "Never!—*That the Sepoys who were learning the use of* "*the Enfield Rifle were to have no more practice ammu-* "*nition served out to them!*"

This supplies material for some humorous remarks, which end with the words—" Everything wears such a "mysterious aspect to us benighted Sealkotians, that "none dare venture an opinion, and we must wait till "time and the *Englishman* enlighten us."

They were to be soon enlightened by quite another agency—by a leading article written in a very different composition from printer's ink. One evening in July, Dr. Graham, the superintending surgeon of the station, begged a friend with whom he was dining, who had remarked on the insolent demeanour of the sepoys, not to let his fears get the better of his senses. The next morning an officer " saw Miss Graham coming in the "buggy, *apparently alone,* screaming and crying most "piteously." He assisted in taking out her father's body.

The Lucknow news in May 1857, consists chiefly in the badness of the road from Cawnpore.

" Soft blankets should be provided in the dawk "carriages, and plenty of them. We have large plates "of strawberries every morning. Calcutta people might "well pay Lucknow a visit. Our hospitality is famous."

---

[1] The Persian war was still in progress, and the prospect of a campaign would have even greater attractions than the retrospect of a consecration.

ALLAHABAD.

Small thought had men of soft blankets and large plates of strawberries on that November day when the English host covered sixteen miles in length of that Cawnpore road, with the sad remnants of the immortal garrison marching in the centre, and among them threescore widows who had been wives when the siege began: —the van hurrying forward under stout Sir Colin to save the bridge from the victorious mercenaries of Gwalior, while the rear stood savagely to bay against the clouds of sepoys who poured from the town to harass our retreat.

At Allahabad, towards the end of March, the weather was—

" Delightful. No news ; no one dead ; many married ; " some about to be born ; some have been ; and some " won't be, notwithstanding the welcome awaiting " them."

The welcome awaiting them ! On the 22nd May—

" We have plenty of cause for amusement here. The " railway people insist on going the grand rounds. One " cadet doing duty with the 6th Native Infantry, walked " in the verandah last night for five hours, armed with " sword and pistol, amidst the raillery of his wiser " comrades."

Two days after these words were written the 6th Native Infantry rose and massacred seventeen officers, including this poor boy and several other young cadets, who were waiting to be attached to regiments. From that time forward the Allahabad news becomes significant. On the 8th July the " bodies of European men " and women were floating down the river lately."

Late in March we find the following paragraphs :—

"We of this generation cannot realize what the effect
"of a real panic would be among the European residents
"in this country, and it would be foolish to attempt to
"realize it."

And again :—

"I fear that the good old days are gone by when we
"were accustomed to quell disaffection by blowing from
"a cannon a few of the malcontents."

So men wrote in the spring. Before autumn had well set in their style had altered. A gentleman at Raneegunge says :—

"I have three pieces of timber, which the taste of
"my engineer would convert into a picturesque gallows
"which would accommodate sixteen of the largest size
"without inconveniencing each other. A coil of whale
"rope, warranted not to have any bullock's fat to offend
"prejudices, will do its work. Having been a sailor,
"I am up to knot-making, and can introduce one much
"approved of by Bolivar, when he sometimes amused
"himself by hanging instead of shooting."

The residents at a station in Bahar would be "all
"right and merry, if we could only get a few people to
"hang."

At Allahabad the Judicial Commissioners, Sandys and Palmer, whom Lord Canning, to his eternal honour, speedily sent back again into private life, "are doing
"their duty well. The day before yesterday one of 'em
"hanged thirteen, yesterday he hanged fifteen, and there
"are still seventy-two candidates."

And again :—

"Palmer and Sandys are doing good service in tuck-
"ing up and scratching the backs of rebels."

Soon afterwards a correspondent from the same place —let us hope the same man—recommends torture for "respectable Mahommedans." At Delhi, four months after the restoration of tranquillity, six men were hung on the information of a single witness, *who himself was hung on the same day for being concerned in the murder of Europeans.* A company of gipsies, against whom no special charge could be found, were strung up together on the indictment of "retarding the peaceable organi-"zation of society." The newspapers teemed with deliberate propositions to raze to the ground ancient and crowded cities—to depopulate vast and thriving provinces—to put to the edge of the sword all the women in Delhi and Cawnpore—to exterminate the inhabitants of every village which a European fugitive had traversed without being entertained and protected; the certain and merited consequences of which barbarity would have been that, in the case of another outbreak, the peasantry would take good care that no European fugitive should escape to tell the line of country which he had taken in his flight. In fact, as a contributor to the *Englishman* remarks, with logic at least equal to his humanity:—

"There was only one prayer, and that was that every "one should meet death after a fair trial, *such as they* "*all get.* How very differently they would have been "treated by any other of the European powers."

O my countrymen! Is there no such thing as British bunkum? Have our Columbian brethren a monopoly of self-appreciation?

When it first began to be whispered in English circles that sedition was afoot, public opinion was strong against the alarmists. The sepoy was everything that could be wished. Faithful and docile, his prejudices were to be respected and his calumniators snubbed.

"We understand," on the 3rd of February, 1857, "that the sepoys of Barrackpore have consulted their "comrades in the upper provinces as to the new method "of making cartridges, and have been informed that "they are determined not to submit to an innovation "which affects their rules of caste. The Government "may be assured that those who are most determined "to maintain their own rights are neither the worst "nor least faithful soldiers. *Even Cromwell's Ironsides* "*would have mutinied if they had been forced to hear the* "*Common Prayer read.*"

"What a pity it is," writes an officer of the 65th Native Infantry, "that Europeans abusing a corps cannot "be strung up."

A few short months, and a Delhi ruffian, stained to the elbows with English blood, was a saint compared to the Englishman of noble and elevated nature, who, amidst the universal madness, preserved one tittle of justice, one spark of humanity. "We earnestly hope," (such was the style of the penny-a-liner of those days,) "and we shall be joined by almost all our readers, that "the sepoys will first sheathe their bayonets in the "bodies of those capable of excusing them."

Here is an art-notice of the period:—

"That indefatigable artist, Mr. Hudson, has just "finished a portrait of Captain Hazlewood, which may "be seen in Thacker and Spink's gallery. The friends "of the gallant officer will at once recognise the like-"ness, and feel confident that no undue lenity on his

"part will be shown to the murderers of women and
"children; for he has a stern expression of counte-
"nance, as if he had just given an order to hang them
"*and their favorers.*"

The Poet's corner in the *Englishman* of that year contains productions the most degraded, morally and intellectually, that ever proceeded from a human pen, not excepting that of the Père Duchesne. These are the terms in which men allowed themselves to speak of the ruler who saved our nation from as awful a crime as any on which the sun has shone:—

> "*Barring humanity-pretenders,*
> To Hell of none are we the willing senders;
> But, if to sepoys entrance must be given,
> Locate them, Lord, in the back slums of Heaven."

Talk of the *New York Herald !* May our Father which is in heaven not lead us again into such temptation!

When but seven years have passed since such a mine lay beneath our feet unheeded and unknown, we should be slow to affirm that we understand the feelings and character of the people of India. Their inner life still remains a sealed book to us. Certain it is that we have a very vague notion of the estimation in which they hold us. It is hardly possible for a man brought up amidst European scenes and associations to realize the idea conceived of him and his countrymen by a thorough-bred Hindoo. On the one hand, the natives must acknowledge our vast superiority in the arts of war and government. Our railways and steamships and Armstrong guns are tangible facts which cannot be slighted. They must be perfectly aware that we have conquered them, and are governing them in a more systematic and downright manner than they have ever been governed before. But, on the other hand, many of our usages must in their eyes appear most debased and revolting. Imagine the horror with which a punctilious and devout Brahmin cannot but regard a people who eat the flesh of cow and pig, and drink various sorts of strong liquor from morning till night. It is at least as hard for such a man to look up to us as his betters, morally and socially, as it would be for us to place amongst the most civilized nations of the world a population which was in the habit of dining on human flesh, and intoxicating itself daily with laudanum and sal-volatile. The peculiar qualities which mark the Englishman are singularly distasteful to the Oriental, and are sure to be strangely distorted when seen from his point of view. Our energy and earnestness appear oppressive and importunate to the languid voluptuous aristocracy of the East. Our very honesty seems ostentatious and contemptible to the wily and tortuous Hindoo mind. That magnificent disregard of *les convenances*, which has rendered our countrymen so justly beloved by all the continental nations, is inexplicable and hateful to a race who consider external pomp and reticent solemnity to be the necessary accompaniments of rank, worth, or power. The Maharajah of Kishnagur on e described to me his disgust and surprise at seeing an English magistrate, during a shooting excursion, bathe in a tank near which the tents were pitched. Europeans who have resided many years in the East seldom fail to acquire some of these so-called Oriental prejudices. Some of my Anglo-Indian friends have told me that nothing would persuade them to strip themselves in a public swimming-bath; and I have seen a high official unable to conceal his horror when a sucking-pig, which by that time was a sucking-pig only in name, was placed on the table directly under his nose.

It is noteworthy that the free and hardy customs of the ancient Greeks produced much the same effect upon the effeminate subjects of Darius and Artaxerxes. The Persian, whose every action was dictated by a spirit of intense decorum and self-respect, could not appreciate the lordly indifference to appearances displayed by the Spartan, accustomed to box, and run, and wrestle without a shred of clothing, in the presence of myriads of his brother Hellenes. Herodotus tells his countrymen, as a remarkable piece of information, that, " among the " Lydians, and, speaking loosely, among barbarians in " general, it is held to be a great disgrace to be seen " naked, even for a man."

Add the mysterious awe by which we are shrouded in the eyes of the native population, which very generally attributes to magic our uniform success in everything we take in hand, and you will have some conception of the picture presented to the Hindoo mind by an indefatigable, public-spirited, plain-spoken, beer-drinking, cigar-smoking, tiger-shooting collector. We should not be far wrong if we were content to allow that we are regarded by our Eastern subjects as a species of quaint and somewhat objectionable demons, with a rare aptitude for fighting and administration; foul and degraded in our habits, though with reference to those habits not to be judged by the same standard as ordinary men; not malevolent withal (that is to say the official fiends), but entirely wayward and unaccountable; a race of demi-devils: neither quite human, nor yet quite supernatural; not wholly bad, yet far from perfectly benificent; who have been settled down in the country by the will of fate, and seem very much inclined to stay there by our own. If this is not the idea entertained of us by an average Bengalee rustic, it is something very near it.

Such is the incompatibility of sentiment and custom between the European and the natives, that even the firmest friends of the latter allow that a complete amalgamation is quite hopeless. The wide and radical difference between the views held by the respective races with regard to the weaker sex alone, forms a bar, at present insuperable, to any very familiar intercourse. We, who still live among the recollections and records of chivalry, horrify utilitarians by persisting in regarding women as goddesses. The Hindoos, who allow their sisters and daughters few or no personal rights—the Mahommedans, who do not even allow them souls—cannot bring themselves to look upon women as better than playthings. The pride of a Mussulman servant is terribly wounded by a scolding from the lady of the house. He takes every opportunity of showing contempt for his mistress by various childish impertinences when the Sahib and his horsewhip are well out of the way. Among the numberless symptoms of our national eccentricity, that which seems most extraordinary to a native is our submitting to be governed by a woman. For a long time they accounted for the presence of the Queen's effigy on the rupee by setting her down as the wife of John Kumpani. Now they probably imagine that John

Kumpani is dead, and that she has come into possession
as residuary legatee. The free and unrestrained life of
an English lady excites the strangest and most unjust
ideas in the mind of an Hindoo. To see women riding
in public, driving about in open carriages, dining and
talking and dancing with men connected with them
neither by blood nor marriage, never fails to produce
upon him a most false and unfortunate impression.
Many gentlemen who are intimately acquainted with
native ways of thought are not often very ready to take
their wives and daughters to balls where the guests are
of mixed nationality. I was present lately at an entertainment given by the Maharaja of Nilpore. The dancing went on in a sort of atrium in the centre of the
palace, while the host, in a blaze of diamonds from
head to foot, inspected the scene through a lorgnette,
from the gallery, turning from time to time to make a
remark to a circle of his friends and hangers-on. He
resembled Lord Steyne at the opera, surrounded by his
Wenhams and Waggs, rather than the received notion
of " the man of the house " of a Belgravian ball-room.
His bearing aroused the most lively indignation among
the older Anglo-Indians. Suggestions to " turn him
" out," and " throw him over " were bandied about in an
audible key. One old campaigner sighed for the halycon
days of the mutiny. " Hang him ! I should like to
" loot him. He must be worth a quarter of a crore of
" rupees as he stands. His cap alone would be a good
" two lacs."

The longer a man lives in this country the more
firmly convinced does he become that the amalgamation
of the conquerors and the conquered is an idea impràc-

ticable, and, to use an odious word, Utopian. But this does not imply that, as time goes on, as the native becomes civilized, and the European humane and equitable, the two races should not live side by side with mutual sympathy and self-respect, and work together heartily for the same great ends. But this consummation is simply impossible until there is a marked improvement in the tone of the European settlers. That intense Anglo-Saxon spirit of self-approbation, which, though dormant at home, is unpleasantly perceptible among vulgar Englishmen on the Continent, becomes rampant in India. It is painful, indeed, to observe the deep pride and insolence of race which is engrained in our nature, and which yields only to the highest degree of education and enlightenment. The lower in the scale of society, the more marked become the symptoms of that baneful sentiment. A native of rank, whom men like Sir John Lawrence or Sir Herbert Edwardes treat with the courtesy due to an equal, will be flouted and kicked about by any planter's assistant or sub-deputy railway-contractor whose path he may chance to cross. On such a question as this, one fact is worth volumes of declamation; and facts of grave import may be gathered by the bushel by any one who spends three days in the country with his mouth shut and his eyes wide open.

Sonepore, the point at which the Gunduck runs into the Ganges, is the most sacred spot in the North of India. Thither, time out of mind, at a certain phase of the moon during the late autumn, devout Hindoos have been wont to repair from hundreds of miles round, for the purpose of washing away their sins. Men discovered that expiatory bathing was not incompatible with business, and a great fair began to be held yearly during the festival, principally for dealings in elephant and horse-flesh. The Anglo-Indians, who attended for the purpose of buying nags, soon took to running their purchases one against another; and the attractions of a European race-meeting were thus added to those which Sonepore already possessed during the sacred week. The whole of Bahar society now makes holiday in that week, and a more pleasant reunion it is difficult to imagine. Men rejoice in the annual opportunity of renewing Haileybury and Addiscombe friendships with old companions from whom they have been separated throughout the remainder of the year by vast distances and vile roads. The complicated family connexions, so general in the Civil Service, render this periodical gathering peculiarly pleasant. The wife of the Judge of Boglipore looks forward for months to meeting her sister, the Collectrix of Gya; and the Commissioner of Benares, like a good cousin, has promised to bring her brother in his train, though that promising but susceptible Assistant-Magistrate has exceeded his privilege leave by ten days' extra philandering at Simla. The desirable young ladies come to Sonepore already engaged to local partners for every dance during the meeting:— a circumstance extremely discouraging to casual swells who may have been attracted from Calcutta by the glowing accounts of the doings at the races put about by Bahar members of the Secretariat. Beneath a vast circular grove stretches a camp more than a mile in extent, where croquet and betting go on briskly by day, and waltzing and flirtation by night. The tents of each set of friends cluster round a large open pavilion, belonging to some liberal planter or magistrate, where covers are laid three times a day for every one who can be cajoled into joining the party. I could talk on for ever about Sonepore; such dear associations does it conjure up of open-handed Indian hospitality and open-hearted Indian friends, from my feeling for whom neither time, nor absence, nor opposed sentiments, nor divided interests, can ever, shall ever, abate one atom of affection and gratitude.

It was there, during one of the principal races, that I was standing at the judge's post, divided by the breadth of the course from a platform occupied by some dozen Englishmen. Close up to this platform crowded a number of well-dressed, well-to-do natives—respectable shopkeepers from Chupra; warm men of business from Patna; gentlemen of rank from Benares and Lucknow. I saw—with my own eyes I saw—a tall raw-boned brute of a planter, whose name I should not hesitate to publish if it were worth the publishing, rush at these men, who had as good a right to be there as the Governor-General himself, and flog them with a double-thonged hunting-whip, until he had driven them in humiliating confusion and terror for the distance of many yards. One or two civilians present said to each other that it was a "shame;" but no one seemed astounded or horrified; no one interposed; no one prosecuted; n one objected to meet the blackguard at dinner, or to take the odds from him at the ordinary.

A Judge of the High Court at Calcutta informed me that he had himself witnessed the following scene, while travelling on the East Indian Railway between Benares

A "NATIVE GENTLEMAN."

and Howrah. When the train stopped at a certain station, a Bengalee attempted to get into a second-class carriage. Some Europeans, who were comfortably settled down for a long sleep, told him to go about his business. He appealed to the officials, stating himself to be a native gentleman. A person in authority told him he must be contented to travel third-class; to which he replied that he preferred to be left behind. By this time he was surrounded by a circle of bullying English travellers; whom *the guard of the train* convulsed with delight by holding up his lantern to the poor man's face, and in a strong Irish brogue bidding the bystanders look at " a specimen of a native gentle-" man."

If I could think that the interest with which you read these stories could be one-tenth as deep as the pain with which I write them, you should have enough to keep you in indignation for the next twelvemonth. But things which, when acted, set the teeth chattering and the fingers twitching, seem childish enough when turned into sentences and divided with commas and colons. Heaven knows, I would give a month's pay or a year's pension to have my will of some ruffians for what I have heard them say with applause, and seen them to do with impunity. Fearful symptoms these of what must be seething below! However kind he might be to his native servants, however just to his native tenants, there is not a single non-official person in India, with whom I have conversed on public questions, who would not consider the sentiment that we hold India for the benefit of the inhabitants of India a loathsome un-English piece of cant. Hence comes the paramount necessity that opinion at home should keep a close watch upon the conduct of the affairs of India. It is not enough that we send her out able and high-minded rulers. While there, they must never be allowed to forget that the eyes of England are upon them. Lord Canning was as brave a man and as good a man as could well be found within our isles. Such he proved himself to be at a crisis when virtue was useless without courage, and when courage without virtue was far worse than useless. Yet even he succumbed at last to the ravening clamour of the friends of indigo. If Lord Canning had been left to himself, the ryot would have been delivered over to his tyrants bound hand and foot by a law illogical, inhumane, and inexpedient in all the highest senses.

What is the meaning of the Anglo-Saxon outcry? We cannot exterminate a wealthy and ancient community of a hundred and fifty millions of human beings, like so many Maories or Cherokees: and, if we do not exterminate them, we cannot continue to humble and to wrong them. If this state of things is disregarded at home, most serious evils must ensue. If it should ever come to pass that for a single period of five years India should be governed under the auspices of a Secretary of State of anti-native tendencies, the certain result would be a wide-spread system of social oppression, degrading and cruel to the native, shameful and demoralizing to us. The apathy of Englishmen to the affairs of India would be venial if our interests alone were thereby placed in peril; but, when the consequences fall on the innocent children of the soil, that apathy becomes nothing less than criminal. While honest men doze, bad men are hard at work. The people of Hindostan, if they be wise, will make it their prayer that they may gain the ear of England; for, if they succeed in obtaining her attention, they are secure of her humanity and her justice.

Yours ever,
H. Broughton.

THE END.